BEVIN

ERNEST BEVIN AT HIS DESK AT THE FOREIGN OFFICE

BEVIN

by Trevor Evans

LONDON

———————————————

GEORGE ALLEN & UNWIN LTD

To

FREDDY CHANT,

the doyen of national British newspaper
industrial correspondents,
nearing retirement, with the affection
of all his professional colleagues,
who are humbled by his modesty

BOOK
PRODUCTION
WAR ECONOMY
STANDARD

THIS BOOK IS PRODUCED IN COMPLETE
CONFORMITY WITH THE AUTHORISED
ECONOMY STANDARDS

PRINTED IN GREAT BRITAIN IN 11-POINT IMPRINT TYPE BY
THE BLACKFRIARS PRESS LTD., LEICESTER

CONTENTS

ILLUSTRATIONS

CHAPTER I

PROFILE

I was with Ernest Bevin, His Britannic Majesty's Secretary of State for Foreign Affairs, in his room in the Foreign Office on the evening the world was told that he was about to visit Moscow.*

It was not an occasion on which one could relax and examine this historic room, although the guest-seat of bright scarlet leather was well upholstered and comfortable.

There were two reasons why full advantage could not be taken of the visit to attempt anything like a full description of Ernest Bevin in his new surroundings.

Firstly, I could see only about one-fifth of that room. It is the way Mr. Bevin himself has arranged its lighting. The famous chandelier suspended from the centre of the room is in the shadows—like the conference table at its far end, with its neighbouring easel for maps, and the great globe on its bronze pedestal.

Bevin has installed a plain, green canopied desk light. It throws its severely circumscribed rays on the square yard of his desk. One other light, an ornate, richly canopied reading lamp on its six-feet high mahogany standard, stationed a yard away from Bevin's right elbow, barely manages to light the ankles and feet of the nearly-double-life-sized oil painting of his late Majesty, King George the Second of England, which stretches from the white marble mantel-piece above the roaring coal fire, two yards behind the Foreign Secretary's back, nearly two-thirds of the way up the twenty-foot high wall.

It may have been accidental, but when Mr. Bevin re-arranged his desk light, he raised the shade slightly, but enough to cause a shaft of the light to strike me straight in the eye. I avoided the strain only by sitting bolt upright, thus permitting the upper edge of the light to strike my cheek slightly below my lower lids. This went on for quite five minutes because Mr. Bevin was pre-occupied though he went on talking, and Mr. Bevin is neither quickly nor easily interrupted.

Secondly, I had been invited to wait on Mr. Bevin to discuss this book. It was not a normal consultation. There was little co-

*Friday, Dec. 7th, 1945.

operation about it. Indeed, all that follows after this introduction had been completed more than two weeks before I was summoned to the Foreign Office. The morning after the script had been completed, I received a telephone call from a friend of mine, who is a closer friend of Bevin's, inviting me to let the Foreign Secretary see what I had written.

He received the typescript next day. And, officially and formally, there had been silence for twelve days. Naturally, there had been whispers. Mr. Bevin, it was said, did not want any biography written about him because in his new position, as Foreign Secretary, a distortion of the man might lead to a misappreciation of his country's policy. There never had been a biography of Ernest Bevin. The first approved outline of his life would be contained, sometime, in an autobiography. Attempts had been made previously at biographies—they had not been published.

Further, he would want to know why I wanted to write about him. This was the most natural suggestion of all. This was in line with the famous Bevin search for motive. Bevin has lived such a life of controversy that he finds it difficult to believe he can be the object of detachment. He has some right to this belief. There is nothing negative or passive about Bevin. Those who know him are hearty in their approval or disapproval. Bevin bases nearly all his actions and sayings on his principles. He believes men should go through life guided by principles. He describes his critics as "irresponsible" when he really means they are not guided by the right principles. He is constantly on the watch for the motives of others. He has become a formidable adversary to all who differ from him, without ceasing to be an uneasy, slightly uncomfortable, colleague to those who work with him. But he is a comfort to those millions who know there must be action in every situation which arises these days without knowing what that action ought to be. He is the answer to all those who condemn the failure of past British Foreign Secretaries to do something—except appease.

Still, there had been silence for seven days. Nobody knew what had happened to my typescript after one of the "office keepers," which is the distinctive Foreign Office name for its uniformed messengers, had been handed the bundle to put into the Foreign Secretary's automobile on a gloomy Saturday evening. The silence was more disturbing than the theories and the speculations.

It led to a pre-occupation which blunted appreciation of the

sights and sounds of the department which shares with the
Treasury the reputation of being the most exclusive branch of the
British Civil Service. It was not for an hour or two that I realised
how beautiful was that statuesque brunette in full-length black
evening gown tripping down the cold, stone steps, as I barged in
through the swing doors from the outer courtyard with barely one
minute to go for my six o'clock appointment with the Foreign
Secretary.

Nor did I realise, as I was escorted by the benign and dignified
office-keeper that the room on my right with the artificial sun-
light was the one room in the whole of Whitehall which keeps
open, fully staffed, for every minute of the year. For it is in this
room that all messages are received from British diplomatic and
consular representatives in all parts of the world.

I noticed, however, that before my escort had uttered a word
to the office-keeper on the first floor, the latter mentioned my
name, asked me to confirm my identity, and then with great
courtesy showed me into a dignified waiting-room. It was the
Ambassadors' Room. Here conferences are held by the senior
permanent officials of the Department with British ambassadors
and consuls recalled for consultation or prior to being posted to
new appointments.

The most arresting piece of furniture in the room is the great
solid oak table, around which are placed thirty massive chairs.
It is difficult to imagine how the room must look about 4-30 every
afternoon, when it is converted into one of the world's most
exclusive tea-clubs. Here come all those of the top-ranking dozen
or fifteen chiefs of the department who can tear themselves away
from their duties to take a frugal tea. It is frugal. It consists of a
pot of tea, two or three slices of thin bread and butter and a piece
of plain cake. Each official marks up his attendance, and pays his
account weekly to the office-keeper in attendance. There is more
in all this than a mere social break. It provides an opportunity for
consultation with colleagues in an atmosphere of relaxation.

Around the walls are gilt-framed paintings of dead monarchs
and statesmen. And dominating them all is Queen Victoria, wear-
ing on the left half of her cape a dazzling display of her most
cherished Orders and decorations. This has forced the artist to
paint the Queen in profile. She looks towards the door. This is as
well. She is unable to see the table. The Queen, who hated tobacco,

would be shocked to see that table. Its solitary decorations now are four massive cut-glass ash-trays.

The private secretary suddenly opens the door, and takes me across the hall to the sanctum. Mr. Bevin sits with his back half-turned to the door. He does not turn round, but I come into his vision half-way between the door and the seat beside his desk. We shake hands, and that to me is a great relief. It shows that Bevin has not been outraged. He speaks quietly, and almost gently. He tells me there are inaccuracies in my script. I tell him I will correct them. He hardly seems to notice my reply, but proceeds to name them. They are not so much inaccuracies as too one-sided recitals of incidents which happened twenty to thirty-five years ago. As he lights his cigar, I tell him how I have had to rely on the evidence of old colleagues whose knowledge of all the circumstances naturally would not be as great as his own, but then he proceeds to explain his attitude to these old-time crises. "I know" he explains, "that what you have recorded was said at the time and was accepted as pretty accurate. During all these years I have taken no steps to correct such impressions. But now people in other countries are eager to find out what sort of fellow I am. They are liable to draw wrong conclusions if some of the things that happened long ago are not put in their proper light."

Then Bevin elaborated incidents of 1911, 1918 and 1923. These are amended in the text. But I mention it here because on no subject is Bevin as fascinating as on his own memories of his early days. This memory is prodigious. He recalls the names of minor characters in the incidents he describes, what they looked like, and what happened to them years later.

Bevin makes no attempt to obscure the humbleness of his origin. There have been times in his career when it has been of value to him to remind his hearers of his experiences. Now, it suffices to him to have it known that when he claims to speak for the people of England, he speaks for those from whom he sprang.

He showed one curious piece of non-co-operation. He says suddenly, "You write about me reading to my employer when I was a farm-boy. You went to the wrong farm. I worked at the farm you visited just over a year. I was also at another farm, when I read the newspapers." He declines to give further information about that, so I am afraid, that slight inaccuracy must remain.

But on other incidents he is much more generous with his help, particularly where they concern the trade union, of transport workers and men and women in thirty other callings, which he took the dominant part in forming. He is devoted to it, and if all its early records were destroyed, I believe he would be able to dictate the main points of all major discussions within its executive council. He was in the middle of recalling a crisis which happened on the eve of the formation of the union when he was interrupted by an official with a reminder of another appointment. "Two minutes," replied Bevin, and he went on with that tiny piece of forgotten trade union history.

Beyond a repetition of my assurance that I would correct any inaccuracies, I had said little. Bevin suddenly stood up. He escorted me to the door of his vast room, and bade me an affable farewell.

In spite of this, I counted the interview a howling failure. True, Bevin's criticism had been more subdued than I had expected, and had been delivered with a mildness that was uncharacteristic. He has always been wont, in the fifteen years I have known him intimately, to express himself with vigour and forthrightness. He is one who has specialised in full tones. No nuances or subtle shades for him.

No, my professional pride as a newspaperman had been injured by the meagreness of the knowledge I had gained of the man in half an hour. I tried to console myself with the excuse that Bevin had given me little chance for an opening. He is extraordinary that way. He will have his say. If there is something he has left unsaid, he will interrupt your question to complete his answer. And he intends no rudeness by it. That is one of his conversational foibles. In more formal arguments, debates, discussions or negotiations he is scrupulously and punctiliously observant of the rules.

Two minutes after I left Bevin's room I was gazing out of the window of a neighbouring room. It looked out, like Bevin's room, over a fragment of lovely St. James's Park. The headlights of motor cars cut swathes of light through the clear wintry blackness of the Horse Guards Parade as they swung from the Mall towards the seats of government. Slightly to the left of the picture, through the bare trees of the Park, lights were twinkling from Buckingham Palace. More to the centre there was the haze of light which was the canopy of the West End. And there, barely fifty yards away, was the man I had left, the orphaned farm boy, who was guiding the world destinies of the race who count this scene the centre of their Empire.

I turned to young Hector McNeil, the earnest journalist who is Under Secretary for Foreign Affairs, who becomes more devoted to Bevin the longer he serves with him. After pointing out that twice before Britain has had Labour Foreign Ministers (first was Ramsay MacDonald, and the second, better remembered, Arthur Henderson), I asked, "why should it appear so remarkable to have Ernest Bevin here now?"

There are at least three reasons. There was a great deal of solid formality about Arthur Henderson. The affection which he inspired, shown by the universal use of the name "Uncle Arthur" by his supporters, was based on his rectitude and loyalty to peace-providing principles. Uncle Arthur was the embodiment of Nonconformist solidity. His public and personal lives were both remarkable for their consistent integrity. Impossible not to feel confidence in such a man.

Bevin has all these things—with a lot more. The extra attributes are, however, those which fill his supporters with increased enthusiasm and his critics with added misgivings. Henderson, though he started as a trade union official with the iron and steel operatives, had devoted most of his life to politics, and years before his Party came to office it was realised that Henderson's prestige would command one of the highest posts in the Administration.

Bevin, on the other hand, did not enter Parliament until 1940, when he was 59. Henderson was Foreign Secretary in a Government which held office without power, and therefore was compelled to observe political orthodoxy.

Bevin takes office in a Government with supreme authority at a time when the new peace has to be shaped, and when old policies must be discarded because his people know they have failed, and will fail again if they are retained. He is a natural experimenter, placed in a huge, unfamiliar laboratory with the rest of the world watching him through a glass panel, knowing that failure on his part will mean misery and may mean destruction for millions.

Had it been possible to mention any of these considerations to

Bevin he would have responded. His imagination is Celtic in its imagery, his outlook is wide, not so much from his own suffering as a youth as from his observation of the misery of others, and his profound knowledge of men is a thousand-fold compensation for his lack of formal education. He murders the English language but mirrors the soul of millions of the English people.

Only one clue had he given me that his new and greatest office had caused any change in his own assessment of himself. He had said, "Now people in other countries are eager to find out what sort of a fellow I am."

That threw me back to a memory of five years earlier. One evening in the summer of 1940, the well-known American newspaperman and broadcaster, Quentin Reynolds, blew into my room in a London newspaper office.

He was almost breathless, as if his flight across the Atlantic that day still "told" on him. He appealed, "You've got to introduce me to this guy Bevin at once." I asked Quent. what all the excitement was about. "Well," he demanded, "who is he? Where does he come from? How far will he get?"

There was a good topical reason for this interest in Bevin. A week or two earlier Winston Churchill had formed his National Government, which was to guide Britain right through the war.

It seems a curiosity now but it was a fact then that Reynolds had been sent across the Atlantic by his magazine because the name of Bevin was unfamiliar among the names of the new Ministers.

It was the third of Reynolds' questions that I answered first. "Bevin," I replied, "will get to the very top if his health holds good, and his age doesn't tell against him. He may even be Prime Minister of Britain." Reynolds got very impatient and excited. He handed me my own telephone, and begged "Get me through to him." It was a pleasant thought that even such an experienced visitor as Reynolds should think life in wartime England was as easy as that. All the same, I telephoned the Ministry of Labour. I spoke to a fascinating character called Sam Richard Chaloner. He looks like the slim younger brother of Mr. Pickwick. He talks quietly, almost in a monotone, and has developed a fantastic trick of training the gleam in his eye to reflect the degree of significance in his announcements. At that time he was the Ministry's chief press officer—one of the best any department ever had. I repeated Reynolds' request.

There was a note of pained surprise in his voice as Sam replied, "You know, my Minister never gives individual interviews to newspaper men, however distinguished they may be." Without waiting for any retort, Sam went on, "Tell him to call in my office at noon tomorrow. The Minister might be free between deputations for a few minutes then. Of course, I promise nothing." I replied, "Tomorrow, Saturday, Sam?" He murmured, "Days and times make no difference to my Minister. He has half-hourly appointments throughout the weekend."

Next morning, little Sam led big Quentin up the impressive marble stairway of Montague House, and at the top of the stairs Bevin happened to be crossing from a conference chamber to his own private room. "Ah, Minister," murmured Sam suavely, "would you care to meet Mr. Quentin Reynolds, of New York?" Bevin nodded his head towards his room, and in the immediate hiatus which followed their entry, Reynolds recalled my prophecy that some day Bevin might be Prime Minister. Quite good-naturedly, Bevin growled, "You can't always rely on his judgment, can you, Chaloner?" Sam bowed almost imperceptibly as he replied profoundly, "Only time, sir, can prove prophets liars."

Reynolds was delighted with the interview. When I saw him later he had become a Bevin "fan." He demanded, "Why haven't you told me about Bevin before?"

I felt a little injured, seeing I had been writing about Bevin for years and years. True, most of what my colleagues and I had written dealt with affairs of the moment. There had not been many occasions calling for a broad review of Bevin's past career. Besides, most British newspapermen assumed that most of their readers had a sound working knowledge of Bevin's past career and of his standing in the industrial life of Britain.

That was the trouble. In Britain we have grown up with Bevin. Today he is not so much a man as a phenomenon. Maybe he is both. A manly phenomenon. Britain has taken him for granted.

Bevin would not be where he is today but for the authority and influence of the trade unions. The reverse holds good. Bevin has done more than almost any other man to bring the trade unions to their present accepted position.

That is a position readily understood by most people in Britain. It was not an explanation which Quentin Reynolds was prepared to take without further elucidation. He wanted to know, for instance, whether Bevin was a "trade union boss" in the sense understood by some trade unions in the United States. The answer is no. Even that has to be qualified. While Bevin has not given orders to his people and expected them to be obeyed blindly and unquestionably, he has made proposals which his elected executive council have almost invariably found to reflect their own ideas. He has been the first to put into words, and shape into policies, vague aspirations and desires which others had held but had been unable to define. This was the secret of his earlier success.

So consistently did Bevin produce this forward-looking sense of his, that over the years it came to be expected. Thus, sometimes grudgingly, sometimes unstintingly, other trade unions came to regard Bevin as their natural spokesman. And, as the unions grew in numbers to more than 8,000,000 members, so Bevin grew in stature as the man who knew what they wanted. His instinct was unerring. It gave him influence, though it never made him wealthy. Until he became a Cabinet Minister he had never earned more than £1,250 (5,000 dollars) a year in salary.

Bevin discovered fairly early in his career that leaders must be prepared to lead and not be content merely to obey the decision of a committee. His skill in judging what the majority of his followers wanted, gave him confidence in asserting himself. This led to many accusations of dictatorship. But whenever he was challenged on this ground, he was always able to produce the authority of his executive council, an assembly of working men who formed the supreme policy-making body of his union, for all his actions.

Because Bevin has won, and likes authority he has been called vain. He has suffered from the adulation of hero-worshippers, who resent any word of criticism against him. Such men have done him a dis-service. They have nurtured the impression that Bevin likes "yes-men" around him. He is much more interested in efficient men.

His authority, when he was chief of the Transport Workers' Union, was unquestioned by the other 500 paid officials of the union. Indeed, they showed him remarkable consideration.

One of his former chief lieutenants tells this illuminating story. "I went into E.B's room in Transport House one day and found him irritable and 'snappy.' After a while he apologised and explained that it was always thus with him when the wind blew from the East. I had to see him again about a month later, and, bless me, it was the same with him again. He told me once more about the wind from the East."

I asked the official if there was any sequel to all this. He replied, "Of course there was. If ever I saw him again, why, I took note of how the wind blew, and if it was from the East, I just postponed my call. It worked. At all other times he was most helpful and encouraging."

All the same, Bevin gave his officials considerable scope for their own initiative—as long as they kept within union rules.

That sturdy character, Dan Hillman, when he was a dockers' leader in Bevin's union, once hired a tug in Plymouth Sound, filled it with his men on strike and took it out in the bay to dissuade some strike-breakers from going on with their job of unloading a ship. The ship was owned by a firm with which the union was in dispute. So fierce did some of the strikers seem and sound on the tug, with their grimaces and their shouts, that Dan had to promise protection to all the strike-breakers before they would clamber down the side of the ship to be taken ashore by the tug—and then made members of the union !

Bevin's memory for this type of incident is tremendous. After hearing one such recital, one of his men observed, "Why, Ernie, we'll have to call you 'The Elephant'." Bevin plainly showed his disapproval of the idea. It was intended as a compliment to his memory—but it was also too pointed a reminder of his growing girth.

All the same, he has a boisterous sense of humour. In the early days of the war, two or three of us were invited to accompany him on a week-end tour of South Wales. He was then Minister of Labour. When we reached the tinplate town of Llanelly, the local citizens, proud of their reputation as singers, honoured him by organising a massed choir to sing Welsh hymns to him. I sat in the front row of the stalls, facing Bevin and the leading local citizenry on the stage. During the community singing I was so moved by the beauty of old hymns which I had not heard for more than twenty years that I joined in the singing, to the pain and embarrassment of Sam Richard Chaloner, who sat beside me.

Bevin delivered a powerful speech, and, while formal thanks were being tended to him, my colleagues and I hurried back to our hotel writing room to prepare our messages. We were in the middle of this labour, when the door burst open, and in dashed Bevin, beaming. He shook me warmly by the hand, and said, "I congratulate you on having been to Sunday school, some time; now you congratulate me for having made such a remarkable discovery."

He continually gives evidence of the most surprising erudition. His mind is filled with scraps of intimate knowledge on the most abstruse topics. Yet at no period in his life did he settle down for an intensive course of study—except once. Bevin left a village school when he was eleven. That was the end of his formal education. He has never developed a passion for any particular author. He knows some books practically off by heart, like Bryce's *Constitution*.

One of his closest and most astute colleagues swears that Bevin is one of those men who learn more from people than from books, who places more value on his own experiences than those of others. Yet, there was an occasion when he applied himself with diligence to the mastery of an unfamiliar subject. It was in 1929, when he was appointed by Philip Snowden, then Chancellor of the Exchequer, to the Macmillan Committee on Industry and Finance. Bevin was determined that he was not going to be a mere figurehead to bolster up the claim that such a committee was wholly representative of all sections of British life.

Such study enabled him to contribute materially to the conclusions of the committee. He even contributed an addendum dissenting from the majority views of the committee on the illness then assailing British economy. He gained knowledge which enhanced his contribution to debates in the annual conferences of of the Trades Union Congress, the central meeting of representatives of more than 200 affiliated independent unions.

Perhaps most important of all to his relations with other people and other sections of his movement, he mellowed his views towards professional economists, theorists, and other "intellectuals." In these categories he includes most people who have not had to do manual work for their living.

Bevin has always written his own speeches. They are broad in

B

their outlook and they are delivered with a force that obscures his cavalier treatment of syntax. He is concerned mainly with putting over his ideas so that they can be grasped quickly by his hearers. He never fails in this. He makes frequent use of colloquialisms.

Naturally, since he has become a Minister, he calls for briefs. But the speech he delivers is his own. No one knows quite what he is going to say. On the few occasions that advance copies of his speech have been provided, his officials have always advised newspaper men to "stick around" if they want to know what he really said. Of course, that applies only to his public speeches. He always sticks to his script when he is broadcasting.

His art of improvisation is inspired by the response of his audience. He must see the people to whom he is speaking to give of his best. He is chilled by an impersonal microphone. He responds well to vast audiences, and to inquisitive newspaper conferences, which, by the way, he never held before he became a Minister.

Bevin has never been mercenary. He has never gone in for big money, although his union provided him with an automobile and chauffeur. His expenses allowance was never as high as his salary, except when he was travelling abroad. No one has ever attempted to bribe him. His incorruptibility was too patent. But he has received many gifts. Always from the men he has led, never from the men he has faced across the negotiating table. Indeed, he was ostentatious in his refusal to meet socially the representatives of the employers.

Yet he is a shrewd business man. He was walking down Whitehall, London, towards Parliament Square, one day with a colleague, and they happened to look over towards Central Buildings, Westminster. This was the home of his union for seven years. Bevin chuckled as he recalled that he had sold Central Buildings to Dorman Long's, one of the leading British steel companies, at a profit handsome enough to have gone a long way in paying for Transport House, the present headquarters of the Union and also the temporary home of the British Trades Union Congress and of the Labour Party.

Although all his energies were devoted for nearly thirty years to the improvement of the position of his trade union and in helping to shape the policy of the whole trade union movement of his country, he did not adopt the attitude of personal austerity.

Nor did he go around after he had ceased to be a manual worker pretending to be a working man. He had an innate sense of dignity early in his career, liked personal comfort, and appreciated the value of good clothes, without being ostentatious about his appearance.

There were two distinct traits so deeply developed in Bevin's character while he was a trade union leader, that they are not likely to be altered now that he is one of the most influential Ministers in a government of his own Party.

1. He has a passionate belief in the sanctity of agreements. That is why he has always been distressed by unofficial strikes, which invalidate contracts entered into between organised employers, or individual firms, and the trade unions.

2. He is not against private enterprise. That does not mean to say he is against the nationalisation of certain basic industries. He believes that a wide field of activity should be left open to private enterprise. He goes even further. He has been outstanding among British trade union leaders for his readiness in discussing improved technique and productive processes to ensure greater returns to industry, and safety to workers. He has not objected to these greater returns, so long as a fair share of the improvement was given to the workers.

The result was that in the later stages of his career as a trade unionist Bevin found many of the more far-sighted and progressive employers ready to co-operate with him in discussions for the improvement of working conditions and earnings. This helped towards the impartiality he achieved when he became Minister of Labour.

He believes in orderliness and progress. One of his most oft-used phrases is, "You must have a thing tidy." He hates loose ends. Therefore, he hates buccaneers of all sorts, especially when their failure can do harm to those whom they employ.

He is not against success as such. He does not begrudge the tremendous ramifications of Britain's biggest concerns, so long as they stop short of becoming monopolies, and keep clear of international cartels designed to maintain high prices. In fact, there are circumstances in which he approves of big organisations. When thousands of men and women work together it is easier to organise them. Further, the bigger the firm the greater the dislocation when there is a stoppage of work, and therefore the keener the disposition to negotiate good working conditions, and maintain efficient personnel management.

He has gone further than most trade union leaders in Britain to urge industrial co-operation between employers and employed. He is one of the great protagonists in Britain of the tripartite partnership, the third being the State. That is why he is such a great supporter of the International Labour Office, whose directorship it was said he wanted, after he had finished his war service as Minister of Labour. That was merely a hunch based on Bevin's known interests, and not on any wishes he had expressed himself. It is significant, however, that he has reached the stature when men cast him only for great appointments.

It was not always thus, even after he had established the union which is the greatest movement to date of his life's work. Many other trade union leaders found him difficult to get on with. He could be harsh and intolerant. He was quick to resent criticism of himself, and as quick to reciprocate with harsher retorts. The result was that some trade union leaders were too prone to attribute Bevin's spectacular rise to fame as due to luck. There was some luck in his career, but it was mainly due to his quickness to develop situations that he rose above other trade union leaders who had equal opportunities. Sir Walter Citrine, general secretary of the Trade Union Congress, was the only trade union leader comparable to Bevin in ability to grasp details and to present a finished case to a critical assembly. Citrine resigned his job, to become a member of the National Coal Board, in June, 1946.

Now that Bevin and Citrine have departed finally from the British trade union scene, it is difficult to name their successors. The obvious choice for leadership is Mr. Charles Dukes, this year's president of the Trade Union Congress, whose handsome, regular features have led to his being called "the centurion from Warrington." But Dukes nears retirement. So do two or three of the other veterans, like Andrew Conley and Joseph Hallsworth. British trade unionism is likely to be entering a new phase shortly, producing scientifically-trained leaders whose principal qualities will be technical brilliance rather than demagogy. They will be even more thorough than Bevin in some of their performances. But not nearly so picturesque. The most forthright leaders in the interim period are Arthur Deakin, of the transport workers, Will Lawther, of the miners, and Jack Benstead, of the railwaymen.

Bevin himself has taken the centre of a greater, wider stage. He once said that he was reluctant to use the word patriotism because its frequent currency had debased its true meaning. But he is a patriot, all the same.

His interpretation of patriotism is more practical than emotional. He holds that in Britain all people can share the four essentials to a good life. Security in jobs. Just reward for labours. Homes in which workers can live in privacy and dignity. Opportunities for cultural and educational advancement. But Britain cannot provide all these, Bevin argues, unless the world, too, is economically healthy.

He is not, therefore, a revolutionary in the accepted political sense of the word. This has made him suspect to the more extreme politicians in his own country. They accuse him of having retreated from an extreme political philosophy which they think he embraced in his youth. They are wrong. There is no evidence that Bevin ever was an extremist by present-day standards. His first incursion into local politics was regarded as an impertinence merely because he was a poorly-paid workman, concerned in the fate of those even poorer than himself.

In the years of his development, he devoted himself almost entirely to industrial and not political organisation. It led to him entering politics late in life—when, in fact, he was on the point of retiring from public life altogether. He was in his sixtieth year when he first entered the British House of Commons—only five years ago. It was late for any man to become a politician—perhaps too late to become Prime Minister.

He brings some prejudices to his latest, most exalted office. He may make some mistakes because he is such a decisive man.

But there is one mistake he will never make. He may appear to be an individualist. In fact, he is a team player. His words and his actions have always either reflected decisions already taken or have been subsequently confirmed by those he represents. He has never acted contrary to the desires of his team, whether that team be his union executive, his political party, or the Government of which he happens to be a member—National or Labour. He prides himself on knowing his people. He never tires of talking about the hopes and aspirations of the Common Man.

He says, "I know them. They are my own people."

He is the most Uncommon Man of them all.

It was Quentin Reynolds who demanded characteristically, "What makes Bevin tick over so effectively?" Obviously, there is no simple recipe. There is only one Bevin. He had vision. That made him realise the value of a strong organisation for his fellows. It gave him courage to experiment in his proposals before the British Trades Union Congress, because failure to carry the majority of his colleagues would not have been total failure. He would have succeeded in turning their minds towards the direction where his own was set.

But he never failed in these experiments, although there were times when his victories were close. He had another quality. It was a sense of realism, which prevented him making extravagant demands. And he had a sense of timing which taught him when to retreat and compromise—and when to return once more to the offensive.

Now all these qualities are instincts. They can be developed but not acquired. They are the compensations with which Bevin has been blessed for lack of opportunity and education in his youth. They are qualities which would have served him handsomely in other branches of human activity, notably in business. The fact that he chose and stuck to his calling has brought him dividends more precious than gold—the faith and trust of hundreds of thousands of those whom he has led during the past thirty years.

Bevin is conscious of this. Sometimes it makes him appear arrogant. It will always make him a force. And that is what he will continue to be, so long as he elects to remain the voice of the people. His people—the members of the trade unions. It is a conception that will doubtlessly lead to such apparent incongruities as the approval of some die-hard Conservatives, and the violent criticisms of many extreme Left politicians. But the idea of the trade union handling of foreign policies is not so ludicrous as some of the conventionally-trained diplomats might suppose. It is more interested in economic advancement than in political advantage, in open discussion than in secret diplomacy, and most of all, in the preservation of peace. Those are the theories. It will be Bevin's mission to put them into practice. It will be a difficult job. But Bevin's life story is not more than a series of difficulties overcome.

CHAPTER II

LAND OF LONG MEMORIES

IN the town of Winsford in Somerset they pride themselves on their isolation and their sense of continuity. There are few changes there. The nearest railroad station is still nine miles away—at Dulverton, and it is doubtful whether such a modern invention as the railway tracks will ever come nearer.

Now all this helps individual and communal memories. Folk live long in the reckless natural beauty of this village. Why, in this month of November, 1945, they tell you with natural pride of the order old Steere, the village builder, has just given his tailor. Steere is 92. Steere has got himself measured for a new suit with two pairs of trousers. He just knows from experience that one pair of trousers is a poor investment for such an active man as he. Besides, getting measured for another suit eats into his time, fully occupied just now in catching up the arrears of house repairs which the war accumulated.

But 'tis not of Steere and his trousers they talk just now in Winsford. A revolution has hit the place. In two short months it has experienced three changes. Three tremendously important changes. A new vicar—a new policeman—a new landlord at the Royal Oak, the only inn in the village, which for six centuries has looked out with almost insolent detachment first across a diminutive patch of green grass, then across the turbulent, musical stream which is given the courtesy title of the "river" Win, and then upwards to the knobbly knoll on whose sides most of the village clings.

Three such vital changes in fewer months make the good folk of Winsford declare in their homely Somerset accents that the world is obviously unsettled.

But they take comfort from the things and the persons that are constant. Like the 'bus service that calls at the road crossing a mile down the valley twice a week, like the old carrier did thirty years ago. And Mrs. Veysey.

What a curious experience Mrs. Veysey has had. For more than eighty years she has lived in these parts. For nearly half that time she has been the village postmistress. All her life she has been a pillar of the Methodist cause in this neighbourhood. She has been, this gentle kindly old soul, a servant of the community. She remains so. The passing years have greyed her hair but left her eyes clear and her memory keen. Which is as well. For in recent years a newer and greater fame has come upon her.

For she was the first teacher Ernest Bevin, His Majesty's Secretary of State for Foreign Affairs, ever had.

As his fame has grown nationally and internationally, so has her's in the little world of Winsford.

True, other inhabitants remember Ernest Bevin being born. No one now living, however, has quite the intimate and direct association of Mrs. Veysey with such an event. It was Mrs. Veysey who comforted the harassed Diana Mercy Bevin in that spring of 1881 when her fifth and last child was born. Diana Bevin, as Mrs. Veysey calls her in contrast to the alternative name of Mercy Bevin by which her distinguished son remembers her, had been left a widow only a few short months before.

It was Mrs. Veysey who kept an eye on the growing family as Diana Bevin resumed the chores by which she and her children lived. Diana Bevin was the village midwife. She gave a hand on special occasions in the administration of the Royal Oak, favoured then as now by sudden incursions of guests. Mrs. Veysey says, "The old landlord of the Royal Oak used to say he didn't know what he would do at times without aid from Diana. She was capable and she was quick and she was a kind soul who would help anyone."

And it was Mrs. Veysey who taught the little boy Ernest in Sunday School. Mrs. Veysey pauses a moment. And then memory helps her to qualify such a claim. "Well," she adds, "that is, if you can call it 'teaching.' You see, Ernest liked to hand the hymn books and the testaments round to the other children. He would get cross if this was denied him. So I always let him do it, and then he would come and sit down beside me, and I am afraid he would pay little attention to the lessons until it was time to collect the books once more. You see, he was only three. He liked to feel he had some part in running the class, I suppose."

Mrs. Veysey looks up sharply. She knows what is in your mind. She knows that you realise she is talking so meticulously about something that happened more than sixty years ago.

So, without a word, Mrs. Veysey leaves the business of the

King's mails to her two friendly smiling daughters and trots off
to her little parlour and returns with a framed faded picture which
she hands over the wire grille for you to inspect for yourself. And
there, defying further doubts, is the inscription recording that the
picture was taken on the annual "outing" of the Winsford Methodist Sunday School on a July day in 1884.

Further, sitting prominently in the front of the group is a little
pale-faced boy in a black velvet suit and a wide-brimmed white
straw sailor hat. And Mrs. Veysey gives a little chortle of delight
as you point to this little boy in the front of the picture, and says,
"Why, you'd recognise him anywhere." Miss Veysey, senior,
comes in from a back room where she has been despatching a
telegram, to say, "Yes, and we have his little oak chair with arms
which we always refer to as 'The Seat of the Mighty,' haven't
we, mother?" And they all laugh merrily as they reveal this great
and treasured family joke.

Mrs. Veysey feels that your prompt recognition of the boy in
the velvet suit entitles her to recall, and you to hear, other
memories of those far-off days.

There came into those wooded valleys shortly after Ernest's
birth a travelling evangelist. This holy man in his frayed, green-
black frock coat had whipped up the south-western counties of
England into the frenzy of a religious revival.

The great natural theatres in the open air at the foothills of
Exmoor were filled with inspired hymn-singing during those
sultry afternoons. The travelling preacher warned his ecstatic
congregations that in the days that would follow his departure
there would be many "back-sliders." He thundered, "You will
return to sin," but the multitudes called back that they were
truly converted and would be steadfast.

Diana Mercy Bevin said little. She was a practical woman. She
realised that if the cause was to be sustained there must be a
larger meeting place than the tiny hall where the faithful few, like
Mr. Shakespeare, Mrs. Veysey's father, and his friends had
hitherto foregathered. And so Diana Bevin took up what was to
become the ruling obsession of her last years. She set about
collecting the pennies of her neighbours, of the families on whom
she called professionally, and even of guests at the Royal Oak to
help the fund for the building of the chapel which stands today
on the high road out of the village towards Devon. It stands at the

foot of the hill on which most of the village is built. Just as the
Established Church, with its bold Norman tower, stands on the
crest of the hill and dominates the whole neighbourhood.

Mrs. Veysey recalls, "There was no trouble which Diana
thought too great. She had a great sense of fun yet she was gentle.
She was thorough in all she did—spotlessly clean she kept her
home, though, poor soul, she worked hard throughout the day
away from it. Her children helped for they were growing up and
there was a great gap in years between the older ones and little
Ernest."

Diana Bevin was in the middle of this mission for her religious
cause when she died in her little home—the last house in the road
which clings up the side of the hill behind the Royal Oak towards
high and bleak Exmoor.

The vicar's disapproval of Diana Bevin's dissenting influence
in the little community went to the length of debating whether he
was called on to permit her interment in the holy ground of his
church, beside the orthodox and faithful Prings, Tapps and
Bristows of the little community. Indeed, at one time the vicar
said he would refuse. His final attitude was not known until the
day of the funeral. It was sealed by the size of the congregation
which had gathered to bid her farewell. The whole village was
there.

Mrs. Veysey remembers that day. She remembers the pathetic
picture of the little six-year-old boy who clung, miserable and
bewildered, to the hand of his grown-up sister Mary.

But here is the curious thing. Mrs. Veysey only barely remembers Diana's husband, who was a farm worker, and the other
Bevin children. Yet they, too, were scholars in her Sunday school
class. She explains, "There was 'something about' Diana and
little Ernest." Thus the memory of the old folk in this community,
as in others, is high-lighted by the distinctive. There are Bevins in
Winsford to this day—children of another brother. Jack Bevin
cousin of the Foreign Secretary, is the gardener at the Royal Oak.
Naturally, he is proud of cousin Ernest's present eminence, but
the ties between the two branches of the family were not maintained after the death of Diana. Jack Bevin is laconic about his
cousin. He straightens himself from his flower beds, pauses and
says, "I reckon Ernest has done well for himself." Once a gushing
visitor to the hotel, discouraged by Jack Bevin's refusal to be

madly enthusiastic about it all, petulantly declared, "Well, Ernest has given distinction to the name." Jack paused, crinkled his nose as he searched the sky for weather signs, and then said slowly and with shattering simplicity, "That is so, ma'am," and went on with his planting. That is the way of Winsford. There is a placid acceptance of the fame of one of its sons. But it hides a deep pride. It is personal rather than political, because in this part of the world they do not vote Bevin's way.

Thirty-two years after the funeral of Diana Bevin, Ernest Bevin drove over to Winsford with one of his trade union lieutenants. By this time he had become well known as a leader of men. He stopped to find anyone who looked like being the oldest inhabitant, and found an old toothless shoemaker, whose eyes were bleary and whose voice was cracked, but who was blessed with the Winsfordian trait of a good memory. Bevin mentioned his own name. The old shoemaker put down his awl, adjusted his spectacles on the bridge of his nose, and demanded, "Be ye Mercy Bevin's boy?"

Bevin nodded, and then turning to his colleague, whispered, "It's my mother they still remember." The old shoemaker murmured, "She was a willing soul and a good woman. Aye, ye don't meet such women often nowadays. I'll say you are a credit to her name." And with that he went on with his job. He had given his greatest praise to Bevin. It was the tribute Bevin appreciated most of all.

He took his aide up the moorland road to point out the house where his mother died. It was dilapidated, and the winds from Exmoor tore through a great rent in the roof into the room where he had slept his childhood. His thoughts were far away as he said softly, "I've got her picture."

For more than twenty years the photograph of Diana Mercy Bevin has been given a place of honour in her son's private office in Transport House, London, headquarters of one of the world's most powerful trade unions. It shows the wide forehead, the clear eyes, the full lips and the firm chin of the mother Ernest Bevin only vaguely remembers but cherishes deeply.

One of the biggest problems created by the death of Diana Mercy Bevin was the future of Ernest. His two brothers and two sisters had grown or were growing up. They were starting their own lives. They were scattering. It is obvious now that Ernest's tender years were an encumbrance to them and to him.

His eldest sister, Mary, had recently married George Pope, a serious-minded young railway man, and because there was no satisfactory alternative, it was to the Popes that young Ernest was sent to live at Bishop Morchard, a beautiful hamlet outside Crediton in East Devon, about thirty miles from Winsford.

Soon they moved to the neighbouring village of Copplestone, nearer Crediton, to a house on the Barnstaple road with the curious and whimsical name of Tiddly Winks.

It was here he spent his boyhood from seven to eleven. It was from Tiddly Winks that he went to school across the valley two miles away to Colebrook.

All that ended more than half a century ago. But Copplestone, like Winsford, remembers. It should. Copplestone is so old that the Celtic stone column which stands in the centre of the village has had its hieroglyphics obliterated by the centuries, and archeologists can only guess that its origin is in the days when the men of Devon were ancient Britons.

I go to Copplestone on the slender clue that in it lives W. Carby Milton, who is a Justice of the Peace, and that Mr. Milton has lived there all his long life, whose span I can gauge only by the fact that he was a young man when Bevin was a boy. Now Carby Milton is a prosperous linen draper, but then was a country postman, whose daily rounds took him past the cottage of Tiddly Winks.

We stand outside the cottage which now bears the more dignified name of Lee Mount. Mr. Milton explains, "It was a stone mason, Mr. Lee, who bought the cottage and he changed the name. He didn't like to be known as the man from Tiddly Winks."

Across the road from the cottage is a field which slopes steeply upwards. Down the face of the field two icy-cold rivulets flow from springs near its summit. They break through the bottom hedge into the gutter of the roadway, and then the combined cascade disappears into a culvert built under the roadway.

Mr Carby Milton looks at this stream with the curious faraway expression of a man throwing his mind back over a span of half a century.

In his pleasant, quietly modulated voice, he murmurs, "Yes, I can see young Ernest Bevin now—standing there where an old water trough used to be doing such hum-drum chores as washing potatoes, cleaning shoes, or something like that."

Mr. Carby Milton pauses. "You may be surprised," he suggests, "that I should remember such trivial things after so long an interval ? The great feature of life here in those days was its orderly regularity and punctuality. We all followed it. I would pass up this road from Copplestone every morning on my post-man's round within a minute either way of 7-30. Young Ernest would be there—at his post of duty, as it were. I would miss him if he wasn't."

In the evening, Mr Milton recalled, the young men would gather to gossip or debate in little groups around the old stone Cross in the village. The younger lads would play around. But they disappeared to their homes on the first stroke of seven o'clock from the chiming clock in the Post Office.

He shakes his head, a trifle sadly. "It may seem dull by to-day's standards, but there was something comfortingly sure about it all," he declares.

I suspect, however, that the real fixative in Mr. Carby Milton's mind was the chapel association with George and Mary Pope, and, consequently, with young Ernest Bevin. Congregations in the dissenting chapels were tiny. Each member felt he belonged to a family. The Popes were good, steady-going members of the United Methodists, and every Sunday, punctually and regularly, Ernest turned up at the United Methodist Sunday School, where Carby Milton taught class.

The mellow and magisterial Mr. Milton sees incongruity in the contrast between the well-remembered, though uneventful, boy-hood of Ernest Bevin and the tumult of the middle years which led first to prominence and then to fame. But Mr. Milton resists any temptation to conjure up forgotten incidents. He sees virtue in the Spartan early years, both of Bevin and himself.

"Whatever qualities later experiences brought out in Ernest Bevin," Mr. Milton continues, "this corner of Devon gave him a sense of continuity which he has never lost. Years after he became famous he passed along this way, and told a few of us that coming down to these parts always gave him a deep sense of contentment."

Mr. and Mrs. Pope now live in retirement in another part of

the West Country. With them, Ernest Bevin has throughout the years kept the closest of his family ties.

Mr. Milton gazes round the village he has never left. He shrugs his shoulders, and humorous wrinkles gather round his eyes as he observes, "It wouldn't do for all of us to go about getting famous. Ernest Bevin's enough for Copplestone, and we are all mighty proud of him." And it is then we meet Mr. Cyril Edwards, a prosperous local farmer, sitting in his motor car outside Mr. Milton's shop. They greet each other cordially, and suddenly Mr. Milton says to Mr. Edwards, "Hey, Cyril, you remember Ernest Bevin as a boy at school?" Mr. Edwards replies that he does, but he still thinks the country should be run by experienced business men, and men like Churchill and Anthony Eden, who have been trained to govern, and, in any case, Ernest Bevin was not a particularly good scholar when he went to Colebrook for all that. "Daddy" Sharland, the headmaster of Colebrook, was one of the very best, though stern, mark you, and had turned out some fine boys. "But," continues Mr. Edwards, breathlessly and ceaselessly, "the country has gone mad to put the Socialists in and they'll be sorry one of these days, though, mind you, if it should turn out that the Socialists can really do the job why, I, Cyril Edwards, will be among the first to take my hat off to them and admit that I am surprised though grateful."

Mr. Edwards stops for breath and decides that he would welcome an audience for his strong political views. So he steps out of his motor car, and a fine sturdy figure of a man he turns out to be. He is broad and strong, and his grey cloth gaiters emphasise the staunchness of his legs. He says, "I'm some years older than Bevin," and he quickly notices the surprise on our faces. His red, smooth face, broad and open, shines with pride as he invites us to test the hardness of his arm muscles.

He explains, "I've always kept fit, and I've gone in for boxing and rugby football all my life. Why, when I was a boy I was known as the enemy of the bullies. Yes, there were plenty of them around here, and Ernest Bevin was one of the small boys who used to wait for me to accompany him from Copplestone to Colebrook school. On the way we used to pass Henderson's, the butchers, and there was a fellow there who used to think nothing of whipping the small boys with a great ox-tail as they dashed by on their way to school. Mind you, Ernest Bevin had plenty of guts and could stand up for himself when the odds against him were reasonable, but he was no fool to run his head into a hammering, and besides, he wasn't an aggressive sort of youngster. He had plenty of fun in him, and used to get plenty of laughs as we played bucking broncho with a donkey which Rector Dampery's sons used to collar near the Rectory. And Bevin used to join a gang of us in swimming in the pool near railway property and many's the time that he with the rest of us had to collect all his clothes under his arm and race across a field nude to a nearby copse because George Pope was after us because we were trespassing on railway property. Yes, believe me, young Ernest was up to all the tricks of country boys who had to make their own fun. Don't forget we had none of these cinemas and theatres then, but as I was saying, Bevin was no fool at school, nor was he a scholar either, and I hold that he hasn't had the training that you'd expect from a man who practically rules the country by all accounts, though I don't pretend to believe all I read in the newspapers. Now, I hold that the right kind of Government we want . . . ."

Just then there is a commotion in the square because a herd of heifers being driven to Crediton Market is getting out of hand. It is the raised voice of the herdsman which interrupts the amplification of Mr. Edward's political views; and the sudden appearance of a slight short middle-aged man, who dashes from his stationary motor car to stop the wayward impulses of the cattle.

This is Albert May, the farmer of Beers Farm, Copplestone. No sequence could have been arranged better.

It was to Beers Farm that Ernest Bevin went at the age of eleven. It was then his boyhood and his formal education ended, and his youth and working life began. His employer was William May, father of Albert, and William May followed his father, another William May, in the farming of Beers.

Beers stands aloofly with its back to the Okehampton road, but the length of its wall and the height of its buildings indicate that its tenant is a man of substance. Indeed, back in the village, they talk with respect of the substantial legacies left, first by grandfather William May, and then by father William May, though no one seems precise about the amounts. There are violent nods of approval when someone hints that they were each about £15,000 (60,000 dollars) to £20,000 (80,000 dollars). But the present

tenant, Albert, is unostentatious and amiable. He agrees that his
father was a stern disciplinarian and a man of hasty temper,
though Mr. Milton who recalls these things shows a sense of
delicacy in mentioning them. Albert is now in his middle forties,
so he has no direct knowledge of Bevin's service with his father.
But Albert grew up with Bevin's prominence, and so from childhood he has heard stories of the days which followed Bevin's not-
too-lamented departure from Tiddly Winks. In recalling the
stories he heard from his father and the other farm servants,
Albert follows Mr. Milton's cue and shows politeness and
restraint in mentioning Bevin's past services to the May family.
Tactfully, he says, "His heart wasn't in farming," which reflects
the May family legend that Bevin was a failure as a farm hand.
There was one farm hand who was a direct link with the days of
Bevin at Beers. That was old John Perkins, whose service with
three generations of Mays lasted more than 60 years and ended
with death only two years ago.

Albert is at some pains to stress this. Its implication is clear.
It means that the Mays can't have been such bad employers to
have kept a man in their employ for 60 years. Of course, there is
another side of this. John Perkins is dead, and he has taken the
secret of his contentment with him.

Albert May pays him this tribute. "Of all the people on the
farm," Albert says, "only one forecast a great future for Mr.
Bevin" (Albert always said Mr. Bevin), "and that was old John
Perkins. He always said that Mr. Bevin would end up in Parliament, and he said it when Mr. Bevin worked here. My father
always admitted that. And old John said it because of the way the
boy talked."

Now the most persistent story about Bevin at the farm arises
from Bevin's own memory. Bevin worked hard for his keep and
sixpence (10 cents) a week which he received in cash wages. He
rose at dawn and worked until dusk. It was, and is, a mixed farm,
raising crops and cattle. Then it was about 100 acres in extent,
but now young Albert farms more than 200 acres and leases other
fields from a neighbouring farm.

As the lamps were lit, most evenings Ernest would sit on a low
stool before the great log fire on the open hearth in the low-
ceilinged but spacious kitchen and read the political editorials
from the *Bristol Mercury* to his employer.

A STUDY OF ERNEST BEVIN BY KARCH, OF OTTAWA

Albert interjects here to say that it cannot be for his father. Doggedly and loyally Albert declares that his father was one of the best scholars for miles around, and would need no one to read to him. And Albert dashes off to produce a framed example of his father's penmanship. It was in a clerkly well-formed hand, written by William May when he was leaving school in 1869. Probably his last effort in school. But then Albert softens and concedes that it was probably to his grandfather, William May, senior, that Bevin read, because the bearded, erect old man became blind in his later years. (As I mentioned earlier, Bevin now says that he read to his master during his service at another, unnamed, farm.)

Nevertheless, whoever was the listener, the fact is well established that Bevin remembers with gratitude the welcome respite and the new interest this political reading gave him. He has gone so far as to say that it was this reading which first awakened his political interest. It is easy to understand how steadfast old John Perkins would have been impressed to hear the boy repeat out in the fields or in the stockyards the comments he had read only the evening before from the *Bristol Mercury*. Those readings were variations on the same theme. On the one hand was stressed the glory, the majesty and the goodness of the great William Ewart Gladstone, then forming the last administration of his long Parliamentary life. Before the end of these Bevin readings the Grand Old Man retired from public life and was succeeded by Lord Rosebery, who was as much the object of sympathy at having to shoulder such a burden as the succession to the infallible Gladstone as respect as the leader of the Liberal Party—the only Party that mattered then in West Country farmhouses.

There were exceptions to these peaceful and elevating political interludes. The farmer had a well-developed sense of sociability, and on the average of one evening a week was visited by his neighbours.

It was then the task of the boy Bevin to unharness and groom the cobs and ponies of the visitors, then sit silently in the corner of the kitchen until shortly before the visitors were ready to leave.

Bevin did not object to these social evenings for two reasons. By this time he had on his own account absorbed the urge to follow the reports of the *Bristol Mercury*. While the others chatted about the affairs of the countryside, Bevin went on with his

c

reading. He was interested enough in the affairs of others. He has always been that. But he dare not run the risk of intervening in the conversation to receive a humiliating rebuke. So he curbed his tongue by concentrating on his reading.

Then, after resaddling the ponies or preparing the gigs or traps he would, as often as not, be given a penny by the guest.

There was little to spend this money on. True, Crediton was barely five miles away, but the boy was given little spare time. Circumstances forced him to become a hoarder of money. It was not a habit he retained. Then, he kept his little store in an old cocoa tin in the corner of his bedroom.

Albert May and his bonny, red-cheeked wife took me to this bedroom. Narrow winding stairs lead directly on to its floor from the outer yard. Like other rooms in the farmhouse it has low ceilings. It is spacious enough and, being at the side of the house, it overlooks the muddy stockyards, flanked by massive though rather depressing outbuildings made of a mixture of straw and mud, called, locally, cob. It is very like adobe and lasts as long.

Now the bedroom is used as a store for the unwanted and redundant toys of the two May children.

Suddenly there is a new voice downstairs, Cyril Edwards has driven up to Beers farm to resume his political exposition and his reminiscences. Mr. Edwards dominates the conversation until he is begged to stop, but in spite of his misgivings about Ernest Bevin's qualifications, he suddenly makes a curious appeal. Adopting an attitude inspired by his half-century-old memories, he says sternly, "Next time you see Ernest, tell him from me that I hope he'll do everything he can to keep friendly with Russia." And with that, Mr. Cyril Edwards, once the protector of a little pale-faced boy, stalks cheerily out to his motor car and is about to drive away. He pauses, and ruins the effect of his unexpected solicitude for Anglo-Soviet relations. He shouts back, "Got to hurry because I have to see a football match in Exeter this afternoon."

We walk out to the garden in front of the lemon-coloured farmhouse. Beneath us the valley first dips and then rises to the sombre heights of Dartmoor, seven or eight miles away, arrogant in its perpetual sullenness.

We can do no more than compare notes on how Bevin came to leave Beers. He stayed there two years. The end came suddenly.

One morning Bevin walked into the store-shed on the outskirts of the farmyard. He was dismayed when he saw the mountain of mangles and turnips which had been pitched into the shed. It was his job to chop these roots for cattle food. It threatened to eat up the whole of that day. The monotonous hand-turning of the grinder's rusty wheel was a dismal prospect. Philosophically, he settled down to it. As his hands turned and his arms and back became sore his thoughts were miles away. He did his task mechanically and listlessly. After an hour or two the pile of unground mangles seemed to have diminished little.

Suddenly there was a roar. Bevin jerked back to his surroundings with alarm.

Beside him stood William May, junior. His face was contorted with rage. The farmer pointed jerkily to the smallness of the work which had been done.

There are two versions of what followed immediately afterwards. One, from Bevin, that William May blindly picked up a stout pick-shaft and thrashed him across the back.

The other, told by old John Perkins to his cronies, that Bevin, anticipating May's intention, seized a sharp-edged tool, like an adze or a bill-hook, brandished it so fearsomely before William May that the latter dashed into the kitchen and locked himself in a cupboard until the irate boy could be heard clumping his way up the wooden stairs to his bedroom to collect his money-box and his few possessions, storm downstairs again, and out of the farmyard never to return.

Albert May was handed down neither of these versions. All he was told was that there was a "rare old barney."

Bevin walked down the steep lane, highly banked on either side by the deep red earth of Devon, half a mile to the railway station. His worldly fortune was small—small enough to stuff into one red handkerchief.

He crossed the Barnstaple road and therefore near the house called Tiddly Winks. He was Bristol bound. He said farewell to his boyhood and too-early youth with few regrets.

CHAPTER III

BRISTOL, CITY OF ANCHORAGE

BEVIN'S earliest days in Bristol had a frightening loneliness about them. He knew one or two people in the city, but they were not helpful. They were preoccupied with their own troubles. They were repelled by the manner of Bevin's departure from Copplestone. Their attitude was quite plainly that Bevin had chosen his own course and must put up with the consequences.

His knowledge of cities had been limited to one or two visits to Exeter. Bristol, the metropolis of the West, seemed huge and unconquerable by comparison.

Not that his thoughts were then influenced by any spirit of conquest. There were many more pressing needs, all concerned with the mere business of existing. For Bevin's worldly wealth was down to six or seven shillings. As urgent as finding a shelter was finding a job.

These were times when Bevin knew despair and hunger. Twenty years later he made a significant defence of theft—in some circumstances. A man who was willing to work but could not find a job, and whose family was starving, was justified, Bevin declared, in stealing food. He had known himself what it was to be one of the unwanted.

The strange, lost boy of thirteen, however, with no binding home ties, no domestic anchorage, was prepared to accept any drudgery as long as it gave him breathing space to establish himself. And the first job he secured reflected this desperation.

It was in the Priory Restaurant on the old Drawbridge, near Bristol Centre. He had to be there early enough in the morning to wash up the soiled crockery left by breakfast customers, and late enough at night to polish the plates left by supper clients. In those days there was no "restrictive" legislation limiting the working hours of the great unorganised. There was only one influence operating. It was the general acceptance that a man who had a job was lucky. There were no shop hours. Establishments kept open as long as there were likely to be customers.

Bevin's pay was a shilling a day. Much more important was the fact that the boy got his meals "on the house."

He stayed in the job just long enough to get the hang of the city and to prospect for new openings. That took about two months. He longed for an open-air job. The boy who had spent his childhood on the edge of the great moors, and his earlier working days on the uplands of Devon was stifled by the confinement and nauseated by the smells of the city restaurant.

He found his escape to freedom as a van boy attached to one of the two-horse lorries which carried the mineral water bottles of the old-established firm of Brooke & Prudencio around the city.

On balance the change did not mean financial advancement. True, his new employers paid him ten shillings a week, but now he had to provide his own food and his appetite was disconcertingly sharpened by his life in the open air.

It was a losing fight. It was impossible for the growing young fellow to exist on such a pittance, so he moved on to his next job. This time he became a conductor on the City's tramways. He got two more shillings a week, but he also made some bitter discoveries. Chief of them was that he was temperamentally unsuited for the job. The youth at that time was introspective and brooding. He was harassed by penury and suffered from the isolation of a series of unsympathetic lodgings. He got an insight into the working conditions of transport workers which helped him tremendously in later years, though at the time he was gathering such knowledge its ultimate value to him was quite unassessable. Indeed, it was only by a process of retrospective philosophy that he was able to invest those dreadful days with any value at all. He was living them when living was the only thing that mattered, and before he acquired a higher motive for his energies.

It says something for his relations with his old companions in the establishment of Brooke & Prudencio that he was able to return to them after the burden of life on the tramways became insupportable. And he went back on better terms—this time as a driver and at 15 shillings a week. He considered this his first real man's job, and he continued at it until he was 18. Then he transferred to a rival firm, of John Macy's, of Old Market Street, and here, on a wage of 15 shillings and a commission on the sales of his mineral waters, he settled down.

His life became fuller than it had ever been. On Sunday afternoons he attended Logan's classes in Newfoundland Road. The pastor, the Rev. J. Moffat Logan, appears to have been a remark-

ably active man. In the days before Nonconformity allied itself
with Labour politics, Mr. Logan was actively associated with
pacifist movements in the city and was personally intimate with
the active spirits of the lively Socialist groups which flourished in
the city.

These activities of Mr. Logan's caused some criticism among
the more respectable members of his congregation, but his
pastoral reputation was retrieved by his ministerial energies. And
"Logan's classes" were the best-known and most popular of
them all.

This was really a mass bible class which was conducted so
attractively and unconventionally that it became a feature of
Sunday life among the thoughtful young shop assistants and
artisans of the city, particularly those who were in lodgings and
had no family associations with other places of worship. It was a
fore-runner of the Young Men's Christian Association. Its main
feature was the discussion which followed the address given either
by Mr. Logan or one of his associates.

Bevin soon became prominent. His questing mind responded
to the stimulus of the discussion. There were no inhibitions in his
approach to any topic. Most of these topics dealt with sociological
problems, because it was Mr. Logan's intention to induce his
students to apply the tenets of Christianity to modern problems.

Bevin's vocabulary, recalling some of the phrases he had read
years before in the *Bristol Mercury*, was unusually large, although
some of the pronunciations gave him some trouble. He had
learned so many of his words by sight and not by sound, and to
this day he betrays this on occasion. But there was no doubt about
what he meant to say. His clarity was outstanding in Logan's
classes, and he himself tasted the first delirious joy of holding and
then swaying an audience. Some of the young men and women
called him "the boy orator," but Bevin himself seems to have
discouraged this description by murmuring one day, "I ceased
to be a boy ten years ago." He was barely 21 when he said that.

There are many in Bristol who remember these classes and
Bevin's part in them. I met two old cronies there the other day,
John Winter, a tobacco salesman, and Tom Ellison, who was a
foreman in one of the great paper works in the city. They were
talking about those old days in Logan's classes, and arguing as
elderly men will, about the precise year in which Bevin first

commanded attention there. They compromised eventually by agreeing that "it was about the turn of the century," and old John enthusiastically asked Tom, "Do you remember that afternoon when young Bevin shouted, 'If the Lord returned to Bristol now His rejoicing would be near the slums where poverty can be beaten only by the personal bravery of mothers whose faith is the only hope of their children,' and how later speakers argued that it was sacrilege to bring politics into the Church?" Tom could not accurately remember that, but he did carry with him the memory of Bevin's voice. He said, "It was a bit harsh, but it was powerful and compelling. He made you listen because of the sense he talked, but he looked a bit odd because his face was always so pale, and he wore very dark clothes which seemed to emphasise his pallor, but, no doubt, he chose them dark because he thought they would last longer."

The worthy teachers at Logan's classes tried to persuade Bevin to enter the Ministry. He compromised and became a lay preacher. One of his favourite pulpits was in Poulton Chapel, at that time a popular centre of the Baptist cause. Tom Ellison heard him preach there, and although Tom does not remember the text, he recalls that Bevin made a great appeal to his congregation because of the facility with which he illustrated his points by homely, everyday experiences shared by all.

It turned out that these exercises in formal religion were not much more than stepping stones to the form of politics which Bevin ultimately adopted.

It was in this period that he married Florence Bevin. There was little formality about the ceremony. Few were invited. Indeed, the intimation of such a momentous event was made to his cronies almost casually—a week or two after the event. The very preciousness of it made him secretive. Its effect on Bevin was tremendous. Mrs. Bevin's folk were artisans about the docks. She herself was endowed with an understanding which continues to this day. Her adaptability to the subsequent changes in her husband's fortunes would be remarkable but for the fact that she has shared all his experiences for more than forty years. The union started in sympathy, and grew in understanding. The country boy had known little affection from the time of his mother's death. On the contrary, all his experiences had been blanketed in loneliness. The great contrast came from the moment they set up their first home in Saxon road, in the artisan district of St. Werburgh's, which they rented at 5s. 6d. (1 dollar 10 cents) weekly. It was the first true anchorage Bevin knew. Mrs. Bevin has always been "house-proud." Visitors to that early home soon realised that. One of their earliest regular callers met Mrs. Bevin recently and recalled, "Do you remember how I used to hop from mat to mat to avoid soiling your shining floor?" and Mrs. Bevin laughingly retorted, "Yes—and how you sometimes slid along on a mat?"

Their daughter, and only child, was born five years later. She is now the wife of the amiable Sidney Wynne, who was a first-class newspaper man and is now in film production.

It was contentment at home that gave Bevin's eager mind an encouragement to observe and ponder on the experiences of his neighbours and of the customers he met throughout the day. His job gave him ample opportunities for such observation. It was a sort of roving commission he had. There were regular customers for his mineral waters, small shops, restaurants and hotels, in the centre of the city and along the water front. But there were private customers, too, and while some lived in working-class quarters, others in suburban and residential quarters also bought from him.

Bevin was not slow to mark the contrasts. His hearty affability made him many friends, and his horse sense won him many confidences. As wages went in those days he felt he was not doing too badly. It was a regular job and John Macy was a tolerant employer. His basic wage of 15s. a week was augmented by his commission, which usually ran to another 7s. a week—sometimes more. This gave him a status comparable to a skilled man. But the most important thing of all was that he had a job. It had such good features as a combination of initiative, personal freedom, variety, and the open air.

Bevin soon realised how lucky he was. He heard much of the troubles of others. So much, in fact, that he was unable to resist his own examination of the causes and the remedies for the current twin curses of unemployment and under-employment. In a static population inevitable in a city as old and historic as Bristol, thesecond was more insidious than the first.

Bevin naturally considered the solace which religion might bring to an unhappy people. He was too much of a realist to believe that formal religion alone could heal the wounds from which huge segments of his fellow citizens suffered.

The congregations which he addressed as a lay preacher were, in the main, self-satisfied, particularly among the middle-aged. The consolation they secured from their religious devotions was purely personal in most cases. Much of their chapel-going was an evidence of social respectability. Men in rags were regarded as outcasts. Many chapel folk, though their own larders were low, felt that such an outward admission of defeat involved the forfeiture of respectability. It was an age when appearances counted for everything.

Victoria's long reign had ended, but in the provinces of England its influences lingered on. The Boer War had ended, and its effects were dire. Trade languished, and so the great ports were particularly badly hit.

This was particularly galling to the men of Bristol, for in this radical centre the war had been loathed and condemned. The Pacifists had been strong, and their opponents, known as "the Jingoes," had been bitter. There had been many fights between the two groups, and even such a well-known benefactor as Joseph Storrs Fry, the chocolate magnate, whose prosperous concerns had given employment to thousands of Bristol people, was howled down by the mob when he tried, first to condemn the war, and then to read to them a chapter from the Scriptures.

There were thousands who had been against the war. They hadn't wanted it, and they felt that it was cruelly unjust that they should suffer because of it.

In spite of the noisy scenes during these stop-the-war demonstrations, the local Labour and other Leftist parties in the Bristol area actually finished the war with a higher prestige, stronger membership and more experienced organisation than they had known before it started. But the new problems which faced them seemed insoluble.

One day Bevin saw notices stuck up on the quayside walls announcing weekly meetings of the Social Democratic Federation, to which all were welcomed. At the foot of the handbill, in tiny type, was a reminder that a collection would be taken at the meeting "to defray expenses."

Ernest Bevin mentioned casually to his wife one evening that he thought he would "drop in" to the meeting the following night just to see what it was all about. She knew what he was searching for. They had talked many hours on what was happening around them. Florence Bevin knew even better than Ernest how wives in the neighbourhood were grey in the service of "making ends meet." There were no State unemployment benefit schemes in those days. If a man had no money and could not find a job he simply went "on the parish." Going on the parish meant seeking relief from local officials whose attitude generally showed that they regarded all applicants as thieves robbing the community. But most horrific of all was the threat of being sent to the workhouse. This meant the break-up of the family. Males were sent to one block of the bare, ugly buildings which served as the workhouse, and females to another. So much depended on landlords. If tenants could not pay their rents they were thrown out of their homes in most cases. So the rent became the first charge on wages. Frequently, this meant "skimping" on food, which in turn meant that children were given a disproportionate share of the inadequate groceries, while parents made a pretence of eating.

When Bevin attended that first meeting of the Social Democratic Federation in the old Shepherd's Hall, he sat in the back seat and no one noticed him. It was a small meeting attended by fewer than 30 men. The air was thick with tobacco smoke, which curled in obscuring columns around the hissing gas jets which tried to illuminate the hall.

Some of the local speakers demanded extreme measures to cure unemployment. The word "revolution" was frequently bandied about in the discussions. In those days the S.D.F. prided itself on its advanced thought. Some of its members claimed it was the extreme organisation of all, save the Anarchists. The S.D.F. men had plenty of evidence to support their belief that Society as it existed had gone sour. The stories they told were well-known to every man in their audience, yet the tale of woe never grew stale. No remedy was regarded as too extreme, but the magnet was that they were discussing and considering remedies. There was no meek acceptance about them. They were out to improve conditions for all who laboured or tried to labour.

Bevin said nothing. In his talks with his wife he contrasted the attitude of the chapel folk and the revolutionaries to this same problem of unemployment. To the chapel folk the great panacea was Samuel Smiles's "Self Help." Its record of the reward of industry, the glory of enterprise, and the advantage of assiduity was the second foundation stone of every domestic library. It was always placed next to the Holy Bible.

While he was never converted to the extreme demands of the Social Democratic Federation, he was attracted by the earnestness of men like Frank Sheppard, Watts Treasure, Sennington and Clothier, the leading lights of the Bristol Socialist Society. Most of them became, a generation later, aldermen of their city. They were all future Lord Mayors, though the promise of such distinction was slender enough in those days.

Nor were their meetings all gloom and depression. Far from it. There was a lively sense of companionship. There was jollity and singing. Indeed, these Bristol Socialists went to the extent of compiling their own song book, and training their own choir.

Then came the night when Ben Tillett was the star attraction at the Shepherd's Hall. The place was packed. The little man with the great forehead and the flowing black hair was a hero to the nation's have-nots. His stature among the masses was in contrast to his size as a man. His fame had grown for 15 years, ever since he had led the dockers of London in the strike which lifted them from serfs to men with a voice.

Ben himself was the voice. Whenever he spoke he sounded the trumpet of hope. Bevin was early at the meeting that night, and when Ben roared that the salvation of the working man was to be achieved, not through political revolution but through industrial organisation there were some in the audience who winced, and suspected Ben of weakening. Others deplored the declaration, but assumed that Ben was merely doing a bit of propaganda for his dockers' union. Secretly they hoped that he still believed in the revolution. But there was one who was convinced in a flash that Ben was right. That was Ernest Bevin.

Bevin said nothing that night, but it was then that his face turned towards the road he was to follow to the heights.

Yet, contrary to the popular belief, Tillett and Bevin never developed for each other any lasting, firm bond of friendship. The theory that it was Tillett who "made" Bevin is simply not true. In their very earliest meetings there was between them the natural gulf caused by the fame and success of the one, and the obscurity and diffidence of the other.

Tillett had developed a thirst for adulation. Bevin has always been one who has found it difficult to fawn on the famous. It was no instinctive sense of partnership that either was able to inspire in the heart of the other, but rather a feeling of reservation. Bevin thought there was a trace too much of the showman about Ben. Ben did not take long to suspect Bevin of being too self-righteous.

Nearly a decade later, when Bevin was urged to become a full-time trade union official, first by his workmates locally and then by such a nationally influential official as Harry Orbell, national organiser of the old Dockers' Union, there was no overwhelming welcome from Ben.

Nevertheless, Ben had enough real achievement behind him to be a real, if unconscious, encouragement to Bevin at the time of their earliest meetings.

He met at these meetings a tall, lanky fellow named Dan Hillman. Dan was then 25, two years older than Bevin. A great earnest giant of a man was Dan, quite 6 feet 3 inches. He had a sense of humour and a natural instinct for loyalty to causes and men, which made him the ideal companion for Bevin. Dan's easy-going confidence in the inevitability of improvement was a foil to Bevin's eagerness to get things done. They became buddies, and have remained that way, with no mental reservations in their relationships, to this day. It was Dan who travelled longest with Ernest. They were associates until Bevin became a Minister 35 years later.

Dan worked as a loader on Bristol Docks during the winter, and in the summer he worked in the ice-house, stacking up the bacon, cheese and butter, then being imported in increasing quantities from the United States and Ireland.

Regularly they met a few minutes before eight o'clock at the old Sceptre Inn on Bristol Bridge. Dan on his way to the docks, Ernest starting his mineral round, met in the bare old inn, both found companionship and rum-and-milk at twopence a noggin a warm jumping-off point for the tasks of the day.

Perhaps Dan's greatest service to Ernest in those days was to give him an insight into conditions at the docks. Men shivered in the dawn waiting for a "call" to work. For every job on offer there were four men waiting. The work was casual. A man might be paid off after an hour and receive only the standard rate of six-pence. It was rare for men to get more than three days' consecutive work, and 15 shillings (three dollars) on which to keep their families for a week. But still the crowds gathered every morning outside the dock gates, and every day three-quarters of them shuffled away unwanted. Some went homewards. No need to tell their families the result of their quest. Their mere presence at home explained all. Many men were too ashamed to return home immediately. They hung around Bristol Bridge waiting for the mid-morning call, and then for the afternoon, and then for tomorrow. There were so many always waiting for tomorrow.

It was as bad in the building trades, where wages were as low as fourpence an hour. There were more operatives than jobs, but their plight was not as obvious as the dockers because the building sites were scattered all around the perimeter of the city. Their misery was not as concentrated and plain for all to see as at the docks.

The depression affected factories, too. There were no means of measuring its extent because there was no register of workless. There was no means of fighting for better conditions for many of these men because there was no unity among them. It was everyone for himself.

It could not go on. Men clamoured for something but did not know precisely what they wanted. It was in this mood of frustration that the men of Bristol decided to establish a Right to Work Committee. In this they followed London and two or three of the great Northern centres.

They chose as their first secretary, Ernest Bevin, the carman. It was a voluntary job. Bevin did his organising in his spare time for nothing. He built up a modest fund for the work of the committee from the pence of men in jobs. He thundered at street corners. He wrote letters to local industrialists, who ignored them. He led deputations to the City Fathers, who listened politely and then replied that as the depression was a national affair there was nothing they could do about it locally. Bevin got three things out of these activities. An insight into the minds of men whether they were out of work or in the seats of authority. Practice in speaking. And a local reputation as a dangerous agitator.

But he was registering little solid achievement. About two years after the Right to Work Committee had been formed, when frustration was giving way to defeatism, a pale little man who had been without a job for more than a year shouted hysterically to the committee, "You've done nothing but talk."

Bevin flushed. He knew how true the charge was. He realised that polite and formal approaches might go on for years more without visible effect. His fist banged the committee table, and he roared, "You are right. The time has come to act. We will act."

The first of the Bevin plans was remarkable for its boldness, its simplicity and its dignity. He disclosed some of it to his committee, but there was a leakage and on the first Sunday morning when he planned to put it into effect he found the Horsefair, a great open space near the centre of the city, strongly patrolled by the police. He had to abandon his idea.

Two Sunday mornings later there was a fair congregation, in spite of the raw weather, in the beautiful old Cathedral church of Bristol. The Dean was conducting the service with dignity. The well-dressed worshippers filled the church comfortably. Their frequent and seasonable coughing was drowned by the chanting of the choristers.

Suddenly, the main doors of the Cathedral were opened. Two files of white-faced, poorly-dressed men tip-toed or shuffled quietly to line the side aisles. Ernest Bevin led the men who flanked the congregation on the left, one of the Sharlands marshalled those on the right.

In the congregation were many wealthy merchants and their ladies. The rustling of silks and satins betrayed their nervousness. The coughs of the men conveyed their sense of outrage. The choir ended its chanting. The Dean ascended the pulpit, and with sonority and detachment delivered his sermon, apparently oblivious to the unorthodox presence of the workless men.

Some of the leading burghers glared balefully at Bevin. They did not know him, but he was obviously the leader of these hungry men. There could be no objection to the conduct of the men. They just stood there, as Bevin had instructed them, as silent witnesses of the poverty which riddled a city whose greatest pride was the success of its merchant venturers throughout the centuries. They were living examples of the inequalities of life.

The Dean finished his sermon, and the congregation joined, some shamefacedly, others defiantly, in the final hymn of praise. The workless men, silent and bareheaded, stood back while the congregation strolled out to their carriages.

Then they, too, marched back in an orderly way, without ostentation or jeering, to the Horsefair where Bevin advised them to return to their homes and await developments.

They did not have long to wait after this church parade of the hungry. The city was shocked. The cathedral authorities did not complain about the invasion of their church. Nor was there any criticism of the conduct of the "invaders." Indeed, they were praised for the decorum with which they had comported themselves.

No, the Bishop, the Dean and the whole Chapter vigorously demanded of their friends and the members of the City Council why something could not be done for these poor citizens. The clergy roundly declared that it was a disgrace to the fair name of the city that so many men should be without work. Many of the leading citizens admitted frankly that until this incident they had been unaware of the extent of the unemployment scourge in Bristol.

Bevin was asked privately by one or two councillors if he had any suggestions to make. Naturally, he was ready. He had waited for years for such an approach. He had worked long for the creation of such receptivity on the part of city councillors. He urged relief work. They wanted to know what sort of work. For years the poor of the city had been treated like felons. They had been given such tasks as stone-breaking and oakum-picking like men who had been convicted of crimes and were serving terms of imprisonment with hard labour.

Bevin demanded the introduction of constructive jobs. He asked the city councillors if they thought the old city was so beautiful and so replete with amenities that nothing more need be done to improve its appearance and services.

At the next meeting of the City Council it was decided to build an artificial lake in Eastville Park, one of the city's spacious though undeveloped playgrounds.

They had to get the approval of John Burns, the old dockers' leader, who was then President of the Local Government Board in the Liberal Government of Sir Henry Campbell-Bannerman. John Burns was handsome about it. He gave a generous grant to the venture and the workless men who were provided with jobs were paid rates ranging from 4½d. (7½ cents) to 6d. (10 cents) an hour—the wages paid to many men in normal productive jobs.

This had its influence on the normal wage rates in the city. Employers soon recognised that productive work should be paid slightly more than relief work. They showed some reluctance about this, but the alternative of protesting to the city council to lower relief rates was unthinkable in the new mood of public opinion. The men who found work on the construction of that artificial lake promptly christened it "Bevin's Lake," and so it is known locally to this day.

It was Bevin's greatest personal triumph to date. Naturally, his reputation grew among the local trade unionists and members of such bodies as the Trades Council and the progressive political groups. In spite of Ben Tillett's oft-repeated advice about the prior importance of trade union organisation, an important section of the local Social Democratic Federation supporters continued to press for political representation on the Bristol City Council. Eventually, they had their way.

It was decided in 1909 to run a candidate in the municipal election for the St. Paul's Ward, a working-class district.

The local committee met to make two decisions. First, they had to select a candidate, and then there was a discussion on the label under which he should run.

They quickly selected Ernest Bevin as their candidate. His achievement on behalf of the unemployed gave him a good claim for support. His election slogan was "Vote for Bevin who fought for the unemployed."

But there was quite a debate on whether he should be called a Labour candidate or a Socialist candidate. Since those days there have been many arguments over the same point, based on the belief that the word Socialist has a more forbidding sound than Labour to the timid, and is calculated to repel the middle-class vote. There were similar notions back in those Bristol days. The debate, for all its duration, must have been so much shadow boxing because when the vote was taken the whole of the committee supported the description Socialist. Dan Hillman commented, "We don't want those who won't back us willingly. We'll have no compromise." The official history of the Labour and Socialist Movement in Bristol, however, records that Bevin was nominated as a Socialist and Labour candidate.

The campaign was conducted with plenty of enthusiasm but with little cash. At the adoption meeting the emptied pockets of all those present yielded less than fifteen shillings (three dollars) and the whole campaign was fought on an expenditure of less than £7 (28 dollars).

Bevin's election address was uncompromising and forceful. He declared, "Docks are a national necessity, and, as a Socialist, I believe they should be nationalised." He ended his exhortation to the electorate, "Think! Last winter in Bristol there were 5,000 heads of families out of work, 20,000 human beings suffering want, and 10,000 paupers, and you will realise the chaos, misery and degradation brought upon us by the private ownership of the means of life. I claim that Socialism, which is the common ownership of these things, is the only solution of such evils."

His opponent was a local business man, J. H. Gibbs, a Liberal, but the biggest thorn in Bevin's flesh was a negro political spellbinder named Quinn, who was especially imported into the area by the Liberals.

Bevin did his electioneering during the midday break, using his mineral water wagon as a platform, and in the evenings. Wherever a crowd was collected, there the mineral water cart pulled up. The candidate would throw his reins over the haunches of his old cart horse, and address the crowd from the driver's seat.

Hardened though Bevin was becoming to dealing with crowds and with hecklers, he had one experience which so discomfited him that he gave up the bout because he could not stand ridicule. It was his habit to wear a short sack-cloth apron to save the wear and tear of his clothes when carrying cases of his mineral waters from his wagon to his customers.

One day he saw a group of working girls standing about outside their factory gate. Beside them were some men and young fellows. Bevin drove up, and as usual stood up to deliver his election speech. Suddenly, one or two of the girls started yelling in derision, "Ooh, look at the big man in the little apron." The fun appealed to the thoughtless girls. Soon they all took up the cry, and chanted the one word "apron" in unison. Even Bevin's powerful voice was unable to pierce this hostile barrage. He drove away, hurt and angry. He was obviously before his time in this district, which for a generation now has steadfastly supported his views and his successors.

Bevin's advent into local politics whipped up the organisation of the old-established Liberal Party. Bevin secured more votes—

D

663—than any previous victorious candidate had secured in that ward. Yet he lost by the biggest majority on record, because Gibbs polled 1,052. In previous elections the electors of St. Paul's were noted for their apathy. It was rare for more than 500 of them to trouble to record their votes.

There was a scene at the declaration of the result. Bevin accused one of the Liberal agents of indulging in illegal practices by divulging the identity of some of his own supporters, and thus invalidating the secrecy of the ballot box.

The point is significant only because of its effect on Bevin. He became a marked man in the rival political camps in the city. He was listed as "an awkward customer." He was soon to receive his first personal experience of the bitterness of an affronted rival political machine.

The local Liberal leaders, totting up all the grudges they had against him—and they included the Cathedral demonstration, the initiation of relief works, the effect of such works on local wage rates, as well as the affront to one of their paid agents— decided that Bevin had to be hounded, not only out of public life, but out of Bristol. Bevin was unbribable. The only known alternative weapon then was starvation.

So Bevin discovered within a week that Bristol had lost its thirst. At least, it had lost its desire for the mineral waters his employer made. It was a boycott.

Every morning Bevin would load up his wagon, and would drive forth on his usual rounds. Every evening he would unload the same cases into the firm's warehouse before parking his empty wagon, and stabling his horse for the night. It went on for weeks. It meant, of course, that Bevin drew no commission above his bare wage of fifteen shillings a week. He had plenty of time to think, and among his conclusions was that it was unfair to his employer, John Macy, who was a Liberal anyway, to have his business ruined. True, John Macy had other carmen, but Bevin, with nearly a decade of service, was the senior salesman.

So after nearly two months of boycott, Bevin stopped John Macy one night and offered to give up his job. The old man put his hand on his carman's shoulder, and said, "Ernest, I know how you feel. Stick it, my lad. I hate those fellows who are doing this to you as much as you do. Besides, we can't give up now. We can't let them win."

So Bevin stayed. It was not to be for long. But he was in his job long enough to have the satisfaction of knowing that he beat the boycott.

The other side weakened, but the determining factor was that most of Bevin's old customers found it difficult to remember the cause of their action. Political passions die fairly quickly in England at any time. In those days the country was in the early stages of a political awakening. There was plenty of evidence that the search for work was as difficult as ever. The more people thought of it the more commendable Bevin's past actions appeared. So those who manipulated the boycott found they had introduced a boomerang. They started people thinking about what Bevin had done, and why he was now being blamed. And in the long run Bevin did not suffer. On the contrary, when his business started to pick up again it did so with a momentum which soon brought his returns up to a higher level than he had ever reached before.

But this improvement occurred when his attention and interests were becoming more and more divided between his job and his hobby, which was getting to know more and more about labour conditions in and around the port of Bristol.

He could sense a growing discontent in the docks in spite of steadily improving trade. Its peak was reached suddenly.

Down in the Tidal Port the management had imported two foremen. They had been working nearly a week before someone suspected they were "Federation" men.

In those days, when trade unions were not recognised by the port employers in any part of the country, there had developed in some ports a system of federated employment. Groups of employers, reluctant to combine for any other purposes, saw the advantages of collecting together teams of workers and minor executives who could be relied upon to work regularly in all circumstances. There may not have been an ulterior motive in the original conception of this plan, but it soon became obvious to some of the employers that here to hand was a team of strike-breakers—if ever there was a strike. And union organisers had been alert to this possibility for a long time. The men in the labour federation became known as "masters' stooges." The term "Fed." became one of contempt among dockers who wished to remain independent of the employers. It was synonymous with blackleg.

The system had been adopted in many of the country's principal ports and the unions had been powerless to prevent its introduction, though they had protested volubly enough. They were on their toes to prevent the extension of the system.

Bristol was one of the most important ports in the whole country which had not adopted the Federation scheme. Jealously the union chiefs watched the port for the first move towards this Federation plan. Hence the significance of two alleged Federation foremen. The men selected a deputation to the management to demand the dismissal of the two foremen. The management was barely civil. It refused to discuss the men's grievances, holding, as has been done so often since, that the appointment of foremen was a purely managerial function and of no concern to the workers.

The men threatened to strike. The management did not take the threat too seriously. After all, alternative work was not too easily come by, and the union's funds still needed considerable building up before a major stoppage could be faced. But when the mighty Ben Tillett and Harry Orbell, one of the national organisers of the Dockers' Union, were called into Bristol by the local officials the whole business assumed a new significance. This, indeed, was evidence of the importance with which the union leaders regarded the "defection" of the Port of Bristol.

Preparations for the struggle were made on both sides. The Port authorities showed their hand pretty quickly. They brought round from Plymouth two shiploads of Federation men to operate the docks. These Federation men were paid one shilling (20 cents) an hour—big money in those days, just about twice the normal rate of pay. They were supplied lavishly with food and with liquor after working hours, and they used the two transport ships, the *Lady Jocelyn* and the *Lady Armstrong*, as floating hotels. The ships were moored well within the dock premises and under adequate police protection.

This was construed by Ben Tillett and Orbell as irrefutable evidence that the two foremen had been used deliberately as advance guards for the federalising of the port, and that the suspicions of the local dockers' leaders had been well founded. Tillett had plenty of ammunition for his oratorical broadsides.

All the same no one was more conscious than he of the perils of calling a strike. It meant starvation in a short time unless strong relief funds could be organised quickly. And this business of organising relief had few successful precedents. Few other unions had grants to spare to the dockers. An appeal to the public was a chancy business.

Still, it had to be faced, and quickly. Tillett and his advisers did an unusual thing. They called on a non-member to take charge of the local relief fund. That was one of the results of the reputation Bevin had established for himself through his work for the local unemployed.

Tillett was in tremendous form. He roared that the high wages and good conditions being given to the Federation men were only a "blind" to smash the union. It was obvious that this approach had a double motive. While he wanted to stiffen the morale of his own members, he was also anxious to wean away the Federation men from what he regarded as their unnatural allegiance. Tillett declared that as soon as the strike ended, if it was beaten and enough Bristol men became federated, the employers would slash wage rates still further and the Federated men would share in the reduction and would have no redress because there would be no free union left to fight for them.

The men of Bristol stood by Tillett. Ernest Bevin, busy at his own job of driving his wagon and delivering his wares throughout the day, and busy at organising relief for the men on strike during the evening, found time enough to be impressed, not only by Tillett's crusading zeal and organising ability, but by the solidarity of the Bristol dockers. Non-unionists flocked into the union. Bevin knew the significance of this gesture from men who had never earned enough to put anything away for personal contingencies.

It was a victory for the Bristol men and for the union. The Federated men were withdrawn. Bristol remained a "free port." It was a victory for principle. For the cost in wages to the men who had been on strike, and the depletion of the union's funds were both disastrous.

But then someone made a shattering discovery. It turned out that the two foremen over whom the trouble had started were not Federation men after all. The strike had really been fought over the refusal of the port authorities to recognise the union. Still, the men showed plenty of rejoicing in the retention of their freedom to organise themselves in their own way.

The victory had another effect. It showed men who followed unorganised callings the weakness of their own position compared with the men inside the unions. Two men were particularly intrigued by the position in Bristol. One was Ernest Bevin. The other was Bill Ellery.

Ellery was the Gloucester organiser of the old Workers' Union. He saw the possibilities of extending his activities to Bristol, about twenty miles from his base. He sent handbills over to Bristol calling on all unorganised workers to attend a conference to establish a branch of his union. That meeting was never held. Because of Bevin.

He took the view that there were already enough unions in Bristol without importing more. The trouble, he declared, was that the unions in the city had not done their job well enough. He saw Ellery and explained the position to him. The settlement which led to the withdrawal of Ellery was amiable enough. Bevin had won his first victory of persuasion in purely trade union affairs. It created a precedent for territorial exclusivity of trade union organisation. Strange that it should have been the Workers' Union which gave him this clue to his abilities. Almost exactly twenty years later, when he had a long record of successes behind him, he was to amalgamate the Workers' Union into the vast organisation he helped so materially to create.

He gave Ellery his word that he would convene a meeting of local workers. This he did within two weeks of making his promise. The meeting was held on a Sunday morning, October 10th, 1910, in the Shepherd's Hall.

Bevin himself was elected chairman of the meeting. In his speech from the chair he enunciated a policy which he was able to follow for thirty years. As Bevin himself repeated frequently in later years no individual makes the policy of a union. Bevin had the instinct, however, of gauging the desires of his fellows with remarkable sureness. What he said invariably found an immediate response and support. He knew his own people.

He adapted some of the basic views expressed earlier by Ben Tillett, but he gave them his own distinctive treatment. He urged the value of industrial organisation as the surest and shortest path to economic improvement.

It was an enthusiastic meeting, and in it was born the carmen's branch of the Dockers' Union. Bevin's prominence in convening the meeting made him a natural choice for first chairman of the branch, although he, like all the others, was a new member.

It was an unpaid job, though there was plenty of work to do. Six months later Bevin was made a full-time trade union official on the recommendation of the carmen of Bristol. The pay was less than £2 (eight dollars) a week. But the job had definite prospects. That is what Bevin thought, and what is more, that is what he proved.

CHAPTER IV

WHEN LEADERS WERE SCORNED

IT was poetic that in his first days as a trade union leader Ernest Bevin should be as concerned with the welfare of horses as of men.

Yet this activity reflects the essential humaneness of the poorly-paid members of Bevin's union branch. The carters of Bristol supported an agreement made by Bevin that their wages should be based on a load limit of three tons. For piece-rate workers this was a definite sacrifice. Many of them had regularly loaded their drays and vans with loads of five tons, and the more they carried the more they earned. But it had been cruel on horses.

A trace horse had been stationed at the bottom of Bristol Bridge for years to help the overloaded shaft horse up the hill towards the Cathedral. Citizens whose business or pleasure carried them into the centre of Bristol naturally approved of such obvious consideration. But the carmen themselves knew of many hills quite as steep in other parts of the wide-flung city where there were no trace horses. They knew that their own horses suffered from strains and dislocations. But the merchants for whom they worked were concerned primarily with the speedy transit of loads. They offered the carmen a bonus of 1d. a ton on every load carried above the basic three tons. In many cases this was short-sightedness on the part of the employers, who had to bear the loss of prematurely-aged horses. Bevin was quick to exploit this argument with the employers he was able to contact. It was a never-ending job. Most of the employers were small men. They belonged to no association. They were suspicious of such federations, and in nearly all cases actively hostile to any organisation of their own workers. Naturally, they regarded Bevin as their arch-enemy.

Bevin had to change his tactics frequently. He soon realised that to convince every individual employer would take years. So he would vary his approaches to employers with frequent recruiting campaigns among his own people. Thousands of the most poorly-paid carmen had doubts about the benefits of trade unionism. The indifference of the men whose status he was trying to raise was more discouraging to Bevin than the rebuffs of the employers. Patiently and painstakingly he made progress. He would argue with individual carmen who were obviously overloading their horses. He won through finally by persuading the biggest employers in the city to sign an agreement which gave their men as much in wages for observing the three-ton limit as they had formerly earned by collecting bonuses on overloading.

From his earliest days as a trade union official Bevin decided that purely local organisation, though essential as a basis for building up the union and his own reputation, was not enough in itself to satisfy his own ambition.

This was quite obvious from the memoranda and the letters he poured into the headquarters of his union in the Mile End Road, in the East End of London. The men in headquarters soon realised that the workers of Bristol had picked an unusual type to lead them. They could see two features in the Bevin correspondence—energy and soundness of ideas. The two most influential leaders, Ben Tillett and Harry Orbell, made separate visits to Bristol. Ostensibly they went down to the great western port on speaking engagements. They were almost equally interested in sizing-up Bevin. And the notes they compared back in the Mile End Road made them enthusiastic. It was Harry Orbell who went to Bristol to persuade Bevin to accept a roving commission for the union over the whole of the south-western counties, and it was Bevin who put forward the qualification to his acceptance. He said he would accept the offer after he had built up his Bristol centre to the point where it could stand on its own feet. Bevin himself confessed to his most intimate cronies that the Orbell offer was the chance he had dreamed of for months. One of them asked him, "Why don't you get cracking at once?" Bevin replied that he was building up from a sound base. He planned that when he left a place the organisation locally would be in a position to move forward and not backward.

It was a technique that he stuck to throughout his career as a trade union leader.

Throughout his life Bevin has sought to put his relationship with Tillett into his own idea of its true perspective. He will probably never succeed in doing this because of the controversy which developed in later years between the two men.

There is little doubt that Tillett's influence on Bevin in these early years was tremendous if indirect. Tillet had been a national figure since the great London dock strike of 1889. He was picturesque and forceful. He was a brilliant orator and a Bohemian character. It was Ben who said, when asked why he dined in a fashionable West End hotel in the middle of a great industrial dispute, "Only the best is good enough for a British working man."

Tillett in those days was an inspiration to all interested in trade unionism for general workers, especially in Bristol, where he was born. He was a great counsellor because none realised more than he that the old craft unions showed a disdainful aloofness towards what was called "the new unionism."

Bevin himself had plenty of vision. Tillett did not show too much enthusiasm about having Bevin as a full-time colleague. He offered no specific objection, but his luke-warmness suggested an anticipation of subsequent differences.

Bevin took only three months to put "his parish" of Bristol in order before taking over the wider diocese of the West Country. These were terms which came easily to him in those days because his interest in formal religion still lingered on.

Barely had he surveyed the western counties of Somerset and Dorset, Devon and Cornwall before he was transferred by Tillett and Orbell to South Wales, whose western region was being organised by the bearded orator, James Wignall.

Bevin was given the great industrial belt around Cardiff and Newport, as well as those important ports, to win for his union. Two factors made his task almost hopeless. There were too many trade unions in the area. They were highly local, and absurdly specialised. Coal trimmers would not mix with the carriers of flour, iron ore loaders were spurned by stevedores, the bargemen of Cardiff were in intense rivalry with those of Newport. Each little union had its own leader, and each leader was fighting all others. There were many Monday mornings when a leader discovered that most of his "flock" had deserted him over the weekend, beguiled by the promises of a rival leader at some hastily-convened Saturday evening meeting.

Bevin found no overwhelming welcome from the Welshmen. Indeed, he was met with some hostility because in those days there was a wave of resentment surging in South Wales against the "invasion" of Irishmen and Bristolians. To many, Bevin was just another Bristolian. Until they heard him talk. Welshmen,

reared to an appreciation of superb preaching, are good judges of
all forms of speeches. Bevin's impulsive oratory, with its flashes of
emotionalism, made an instant appeal to the Cardiff dockers. One
of them shouted to him, after he had harangued them outside the
dock gates, "You are better than Spurgeon, my boy." This
comparison with the greatest preacher of the day was intended to
be the highest tribute that could be paid to any speaker. So Bevin
made quick progress with the men.

But not with the masters, as all employers were described in
those days.

The employers of South Wales were quick enough to size up
the potential menace of Bevin. This made them more truculent
than co-operative. They were not more reactionary than the
employers of Tyne and Clyde, but, in the main, they were more
highly organised. They were more subtle, too, than employers in
most other parts of the land.   They knew when to make slight
concessions to their own men. But they always made direct association between an employer and his own workers a condition of
such concessions. No union interference for them. Indeed, they
developed into an art the campaign against paid agitators. They
exploited, for this reason, the origins of these organisers. There
was Bevin from Bristol, and a local official, John Donovan, from
Ireland. It seemed improbable then that John Donovan should
become one of the most respected Lord Mayors of Cardiff a
quarter of a century later.

Bevin's comfort was his success with the men. His scourge, the
hostility of the employers.

One of the employers' associations banned Bevin formally and,
as they thought, finally. They announced they would not have
him in the same room as themselves.

Bevin discovered that one of the clerks employed by the
employers' federation was sympathetically disposed towards
Bevin's views. Bevin arranged a plot with this clerk.

The employers were meeting in conference in their office in
Cardiff. They filed in to the meeting and as they sat down around
the chairman in the board room, the clerk deliberately left the
door of the board room open. It happened to be a warm afternoon,
and some of the employers assumed the door had been left ajar
to stimulate a welcome breeze.

Suddenly the progress of the meeting was shattered by a voice from the corridor. It was Bevin. He stood on the doormat, and reminded them in his first sentence that he, too, accepted for the moment their wish not to share the same room with them. "But," he added, "let me ask you to consider this. Half an hour's conference with our representatives will save you half a year's worry. We will ease your labour problems with our constuctive proposals." Then the door was slammed in his face—as he knew it would be. But he had put his message over. Carefully he had selected the statements he threw at them. Rightly he guessed he would be able to put over his three sentences before they recovered from their surprise. Within a month there was a joint conference between representative employers and the men's spokesmen.

But the careful, building-up period of that phase in Bevin's life was held up by the great transport strike of 1912.

It was the first strike called by the Transport Workers' Federation. Most of the transport unions belonged to this federation for the discussion of problems of mutual interest, though each union maintained its own autonomy. Bevin soon saw the value of the Federation though he realised its structural weakness. It was on both that he subsequently built up his own idea of how union amalgamations should be carried out.

The 1912 strike was bitter and protracted. The dockers and the carmen answered the strike call to a man. There was paralysis over the whole country. The press reflected the mood of the employers and of the middle classes. Tillett and Robert Williams, who was secretary of the Federation, were called bandits and highwaymen. They were called reckless and irresponsible. But the men they led were desperate in their desire to achieve better wages and shorter working hours. Over a wide range of industry working hours of 70 a week were not unusual. There was little newspaper criticism of Bevin. He had not yet reached the prominence of public censure. But he was desperately busy. He saw little of his home in Bristol, although he had gone back to the south-western counties to rally the strikers.

The men lost that strike, but the employers showed no magnanimity in their victory. They gloated and they victimised any men who had taken any share, however humble, in the strike organisation. Men whose greatest crime had been the distribution of handbills to announce trade union meetings found themselves on an employers' black-list.

Bevin was sick at heart from the viciousness of the employers' reprisals. He was so moved that he wrote a personal appeal to the great Lord Devonport, chief of the Port of London, the most powerful of all the spokesmen of the dock employers. He urged Lord Devonport to advise the employers everywhere to show some sense of conciliation. Lord Devonport regarded Bevin's letter as an impertinence. He did not take the trouble to acknowledge it.

All this had a disastrous effect on the membership of the union. Thousands of members left it. They said membership was more a hindrance than a help. Bevin had to do some hefty rebuilding. He trudged all over the West Country, establishing centres at Bridgwater and Plymouth, and addressing meetings in remote moorland towns in Devon and Cornwall.

His success in these years was solid rather than spectacular. He was made assistant national organiser in 1913, and succeeded the genial Harry Orbell, who died in 1915, as national organiser. That was the job he held until he became assistant general secretary to Ben Tillett in 1920.

But the titles of his offices gave no idea of the range of his work and his interests.

Bevin accepted the Great War without enthusiasm. He was no Jingo. But neither was he against the war. He was no admirer of the Pacifists like Ramsay MacDonald because he thought them unpractical and remote from reality. He was pre-occupied with the organisation of his own people and the protection of their standards of living. And his success was recognised far beyond the confines of his own union.

In 1915 the Trades Union Congress held its annual conference in Bristol. It was natural by this time that Bevin should be elected one of his union's delegates to the conference. It was his first conference and it was here he made his maiden speech to the T.U.C.

Everything about it was inauspicious. Even the position given to the Dockers' Union delegation. They sat right up in the gallery of the conference hall, remote from the platform and from the miners, the railwaymen, the engineers and the other old-established, slightly superior craft unions.

And Bevin did not get his chance to speak until the Friday morning of conference, the time when the whole membership get restive about catching trains away to their homes, when the organisers want all the outstanding resolutions galloped through, and when president and delegates are impatient of long speeches.

Bevin, with the eyes of the old maestro, Ben Tillett, on him, rose in his place in the gallery and bawled his debut to the conference. He had to shout in those pre-microphonic days.

But the subject of his contribution to the debates of conference makes the incident one of the most fascinating examples of prevision in the whole annals of the Congress.

Bevin got up to move, "This Congress calls upon the Government to appoint a Minister of Labour with full Cabinet rank; that all departments of Labour shall be co-ordinated under the said Minister's supervision, and to include a statistical department which shall enumerate the number of persons employed in the United Kingdom, stating sex, young persons and children engaged in industrial occupations. The Department shall prepare a monthly statement indicating (1) the number of persons employed, (2) (a) number of persons regularly employed, (b) casually employed, and (c) the number employed in any one week. A statement to be prepared monthly dealing with the average wages of persons permanently employed, irregularly and casually employed. A statement also to be prepared of the changes in wages and conditions of employment."

The resolution went on wordily and without attention to syntax to demand closer supervision of dangerous and unhealthy occupations, the administration of local employment exchanges, the establishment of a national department of industrial arbitration and conciliation, of a legal department dealing with trade union law and the registration of trade unions, the introduction of work-providing schemes like afforestation, land reclamation, and canal deepening, and the provision of relief of distress.

Such wide terms of reference would, in later years, have given Bevin scope for an oration commanding nation-wide attention.

On this occasion, however, there was almost a note of apology for daring to call the attention of conference to such a matter at such a stage in the proceedings.

Bevin's speech was much shorter than the terms of his resolution. He said, "In spite of the fact that this resolution is being considered on the last day of Congress, I hope it will be taken quite seriously. As Mr. Lloyd George said the other day, the war has imposed such tremendous duties on the State that, even in his own department (Munitions) it is by far the largest employer of labour in the country. Delegates will know the difficulty we experience in going to one department after another in regard to our interests. We often have to end up where we began before we can get all our wants attended to. In view of the changing conditions which the war is imposing on the industries of the country, I hope the Parliamentary Committee will press for this resolution to be put into operation at once. It has been said that many of the resolutions passed at this conference cannot be dealt with until after the war, but so far as this reform is concerned I suggest that the new conditions forced upon labour make it additionally imperative that this Ministry of Labour should be set up immediately."

Another docker jumped up to second the proposal formally and almost before he sat down the whole conference yelled its agreement. They wanted to finish the business to get away.

There was none of the later Bevin fire in the speech. It was not more than the 'prentice flight of a tyro. Still, through its adoption by the Parliamentary Committee of the T.U.C. (later to be reconstituted and renamed the general council), it was accepted barely a year later by Mr. Lloyd George, who had become Prime Minister in the meantime.

That Bristol 1915 conference was important to Bevin for another reason. War or no war the Trades Union Congress clung to its practice of sending two delegates to the annual convention of the American Federation of Labour. The exchange of delegates had gone on annually since 1894.

There had been only one interruption. That was in 1914. The war had led to the abandonment of the T.U.C's annual conference in that year. Now, in the very next year, the T.U.C. were determined to resume their fraternal association with the American Federation. But earlier that summer the passage across the Atlantic had become a death trap. The U-boat campaign was winning such spectacular successes as the sinking of the *Lusitania*. There were few applicants for the honour of representing the T.U.C. in America. But one of the few was Ernest Bevin. He was selected to accompany Charles Ammon (now Lord Ammon).

It was the first time Bevin had ever left Britain. He had two weeks to prepare. He was ready and eager to visit the New World.

The Convention of the American Federation of Labour was held that year in San Francisco. Bevin was in the United States barely a month on this occasion, but the visit gave him his first interest in international affairs. It was an interest he never lost entirely, although there were long periods in his life when pre-occupation with purely internal industrial affairs gave the impression that he had lost his enthusiasm for the affairs of other nations. Incidentally, it was this curious departmentalisation of Bevin's pre-occupations which was to lead, thirty years later, to some surprise when he was appointed Britain's Foreign Minister.

Bevin, even in his early days, showed a remarkably quick grasp of essentials. So, although he was able to see little of theUnited States because of the time spent in the rail journey across the continent and back, he came back full of the ideas he had assimilated in social contacts with A.F.L. delegates at San Francisco. He was particularly impressed by the educational programmes which some American unions, notably the garment workers, were preparing for their members. It was natural that the American leader of those days who impressed him most was Sam Gompers. For years afterwards he recalled the surprise he felt at the easy unconventional handling of the Convention by Gompers. It was in fantastic contrast to the way he had seen Seddon, the shop assistant, handle the British T.U.C. conference a month earlier in Bristol.

Seddon, a precise and formal character, had stuck rigidly to a time-table which limited most speakers to five-minute speeches. It had to be so to complete the conference agenda within five days. And it has always been so in the British conferences.

But the American conventions have always been marked by a spaciousness and diffuseness strange to British fraternal delegates. Bevin gasped when he first saw Gompers vacate his presidential chair in the middle of a delegate's speech to saunter round the great convention hall chatting amiably with old friends on the floor of conference. But he recognised Gomper's forcefulness and command of the conference. When Gompers paid his third fraternal visit to England three years later, Bevin contributed much to a restricted British effort to repay that American hospitality which remains a legend in British trade union circles to this day.

WHEN ERNEST BEVIN WAS A STRIKE LEADER
A scene in the Covent Garden Strike, 1924

Bevin's formal report to the T.U.C. of his impressions was necessarily restricted in those days by the newsprint shortage caused by the war. And, of course, by the fact that Bevin was a comparative newcomer to wider trade union circles and therefore reflected a modesty which his later, greater fame was to obscure.

There is, however, a touch of the prophetic in the joint report of Bevin and Ammon. It says, "We would call attention to the resolution carried which expressed the desirability that the international movement should meet simultaneously with the diplomats to discuss peace and in the same town or city to use every means that the organised labour of the world has at its disposal to leave Labour's impress upon the new peace of the world."

Bevin put that into his report because it was the American decision which impressed him most. The form of the sentence is pure early-Bevin.

Yet in this same city of San Francisco exactly 30 years later, Bevin's great rival, Sir Walter Citrine, was kicking his heels and bruising his knuckles knocking at the doors of diplomats who paid no attention to the attempt of organised labour to have a say in leaving "Labour's impress" on the newer peace of a more shattered world.

And Bevin was one of the most influential members of a Government which spurned Citrine's efforts—a fact which Citrine was not reluctant to emphasise when he returned to England.

Still, no one could have foreseen in those other-world days of 1915 that any observations of Bevin's would have had significant sequences. But Bevin's habit of spotlighting the essential was being established even then.

Incidentally, in those days, Citrine had not entered the representative circles of trade unionism. He was still an electrician on Merseyside.

For Bevin, on the other hand, the story was one of progress all the time. Britain was in a tight corner for supplies because of the ravages of the U-boats. The speedy discharge of cargoes and the turn-round of a dwindling fleet of merchant ships became one of the most important defence lines of the nation. And one of the most difficult to weld into efficiency.

Lloyd George set up the Port and Transit Executive Committee

E

in November, 1915. An authority of this kind was urgently
needed, for there was no one body in existence which was
empowered to take concerted action on traffic questions connected with the ports of the United Kingdom. There was no
means of securing a bird's eye view of port activities as a whole.

When, therefore, the normal flow of trade began to be disturbed
by war conditions the various parties concerned with the ports
acted independently of each other, and there was the usual waste
and overlapping.

The Admiralty set up one committee to deal with the diversion
of shipping, the Board of Trade another to handle the congestion
in the docks, while the War Office was vitally concerned in the
transport of men, munitions and food supplies. The Port and
Transit Committee successfully superseded these rival interests.

Naturally, the question of labour was of paramount importance.
Great inroads had been made into the ranks of the port workers
by recruitment, and very soon the committee had to recommend
that workers in this category should be exempted from call-up to
military service.

The diversion of incoming ships from one port to another for
reasons of safety was another of its problems. It often meant that
the already limited supplies of labour in a port were totally inadequate to handle the glut of work that resulted and there was,
therefore, dangerous delay at times. The committee, therefore,
made a bold proposal to the Prime Minister and the War Office
in December, 1915—within a month of its formation.

It was that special transport workers' battalions of the Home
Defence Army should be formed for use in the ports as needed.
The proposals were adopted but not put into operation for some
time. Eventually, however, a corps of 20,000 men was formed,
which, while doing this special work, retained its military
obligations.

Bevin was a member of this committee as soon as he returned
from the United States. It gave him his most important national
job in the last war. It did more than that. It gave him an insight
into administration problems which no other dockers' leader had
ever been given. True, many years were to elapse before Bevin
was able to apply this knowledge, but its possession gave him a
confidence which many of his enemies were to misconstrue as
arrogance.

One of the things which Bevin insisted that the committee steered clear of was the "invasion" of the military into civilian work while civilian labour was available. These transport workers' battalions were paid civilian rates by the employers for all the work they did, were only brought in during an emergency, and were sent away again as soon as it was over. They were the shock troops of the water front.

The Port and Transit Executive Committee also set up local committees in each port to advise on the supplementing of civilian labour where necessary by the transport workers' battalions. These local committees included representatives of the Admiralty, the War Office, the Port Authority, and Labour.

Naturally, the committee had its teething troubles. Britain had never tried this tripartite administrative experiment before, and there were many susceptibilities and vanities to be considered. Within six months the committee proved a complete success.

It even persuaded the coal-trimmers of South Wales to work on Sundays.

The committee sent its teams to these Welsh ports. While Bevin and a colleague were supervising Bristol and the ports of the south-west, Robert Williams, one of the leaders of the Transport Workers' Federation, and Colonel Hawkins went to Cardiff, and Harry Gosling, later to be president of Bevin's own union, and Commander Underwood went to Newport.

It was Harry Gosling who recorded the incident which won the battle of Sunday work. He said, "My colleague, Commander Underwood, who was in naval uniform, talking the matter over with me in the train said he had never addressed a gathering of this kind before and asked what he ought to do. I advised him to say what he had to say just in an ordinary manner."

"As I expected," continued Gosling, "we found the men were opposed to working longer hours, because in addition to being Welsh and strict Sabbatarians, they felt they were only piling up enormous profits for the shipowners. It was our duty, therefore, to put before them the need of the troops across the Channel. Commander Underwood had not progressed very far in his speech when the inevitable voice was heard, 'And what about the shipowners?' Like a shot the reply came from Underwood, 'Damn the shipowners'' He could get no further. The audience cheered him

enthusiastically and the resolution to work was carried unanimously."

This incident was symptomatic of the uneasy relationships
which persisted throughout the war between employers and
workers. In some areas, like the Clyde, it broke out into open
strikes. In others, like the coalfield of South Wales, it needed the
personal intervention of Lloyd George to keep the wheels turning.

Bevin clearly foresaw that no permanent improvement of men's
economic standards was being attempted. He knew from his frequent visits to Bristol and Plymouth that the high wages being
taken home weekly by the dock workers were entirely due to
excessive overtime and occasional bonus payments. There was no
stability about it all. He could see that a fight was coming soon
after the war ended. So he kept closely in touch with the movement Robert Williams was sponsoring to have wages agreements
for dockers and transport men made on a national basis instead of
on the ragged local basis which had led to so much trouble in the
past and would lead, inevitably, to a recurrence of friction in the
future.

Bevin spoke at a great national conference of unions in Man-
chester, called by Bob Williams in 1916, to formulate this national
wages policy, but he himself had to become the architect of its
application four years later before any real progress was made.

His personal position grew more and more influential, yet there
was no loosening of his intimate bonds with the workers of Bristol.
His home was still there, though much of his time was spent in
London, in Effingham House in Arundel Street, off the Strand,
to which his union had moved in 1916, in meetings of the Port
Transit Committee, and even on a deputation from the Labour
Party to discuss with Lloyd George the entry of Labour into the
Government.

More and more of the actual administration of union affairs
devolved on him even though Ben Tillett was the titular head.
Ben was still a great national figure, and his visits to the troops in
France brought flattering evidence of his fame among the men in
the trenches.

There was no softening of Bevin's rugged approach to problems
even though his activities brought him into the urbanity and cool
deliberation of State councils. He won the respect of his new

associates on Government committees without sacrificing the affection of his own people.

One evening in late 1917 he was travelling down from London to Bristol with his old colleague, Dan Hillman. As the train drew out of the Paddington terminus, Bevin pulled a letter from his pocket and handed it to Dan.

It was a flattering letter from Lloyd George inviting Bevin to accept a Government post as a labour adviser. Dan said characteristically as he handed the letter back to Bevin, "There you are, Ernie, as soon as you start making an impression they try to 'nobble' you by getting you into Government service."

All the same, Bevin was flattered by the invitation. It showed that he was beginning to force the highest in the land to take some notice of him.

As the journey proceeded, Dan asked casually, "What are you doing this evening?" Bevin replied that he was going to speak at a dockers' rally in Bristol. Dan asked if there was any special importance in the meeting, and Bevin replied that he knew very little about the details except that the organisers had pleaded with him to make certain that no other invitation or business should be allowed to absent him as a big crowd was expected.

Actually, there had been a friendly conspiracy to keep the details secret from Bevin.

That evening he was presented by the dockers of Bristol with an illuminated address and a cheque for £350 (1,400 dollars). It was their thanks to Bevin for all his past efforts on their behalf.

The next day Bevin replied to Lloyd George, declining his invitation with slightly more firmness than he would have done but for the gesture of the dockers of Bristol. Bevin had given no indication that he would have accepted the invitation in any case. There is, however, little doubt that his rejection had not been peremptory. The recognition of his services by his own people was an inspiration to Bevin. He had experienced his fair share of the lot of trade union leaders in sampling more kicks than halfpence.

Not that Bevin was intensely interested in the money. He is curiously indifferent to personal wealth. He is interested in the good things of life for himself and for others. But the mere acquisition of money leaves him uninterested. It has been said with effect that Bevin may be softened with a good cigar but cannot be bought by a million. As a reflection of his attitudes, that is a neat summing-up.

This appreciation of the value of what money can buy was sharpened when the last war ended by his knowledge that the soaring cost of living in Britain meant poverty for millions.

Bevin was acutely conscious of the weakness of the trade union machine to cope with this problem. True, the war had forced many amalgamations. There were hundreds fewer unions. Their wasteful overlapping had been eliminated. But the transport unions, though federated, were still too loosely knit to be really effective against the closer policy-making bodies of the employers.

The employers were aware that a fight was coming, and they calculated that Bevin would be near the spearhead of the attack from the workers. He was emerging from the war with the most enhanced reputation of all the trade union leaders, but most of them had national reputations before the war. Bevin had started from a lower rung and had climbed highest. Naturally, the employers singled him out for close attention.

And when, at the end of the war, he decided to attempt to enter Parliament as a possible short cut to improving the wages and conditions of his people the misgivings of the organised employers were converted to their political wing, the Conservative Party, whose staunchest newspaper supporter was the now defunct *Morning Post*.

The *Morning Post* sent one of its star reporters to Bristol, and the following day the die-hard Tory newspaper announced that there was "dirty work in Bristol."

Its report said.

"There are four Labour candidates in Bristol all coated with the white paint of Pacifism, but you have to scrape well below the surface of their speeches to get at it. Of the four, the only one who is likely to get within measurable distance of Parliament is Mr. Ernest Bevin, of the Dockers' Union, who is contesting the Central Division against Mr. T. W. H. Inskip, K.C., son of one of Bristol's best-known citizens." Incidentally, Mr. Inskip became Lord Caldecote, Lord Chief Justice of England.

Then there was a "cross-head" which said, "How Jacob Jockeyed Esau."

The report continued, "Last year's Lord Mayor was Alderman Frank Sheppard, a local Labour leader, so generally respected that when, under the new Act, the city was cut into four electoral areas and he was chosen as the Labour nominee for the Central Division, the other political parties agreed to stand aside and give him a walk-over. But at the Labour Party conference, which demanded the retirement of Labour Ministers from the Government, his union (the Boot and Shoe Operatives) voted in the minority. That sealed his fate. The Independent Labour Party threatened him with the usual pains and penalties if he continued his candidature, and in the end he had to withdraw. And Mr. Bevin, who is credited with having all along had his eye on this particular constituency, but to whom, as I heard him declare at a meeting tonight, a seat in Parliament was the very last thing he had in mind, was nominated in Mr. Sheppard's stead. The Coalition Party, disgusted with such jockeying, has determined to upset this pretty little pacifist plot."

This suggestion that Bevin had "muscled in" to the constituency was completely false. Alderman Frank Sheppard, one of Bevin's earliest friends in Bristol, had been ill and was unable to take part in the general election of 1918. His union invited Bevin, who had not intended taking part in the fight, to stand in Sheppard's stead. Bevin consented. It was natural that he should have been considered for the candidature, because during the preceding seven years few local men had gained greater fame than Bevin.

He did not deny the *Morning Post* version at the time. It was accepted, then, as one of the natural features of a political fight. Distortion from political opponents was part of the natural fun of the election.

Here is another cross-head which says, "The Road to Complete Control."

"Mr. Bevin, when I called on him this morning," the report goes on, "was very shy on any subject other than his political programme."

"My attitude to politics," he said, "is this. I look upon the Labour programme as capable of immediate realisation as a basis of reconstruction. The most important point of all I value is that a minimum standard of life must be assured. If that can be brought into existence you can begin to develop a very much higher standard of intelligence among the people and produce the

necessary capacity to assimilate ideas leading them on the road to
advancement."

The newspaper asked, "In what direction?" And Bevin replied,
"A further development both of the standard of life and in
opportunities for culture and for fostering the necessary responsibility for exercising more and more control. What I feel is that
while the great mass of the working people are concerned from
one year's end to another in the question whether tomorrow will
bring unemployment or sickness, and cause them irretrievable
loss in the home, you cannot develop the high standard of
mentality which is necessary, nor can you produce a democracy
that is really physically effective. I cannot see how you are going
to build up a higher civilised State unless there is a fundamental
change in the present organisation of Society."

"That is," the reporter countered, "bring about the revolution
which your party is preaching?"

"If my principles are accepted it is a revolution," Bevin retorted. "I stand for a social revolution brought about by a freely
elected Parliament."

Bevin revealed that the oil and seed-crushing men in the Port
of Bristol were threatening to strike, but were only holding up
their strike while Bevin was fighting his election. There were
delays, he said, in having labour problems considered by the
Government and its departments. "And," he added, "the men
are losing confidence now in arbitration."

The reporter said, "But they agreed to it at the outset?" "Yes,"
admitted Bevin, "but there again there is no basis, no standard
accepted. Every arbitration adjusts wages purely on a subsistence
level. You cannot have the schoolmaster ahead for fifty years and
still keep the working classes at only a living wage. It is like
calculating the cost of keeping a horse simply on a fodder basis.
I have been able to get an insight into art, literature and music,
and to enjoy some of the social amenities; and there are thousands
of workmen who value these advantages as much as I do. Why
shouldn't they have them? I have classes running every Sunday
in the different halls of this city, and I find a real greediness among
men for learning."

The *Morning Post* man asked, "What do you teach them?"
"They can take any subject they like, history, politics, anything,"
Bevin replied.

"Pure Socialism?" the reporter demanded. Bevin responded, "Why not? It is a very good subject. You see you can't go on peopling the world with only the two divisions—millionaires and paupers. Both are anomalies in civilised society."

The reporter argued, "Take your own case. You are neither one nor the other." Bevin beamed, "I suppose I am generally regarded as an argumentative kind of cuss who is fairly level-headed. I am connected with twelve or thirteen industrial councils set up through the Ministry of Reconstruction and the Ministry of Labour, and I have really tried to see whether there has been any chance of the employers meeting us fairly. But I do not see any response. All they want industrial councils for is to get us to agree to join them in increasing production so that they may get more profits, and they will pay a little more wages—not real wages, mind, but a few more shillings. That is the sum and substance of the employers' attitude. Talk is useless. You have to use the threat of a strike weapon at nearly every conference in order to get anything."

Mr. Lloyd George, the Prime Minister, had visited Bristol the previous day on one of his great election tours. Bevin commented, "The Labour Party must be doing well here or they would never have brought him down. I think the four of us are going to win."

The *Morning Post* man ended his report, "I was unable to share his confidence, but the Labour candidates, all of whom are camouflaging their Pacifist tendencies very successfully and trying to pose as the Four Just Men, are making a vigorous fight of it."

That report is interesting for several reasons. It reflects the bitterness with which Bevin ended the war—which had been over a month and two days when that report was published. Bevin was the only one of the four Labour candidates whose name is considered worthy of mention by the *Morning Post*.

Bevin was soundly defeated. Inskip with 12,232 votes had a majority of 5,095 over Bevin, but the campaign had given Bevin, as his *Morning Post* interviews shows, good preliminary practice in marshalling the arguments he was to use so effectively within eighteen months when he gained his first great triumph before the Shaw Commission of Inquiry.

Bevin set up his home in London about this time, and he and Mrs. Bevin took a house in Golders' Green, but they changed homes fairly frequently in the next ten years, staying for a short while in a flat above an hotel in Oxford Street, before settling down in the western districts of the capital.

But the greatest change in Bevin's outlook and daily practice came, surprisingly, from a new secretary. Miss May Forcey gave her name to an era in Bevin's life among his old cronies and his trade union lieutenants.

Miss Forcey was small, spare and energetic. She had been, before the war, of all things, a publicity agent for a London theatrical magnate. During the war she had served with the Ministry of Information, and in this capacity she had organised the visits of such well-known Labour leaders as Ben Tillett to France. It was Ben Tillett who quickly appreciated her vitality and her efficiency. While other officials dithered and dallied, Miss Forcey not only made up her own mind but saw her decisions through, frequently with some unorthodoxy in a Government department. She developed quite a reputation for getting things done. It was this which led to her appointment as an official of the Dockers' Union. Ben appointed her, and it was Ben who persuaded Bevin to utilise her services as a personal secretary. The two worked as a team for more than fifteen years.

Miss Forcey quickly realised that Bevin was good-naturedly dissipating his energies by always being "at home" to any casual callers at his office. Old pals from the West Country would naturally pop along to Effingham House when they had time on their hands to "have a yarn" with Ernest. It is a habit provincials have in London. And, then, most of Bevin's closest acquaintances were provincials.

Miss Forcey brought orderliness into Bevin's routine. She instituted the new-fangled notion of making appointments even for his old Bristol colleagues. They took it badly at first. But Miss Forcey, in her outer room, was firm. Ironically, Bevin, when he had time to think of it, wondered if some of his old pals were neglecting him. Certainly it was a change for the better in his working life. He was able to get through much more work.

It was a change which came at the right moment. Bevin's cares and plans were multiplying. He was at the great division in his life, between the field officer whose job took him all over Britain with a roving commission which engendered a free and easy comradeship within the working-class movement, but also brought many embarrassing rebuffs and discouragements, and the centrally-situated administrator with all reins in his hands and a research department at his elbow.

Up to that time it was not the custom of trade unions to develop card index systems for filing any information except the financial returns of membership from the district offices. Such features as reference libraries, files of economic trends, and records of wage negotiations were considered something of a concession to the office efficiency experts who were elbowing each other for public attention at the end of the war.

Miss Forcey was quick to see the handicap in which the absence of these aids placed Bevin. Especially as he was approaching the greatest test of his life.

There was unrest in all the docks of England and Wales. Bevin's war-end fears were coming true. High wages and overtime had gone. There were too many men scrambling for the jobs on offer. The old animal rush for subsistence was re-appearing outside every dock gate in the land.

Bevin secured a concession in working hours for dockers from the employers in November, 1919, but they would not agree to wage increases. They suggested that such claims should go to arbitration. To the surprise of all, including his own colleagues among the trade union leaders, Bevin accepted the suggestion. He agreed to a public inquiry. There had never been such a thing in England before. Wage claims had always been argued behind closed doors. But Bevin knew what he was about. His claim for higher wages in an open court was a platform to appeal to the conscience of England.

The employers hired Sir Lyndon Macassey, King's Counsel, one of the most experienced advocates in the country, to prove why wage increases could not be granted without the ruin of Britain's invaluable overseas trade. Higher wages, they argued, meant higher freight costs, and these in turn would undermine the competitive power of British exporters in the world's markets.

Bevin was not the slightest whit abashed by the briefing of such eminent counsel. He and Miss Forcey set about the business of co-ordinating the evidence which every district secretary had been instructed to supply. With their colleagues at union headquarters they worked into the small hours of the morning for weeks before the case opened.

And when, on Tuesday, February 3rd, 1920, Bevin marched into the gloomy, venerable courtroom in the Law Courts in the Strand to face the distinguished Lord Shaw of Dunfermline, the President of the Court, Miss Forcey trotted behind him, her arms full of documents, graphs and statistics.

Bevin observed all the formalities. He bowed to Lord Shaw and to his adversary before stating his case. He interpolated the accepted legal phraseology in precisely the right places in his statement.

Up beside Lord Shaw, flanking him on both sides as members of the Court were the three elder statesmen of the transport unions, Harry Gosling, Ben Tillett and Bob Williams. Sir Joseph Broodbank, Sir Lionel Fletcher, and Mr. Frederick Scrutton, three of the most influential port employers, represented the owners, and the Minister of Labour was represented by Mr. John Smethurst, President of the Master Cotton Spinners' Federation, and Arthur Pugh, chief of the Steelmen's trade union.

The four union men blinked as they saw the new trade union star settling himself complacently into the role of barrister. He opened with becoming diffidence.

"The Court," he said, "will appreciate that this is rather an unusual environment for me to be in, and also that the proceedings are very novel for the whole Labour movement of this country. We have agreed as transport workers to submit our claims to the test of public inquiry, first, because we are convinced of the justice of our claim, and, secondly, because we have no objection to the whole question of the standard of life being open for public inquiry. We hope it will serve not only to obtain what our men desire, but to influence public opinion to a higher conception of what that standard of life ought to be."

Calmly he submitted numbered documents to the Court and to his opponents.

He was asking for a minimum wage of sixteen shillings a day for his men. He traced their wage record through generations. He showed that from Ben Tillett's famous victory in 1889, when the dockers secured sixpence (10 cents) an hour for their labours, they had made no progress until 1911. They were getting five shillings and threepence (one dollar five cents) a day to 1915, and then during the war they secured five increases, strictly classed as war wages and therefore liable to be lapsed at any time, until when the war ended their wages had increased by 104 per cent. to ten shillings and ninepence (two dollars fifteen cents) a day.

But Bevin was able to show by the Government's own statistics the cost of living had risen by 136 per cent.

He put in another document showing the profiteering which had gone on in ships during the war. He named ships whose value had risen from £14,000 to £70,000, from £21,000 to £120,000, and from £30,000 to £215,000.

He calculated that during the war the shipping industry had made a profit of £350,000,000.

He argued for a universal working week of 44 hours. In some ports men had been working 60 hours to live—when they could get jobs. He produced a new plan for the registration of dockers through the trade unions so that the old evil of always having more men hanging round the dock gates than there were jobs could end.

He suggested a new plan for the co-ordination of all forms of transport so that great inland cities like Nottingham and Birmingham should never again undergo their wartime experience of being short of food while whole warehouses of perishables were rotting in the ports.

For three days his case went on. The court became more and more crowded. The newspapers stopped their vilification and wrote up his performance as the sensation of the day.

The *Daily Mail* announced, Mr. Churchill, the Chancellor of the Exchequer, who had recently created a stir by declaring that Labour was not fit to govern, "may be interested to know that the list of possible Labour candidates for the seats of Government has received the addition of another notable name. By his masterly statement to the Court of Inquiry of the transport workers' claim for increased pay, leisure and dignity of life, Mr. Ernest Bevin, of the London dockers, has pegged out for himself a place in the front rank of the men who count in social politics."

The newspaper went on, "He spoke for fully eleven hours, and in the course of his speech presented a formidable array of facts and figures which it must have taken months of study, research and analysis to compile, and which he expounded with a fluent ease and clearness that a Chancellor of the Exchequer might have envied. There were touches, too, of intense human sentiment in the orator's plea for his clients' right to the decencies and comforts of life."

As a matter of fact, when that comment was published, Bevin still had to go through the last hour of his opening statement on the third day of the hearing.

He concluded, "The claim covers practically all classes of dock work. I challenge counsel to show that a family can exist in physical efficiency on less than I have indicated. I say that if the captains of industry cannot organise their concerns so as to give Labour a living wage, then they should resign from their captaincy of industry. If you refuse our claim, then I suggest you must adopt an alternative. You must go to the Prime Minister, you must go to the Minister of Education and tell him to close down our schools and teach us nothing. We must get back then to the purely fodder basis. For it is no use to give us knowledge if we are not to be given the possibility of using it, to give a sense of the beautiful without allowing us ever to have a chance to obtain the enjoyment of it. Education creates aspirations and a love of the beautiful. Are we to be denied the wherewithal to secure these things? It is a false policy. Better to let us live in the dark if our claims are not to be met."

The decorum of the old building was shattered. The crowds in the courtroom roared their delight as Bevin sank back on his seat to grasp the tumbler held for him by the faithful Miss Forcey.

The four union leaders on the bench beamed as they heard Lord Shaw lean forward and say warmly, "I desire on behalf of the Court to thank you for the care and cogency with which you have presented the case of the workmen. The Court appreciates very much the illuminating way in which it was made."

When Sir Lyndon Macassey rose to open his case he, too, paid tribute to Mr. Bevin. His overwhelming suavity suggested his tribute was a polite formality, but actually Sir Lyndon spoke warmly to Bevin when the court adjourned that day. "I think," said Sir Lyndon in court, with a touch of pomposity, "we might predict for Mr. Bevin a very great future in the cause he has so much at heart."

Sir Lyndon had prepared his case with care. He resisted the idea of a national agreement, arguing that conditions varied in every port and, in any case, local agreements had always been the custom of the industry.

But he made the fatal blunder, as it transpired, in seeking to prove that dockers could live adequately on the wages they were receiving. He ignored Bevin's argument that in hundreds of cases dockers who had been unemployed had started work without breakfast. Bevin had shouted, "How can you expect output from hungry men?"

Sir Lyndon tried to prove in subsequent hearings that even hefty dockers could get enough to eat on their present wages. He reduced their meals to calories. This gave Bevin his chance to ridicule his adversary's case.

Sir Lyndon submitted a family budget for £3 17s. (15.40 dollars) to the court. Next morning, Bevin turned the court into a cookshop. He smilingly pointed to his wares. He said, "Sir Lyndon Macassey in his budget allowed a shilling (20 cents) a week for vegetables other than potatoes. I have here five plates of cooked potatoes and cabbage, and five portions of cheese. Here is some meat, which I have not cooked. I am willing to cook the whole budget to show the court how much counsel allows to sustain a docker for a day."

Then Bevin called his next witness, a burly docker named Brammell, from Birkenhead. "I would not sit down to such a meal," declared Mr. Brammell. "There would be a row in our house, I am certain. As to the cheese, if I got to the table first I should have the lot myself."

Sir Lyndon had estimated that the weekly rent of a docker's home was about 6s. 6d. (1 dollar 30 cents). So Mr. Bevin put Mr. Buckner, clerk to the Tilbury Council, into the witness box. Thousands of London dockers live in the Tilbury area. Before the war, Mr. Buckner declared, the cheapest house in Tilbury had been let at 8s. (1.60 dollars) a week. Post-war houses were costing three times the pre-war cost to build, and now a rent of 17s. 9d. (3.55 dollars) to £1 (4.0 dollars) would be charged.

Next day, Sir Lyndon put Professor A. L. Bowley, the famous Cambridge economist, into the box to discuss the calorific value and the price of food.

Promptly, Mr. Bevin produced a "ration" of bacon divided into the rashers provided in Sir Lyndon's model budget. "Do you think," Bevin asked the professor, "this will be enough on which a docker can work? We are dealing with dockers not scientists."

Professor Bowley replied, "He does not eat bacon and nothing else. He might prefer fish."

Bevin demanded, "Is a Cambridge professor a competent judge of a docker's breakfast?"

Bevin produced the menu of a 7s. 6d. (1.50 dollar) meal at the Savoy Hotel. "This," he observed grimly, "is the sort of meal a shipowner would eat. What is its calorific value?"

"There are 50 different items here," protested the Professor, "and I don't know what the shipowner ate."

Next day, Bevin produced another parcel. "Yesterday," he reminded Professor Bowley, "you said a docker might prefer fish for breakfast, and you allowed 6d. (10 cents) for it in your budget. Well, here is sixpennyworth of fish bought cheaply at a Canning Town stall last night. Does that, divided up for breakfast for a family of five, provide sufficient for a docker doing heavy work?"

The Professor responded, "It all depends on how much bread is eaten, whether the children eat the fish, or bread and margarine."

Bevin next questioned the allowance of flour, and Professor Bowley confessed that he did not know how much fat was used in a pound of flour to make a cake.

"Do you know," thundered Bevin, "that in a workman's home there is never less than three ounces of fat to a pound of flour for cake?" The Professor retorted, "It does not matter much where you put the fat so long as you get the children to eat it." "If you did not put it in the cake," Bevin explained with mock gentleness, "the children would not fancy the cake."

It went on for days. Bevin succeeded in reducing the whole argument to absurdity. He ridiculed the idea of a docker's wife turning herself into a scientific dietician.

Bevin's elation while awaiting the award of the court led him to make some remarkable personal disclosures about his early life. He was in tremendous demand as a speaker in all parts of the country. His title of "the Dockers' K.C." had stuck to him from the very first day of the inquiry.

To the dockers of Canning Town, East London, he declared, "I was secretary of a West of England unemployed movement from 1905 to 1909 and I found myself walking the streets unemployed and having to steal for my living. I make no apology for that. I will never starve if work is refused me. Neither God nor nature demands it of us, and if man demands it, then I will violate the social laws he has made."

This caused quite a sensation and the next day he amplified the statement in an interview. "I make no apology," he said, "for what I did then. I never went without—that is all. I have always been an energetic man, and I was always willing to work when I could get work to do. But hard times came, and I was unemployed. I had to use my head to live. I never made any bones about it. One had to get food so I stole. Frankly, if I were in a similar position today I should do the same thing again with a clear conscience. I have always gone on this principle—here is a world furnished with every opportunity for us all, once you remove the artificial limitations imposed upon humanity. No one man, duke or capitalist, has any right to make another man starve. If labour was refused me, I knew that not only myself but those dependent on me would be starved. Therefore, I had to steal. I followed that as a religious law, and I should obey it again were I placed in similar circumstances."

His greatest reception he received at a huge demonstration organised by the Transport Workers' Federation which filled the Albert Hall, London's biggest meeting place.

"This Court of Inquiry," he reported, "novel as it is, curious as it may be taken as a method of settling a dispute, is something bigger than merely an inquiry into sixteen shillings a day. It has been a platform on which it has been possible to open a page of history that tells of the struggles of the men and women we represent. It has been an opportunity to unfold the great human tragedy of men and women fighting year in and year out against the terrible economic conditions with which they have been surrounded. Although my speech took eleven hours, let me say that no tongue exists, no voice is capable, no pen can write, no artist can paint the real human tragedy that is behind it all."

He thought this was the first dispute in which the capitalists had not only stated how much money the workers were to get, but also how much and what they were to eat.

Scathingly, he declared, "Professor Bowley and his budget are a revelation of the prostitution of a great institution (Cambridge University) which was formed not to keep the workers in slavery, but to develop knowledge so that the human race might be made happier."

F

Before this great audience, always a spur to his oratory, Bevin announced his attitude to strikes.

He said he did not want a strike for anything but a really great object. "When the times comes," he added, "if ever it does come, for a great struggle between Capital and Labour, I want it to be for something bigger than a penny an hour."

He prophesied, "The world of labour is full of ominous signs. The great miners' movement is on the rumble, the textile movement is full of discontent, the carters are badly paid and overworked, the busmen, the tramwaymen, and the engineers are all at the point of disruption with the capitalist class. I don't want to see a volcanic eruption of labour, followed by a mere falling back into the same old grooves. It won't be worth it. I don't want a mere blind struggle. I want it to have a definite object—that of achieving for those who toil the mastery of their own lives."

Lord Shaw and his court did their job thoroughly. They visited the docks to master the technique of the call-on every morning. They watched men at work to understand the significance of the various grades of workers employed on the docks.

But something even more unusual happened after Bevin had made his memorable speech and before Lord Shaw announced his award. So impressed had he been by Bevin's performance, that he invited the dockers' leader to his own home in London. And together they spent the evening, talking mainly of Bevin's past and his hopes for the future.

When the award was made Bevin could justly claim a 90 per cent. victory. His men got their sixteen shillings a day. They got their 44 hours. They got their national agreement. Bevin did not get his full claim on his plan for the trade union regulation of labour supply at the ports.

His triumph gave him an impetus to increased outspokenness. He warned his own dockers in Bristol to stop "working slow." "Deliberate reduction of output or failure to render proper service is a mistake," he said, "because it becomes a habit and a policy. We experience that when Labour gets into power on the municipal bodies. Some of the men expect to be treated in such a manner that it would be impossible to carry on industry. If Labour is to come into power and hopes to be successful we shall have to call for greater service to the community, not less."

His new prestige protected him from any retort from his men.

He was at the height of his authority inside his own movement. But it brought fresh responsibilities.

The war against Germany had been over nearly two years. The Bolsheviks had been in power in Russia nearly three years. But Poland was restive, and there were deep suspicions in Britain about the policy of its own Government towards the Soviet-Polish dispute.

All sections of the Labour and trade union movement in Britain combined to form a Council of Action to watch developments in connection with the eastern crisis.

On the morning of August 10th, 1920, a deputation of seventeen leaders went to 10 Downing Street to see Mr. Lloyd George, the Prime Minister, who was accompanied by Mr. Bonar Law.

Incidentally, of the seventeen, two only, Mr. J. R. Clynes and Bevin, remained active in the public life of Britain. Bevin had no official standing on any of the bodies represented on the deputation. Yet he had been taken along to act as spokesman.

Bevin bluntly told Lloyd George that the resolution of the conference which had sent them there was not merely one in opposition to direct military action—the use of soldiers and sailors in actual fighting—but it was a declaration in opposition to an indirect war, either by blockade or by the supplying of munitions or by assisting the forces that were now at war against Russia. "The resolution," Bevin added, "expressed the feeling of the overwhelming majority of the six million trade unionists in the country. The decision also, we think, arises from the inherent sense of British democracy for fair play."

Bevin went on, "We are of the opinion that hidden forces have been at work in Europe, especially in Paris, and have been responsible for the prolongation of the terrible conflict with Russia. In this connection some of our delegation have been to Russia, and the statements of the people who have made investigations, and the public declarations all indicate that Soviet Russia has been endeavouring to establish peace with the rest of the world, and that this Polish venture is but a climax—we hope the climax—of the series of wars promoted by outside influences against Soviet Russia. We also feel very strongly that these reactionary forces have been endeavouring to manoeuvre the diplomatic position to make Russia appear in the wrong the whole time, so as to find an excuse to declare war with all the Forces of the Allies against her."

Bevin admitted to Lloyd George that the latter's public speeches appeared to have been in the direction of peace, but the directions of at least one of his colleagues, meaning Winston Churchill, had been in the direction of war. "That," Bevin commented, "indicates an internal conflict within the Government."

Bevin went on to trace the attitude of this country to the new Soviet Government from the time of its establishment.

Lloyd George interrupted him impatiently, "That is a long while ago. Let us get to business. I would not mind if I had time."

Bevin persisted, "We are not going to stand idly by and see the nation's wealth and armed forces spent on stamping out what some are prepared to call a terrible menace."

Bevin declared, "If war with Russia is carried on directly in support of Poland or indirectly in support of General Wrangel there will be a match set to an explosive material, the result of which none of us can forsee today."

"Does this mean," demanded Lloyd George, "that if the independence of Poland is really menaced, if it is really destroyed, and if Bolshevist Russia does for Poland what their Tsarist predecessors did a century and a half ago, we cannot send a single pair of boots there, otherwise Labour will strike?"

"The hypothesis does not hold good," retorted Bevin. "The independence of Poland is not at stake."

Later, Lloyd George repeated his question. Would Labour not permit the Government to send a pair of boots to Poland if she were menaced by the Soviets?

Icily, Bevin replied, "We will consider our position when that occasion arises."

There was no doubt about the mood of the British people at that time. There were incidents like the refusal of the dockers to load the *Jolly George* in London Docks. There might have been a general strike. Many people on the labour and trade union side were prepared to urge that, to refuse support to the British Government in any further adventures against the Soviets. It was not that the British trade union leaders were so rabidly pro-Soviet. They were heartily sick of war. They wanted peace. Almost at any price just then.

Within five days Lloyd George and Bevin were embroiled in

another argument. Lloyd George announced that he had discovered a "plot" between the Soviet authorities and the directors of the Socialist *Daily Herald*. The Soviets, Lloyd George alleged, had offered £75,000 to the *Daily Herald*, then in low water, and the directors of the *Herald* and its editor, George Lansbury, were guilty of concealing the offer from the British public.

Ernest Bevin was one of the newspaper's four trade union directors. He promptly wrote Lloyd George a letter declaring, "You are, of course, aware that four of the directors are responsible trade union officials, who at any rate enjoy the confidence of a combined membership running into millions. Am I to understand, therefore, that the four trade union officials, together with Mr. Lansbury, are charged by the Government that they would have taken this money and withheld the knowledge of such a transaction from the public and the trade unions if they could have done it without fear of being found out?"

Obviously, Lloyd George welcomed the challenge. He sent Bevin a long eight-pointed reply. (1) It was known that the *Herald* was in pecuniary difficulties. (2) M. Chicherin, representing the Soviet Government, had disclosed as far back as February 11th (six months earlier) that Mr. Lansbury was soliciting help for his paper overseas and that the Soviets were prepared to grant a subsidy for the preservation of control of the paper. "All the directors," Lloyd George added, "if they faithfully discharged their trust to their shareholders, must have been aware of these financial transactions." (3) On August 20th, the *Daily Herald* published an article declaring it had received "not a bond, not a franc, not a rouble." (4) "It is now known," Lloyd George went on, "that one of your fellow directors had for some considerable time been in direct negotiations with representatives of the Soviet Government for a grant of money to be devoted to the assistance of the *Daily Herald*." (5) Lloyd George added, "It is also known that a sum of £75,000 was paid to this director as a result of these negotiations."

(6) "Three days before the publication of the statement I have referred to," the Prime Minister pursued, "some jewels received from Bolshevist sources had been sold in London and paid for by notes." (7) The police tracked these notes to the possession of the editor's son, while others reached the possession of Mr. Meynell, a director of the *Herald*. (8) Mr. Lansbury, junior, knew the

police had tracked the notes. Three weeks after their "not a rouble" article, the *Herald* made the first announcement of the Soviet offer and invited the opinion of its readers as to whether it should accept this sum and "thus complete a notable episode in International Socialism."

Lloyd George concluded to Bevin, "If you were ignorant of these transactions, such ignorance of matters of vital moment is a sinister comment on the amount of control exercised by the Trade Union representatives on this organ."

Bevin sent another letter, in which he said, "I note your letter does not deal with the point raised in my earlier letter in which I asked you to give me your charges definite and explicit, but with your usual ability to sidetrack the issue you have merely rehashed the whole story, which has been the subject of controversy in the Press for days . . . . The directors of the paper, as soon as it came to their knowledge and at their first meeting, declined to accept the offer. The real point at issue is the aspersions upon those of us who are responsible, as directors of the *Daily Herald*. You say that if the directors are really exercising control over the concern they should have been acquainted with what is going on, but if the matter was not known to us, and no money was received— not a rouble to our knowledge—and when it became known they declined to accept, surely they were exercising control."

Bevin continued, "Further, would you say that your predecessor, the Right Honorable H. H. Asquith, failed to exercise control because he was not made aware of the Marconi business, and when he was made aware, instead of taking the resignation of those concerned, as was done in the case of Mr. Meynell, he appointed a committee to inquire, and would he be content to accept a statement from at least some of his colleagues that it was an unfortunate error of judgment? Would it have been right to have cast aspersions upon the remainder of the Cabinet because they were aware of what was happening? Further comment is superfluous."

That ended the public correspondence, but started a feud which went on for years. It showed Bevin's resentment of any imputation against his conduct in any of the many roles he occupied.

But his main preoccupation at this time was the welding of about twenty organisations in the transport industry into one great union. It was a delicate job. There were clashing interests, there was jealousy and prejudice between some sections of workers and others, and, perhaps the most difficult of all to negotiate satisfactorily, there was the delicate personal position of all the leaders of all the unions.

There seemed little doubt as to who would be leader of the leaders. There were hopeful aspirants for the position. No one could, however, be seriously considered as a rival to Bevin.

Bevin's fears that a great attack on wage standards was coming was his main argument in persuading the reluctant unions into his great new union.

Bevin's speech at the inaugural meeting of the new combination was a skilful blend of appeal and threat. In the first place he told the delegates to the conference at the Premierland Hall, in the East End of London, that whatever the future of modern industry might be, however powerful trade unions might become, or in fact, if Unionism obtained control, which must be its ultimate end, if it attempted to crush out the pride of calling or omitted to recognise it, it would defeat itself. Dockers were better organised, he admitted, than they had ever been previously.

"But," he added, "there is going to be an attack on the sixteen shillings a day, and I will say that I will not lead another dockers' movement with the present state of organisation. I am not going to lead any men to disaster, and if you do not put your backs into the scheme you will touch another 1912 some time or other. They (meaning the employers) will try and break us after all the work we have done. I hate strikes, but as a leader it is my duty to lead. We are going to lead, but if you do not follow, if you place your pettiness, your personality in the way of the consummation of the scheme you will have committed a crime against the men who are compelled to go forward."

There were nearly three thousand delegates at that meeting. They included all the men who had been local or national leaders in the movement—some before Bevin had emerged from his obscurity in Bristol. Whatever the opposition might have been, he swept it aside. It did not show itself that day. The scheme was accepted unanimously. Bevin assumed the leadership of nearly half a million workers in a wide variety of callings.

None the less, there were nostalgic regrets in the hearts of many at the passing of old unions which had developed a tradition

of their own. There were disappointments among some of the
leaders, too, that they were no longer to be chief executives of
their own unions.

In his final report to the old Dockers' Union, about to become
part of the new Transport and General Workers' Union, old Ben
Tillett made some revealing statements.

"In the debate on the new amalgamation," old Ben recorded,
"I had to make a very frank statement regarding my own position.
I had to make it plain that throughout my career, while I had been
the originator of many great movements, I had put other men
into positions of responsibility, and had not been self-seeking. I
pointed out that on occasion I had dragooned younger men into
taking responsibility, but that at all times I had been against any
one-man show and would be always."

Tillett continued, "I had been nominated for the position of
President, for which naturally I had ambition. Brother Gosling
was also nominated, but had informed the election committee he
would not run against me. The opinion was expressed that it
would endanger the whole amalgamation if we both went to the
ballot. I did not agree, but Brother Bevin and the others were
obviously so impressed that this would be the case that, after a
further reiteration that I would rather go to the ballot, I decided
to withdraw my candidature. This movement has to go on, and I
would sacrifice myself for it if necessary."

Ben Tillett found it hard to give way to other men. Like all
other leaders he has found a place in the new organisation. It was
not much more than a sinecure. He was to live more than another
twenty years. He was to spend much of his time recalling his
former glories, and lamenting his eclipse.

Ben Tillett's version of what happened behind the scenes was
palpably one-sided. It was a direct criticism of Bevin. It implied
that Bevin was so ambitious—indeed, so unscrupulous—that he
was prepared to sacrifice as distinguished a pioneer as Ben Tillett
merely to create a vast new organisation for himself to "boss."

Tillett's version must have been distorted deliberately. He
suppressed a visit paid to him by Bevin on the eve of the conference which formally approved the amalgamation.

Bevin asked Tillett, "What's the trouble, Ben?" and Ben
bluntly replied that he wanted to be president of the new organisation. Bevin pointed out that there were 14 major organisations

concerned in the negotiations. He added, "There seems to be a general agreement that I am to be the general secretary. It is unreasonable for us to ask for the presidency as well. The Watermen and Lightermen demand it for Harry Gosling."

Ben was still truculent. He demanded that his name, as well as Gosling's, should be submitted to the ballot. He said, "Let's see who'll get most support." Bevin replied that even if Ben won, so much bad feeling would be created that the success of the amalgamation would be jeopardised. Bevin had set his heart on his plan to weld all those unions into one. Suddenly, he made one of the most generous gestures of his life. He offered to withdraw his own name, and to support Tillett for the general secretaryship of the amalgamation. Ben was tempted to accept. Then he decided to decline. With an ungraciousness alien to his usual character, he never disclosed Bevin's offer.

His final severance from his trade union came in 1930 when he was 70. He received a pension from his union. He lived long enough to see his protege, Bevin, become a powerful Minister of State. But not long enough to forgive.

Bevin's decision not to support Ben for the presidency of the new union was based solely and detachedly on the interests of the union. Naturally, he signed the final letter acquainting Tillett that the executive council proposed to exercise the retirement rule, which, it so happened, had been especially extended to give Ben five years of office beyond the retirement age for all other officials, including Bevin himself.

But Ben could not reconcile himself to rules which seemed to him to ignore the warmth of human fellowship and recognition to the founder of the "new unionism." Thus, the old association ended in feud. The glory of joint achievement gave way to the bitterness of recrimination. When the remains of Ben Tillett were cremated in 1943, the funeral oration was delivered by Ernest Bevin, His Majesty's Minister of Labour and National Service.

He spoke only of the great years of long ago. They were the happiest to recall.

CHAPTER V

ARCHITECT OF THE "OCTOPUS"

BEVIN found that creating a mighty new trade union was not the end of his troubles. Indeed, in one way, his achievement was mistimed. His creation started to function in the middle of the most disturbing slump Britain had ever known. True, back in the '80's of the last century and earlier, as in the hungry '40's, slumps had caused greater distress among the people, but no previous depression had ever hit the country with such suddenness and such intensity. At one moment in 1921, men in the shipping world of Cardiff and South Wales were millionaires. Speculators in Lancashire's cotton industry were making fortunes in a week. On the London Stock Exchange there was a repetition of the hectic old days of the South Sea bubble and within a month the bubble burst.

Bevin's union, formed with enthusiasm and quite a degree of emotionalism, was suddenly faced with the disturbing reality that in order to hold its members there had to be excessive, vigorous leadership, and that meant strikes.

Bevin was not averse to the rough and tumble of strike leadership, but he himself would have chosen another time for these displays of rugged bludgeoning. Bevin would have preferred a respite of two or three years, so that he could have devoted himself exclusively to the consolidation of his new union. That called for diplomatic, very skilful, very gentle handling of different sections, some of which were not altogether certain that they wanted complete harmony with their new colleagues.

Still, Bevin had devised an ingenious organisation which miraculously achieved the double purpose of satisfying most of the requirements of each separate section, yet was practical as a whole. Even more miraculous, it has, in all its essentials, gone on towards its quarter-century without any great change. Bevin undoubtedly laid a strong foundation.

To govern the whole union there was a general executive council. Some were elected on a trade basis—that is, dockers chose their own representatives, so did busmen, so did operatives in the great public utility concerns—and others were elected on a

90

territorial basis. Generally, one local leader was elected to the executive council for every 50,000 members. All these executive councilmen continued at their trades. They were not paid officials, beyond receiving their expenses and loss of earnings through attending council meetings one week in every three months. These members chose eight of their number to form a general purposes committee, to meet every month. This committee, among other duties, appoints every national officer from a short list elected by the interested membership. That is, every national officer except the general secretary, who is elected by a ballot of the whole membership of the union.

But, in addition, there were, and are, trade groups roughly corresponding to each of the old separate unions, with their own committees and officers. Thus Bevin harnessed old loyalties and interests to the newer function of making their contribution to the bigger, greater amalgamation. It all needed time to settle down. That was why Bevin, the chief architect, hoped for a period of industrial peace.

All the same, Bevin was not the sort of man to run away from a fight. The most disturbing threat of all came from the docks of London. Three years before, Bevin had won his greatest triumph. He had established his reputation as the nation's ace labour negotiator. Flattering and satisfying though this achievement was to him personally, it had the solid merit of having given to the dockers the security of a half day's work at a time and a wage of 8s. (1.60 dollars) for that half-day. That award had been won in a boom. Now, the port employers were able to muster as their strongest weapon the continuation of the slump. So they proposed the vicious reduction of wages to 5s. 6d. (1.10 dollars) for the half-day. It was reduction of $37\frac{1}{2}$ per cent. The natural reaction of any trade union leader to this proposal would have been to reject it and fight the employers.

But Bevin worked more subtly than that. He wanted to establish before the employers of the nation the fact that a new type of trade union leader had risen. He wanted to prove that he was justified in asking for an increase when times improved, that he also wanted to demonstrate that he was prepared to consider a reduction when times were bad. And so, he advised his Executive to enter into negotiations with the employers. It took quite a lot of doing. It was a bitter pill for his colleagues to swallow. But they did it, subject to the dockers themselves giving their approval.

This is where Bevin relied on his magnetic oratorical powers to pull him through. He failed because he was not given a chance to exercise these powers.

The dockers of London revolted. They were convinced that their arch-enemy, Lord Devonport, head of the port employers, was deliberately exploiting the national situation in order to revenge himself for their victory in 1920. And as most of them worked and lived near enough to the palatial offices of the Port Authority near the London docks, it was easy for them to imagine the impressive austere figure of Lord Devonport gloating in his mahogany boardroom, their fury was easily fanned. The old fighting tradition of the dockers was dying a hard death. Greatly though they admired Bevin, they could not accommodate themselves to what they regarded as his mysterious velvet glove technique.

And so, in spite of Bevin's orders and pleadings, they struck work.

Bevin took his President, Harry Gosling, down to the East End to meet the dockers. It was in the massive building known as Premierland, Whitechapel, which was in Harry Gosling's own Parliamentary constituency. Harry Gosling subsequently recorded :

"We had called the meeting to give the unofficial strikers some account of what was really happening, and to show them as clearly as we could what their action was leading to. The hall was packed with a mixed audience of 2,000, but they had come, as we very soon found, not to listen but to shout us down. We were two against two thousand, and, of course, they had an easy run. We tried to speak, but it was impossible.

" 'Traitors—blacklegs ! false leaders—clear out . . . . ' were shouted at us from everywhere at once, and when the audience was tired of that, or rather, to put it in official language, had 'shewn it had no confidence' in us, it withdrew in a body and left us as we were.

"I felt the only thing to do was to smile, but Bevin thrust out his underlip and let his face boldly say what his tongue was not allowed to express.

"It was a strange experience for us both, leaving a bitter taste at the time, and yet urging us on, for the pity of it all, to greater efforts than before."

Next morning, the *Daily Express* reported. "Mr. Bevin went white to the lips. Mr. Gosling, usually rosy, looked haggard and sad. Little wonder. The men he had worked and fought for all his life were turned against him in their ignorance. The commotion had been carefully organised. It switched off abruptly at a given signal. Mr. Coombes, chairman of the unofficial central strike committee, rose to propose a resolution declaring that the lighter-men, stevedores and dockers had ceased to have any confidence in Mr. Bevin and his colleagues. It was carried unanimously. The audience, without another word, left the building at Mr. Coombes' suggestion. They marched out, leaving the union officials alone on the platform."

Later that night, Mr. Bevin thundered. "The organised uproar proves that the one thing the strike leaders did n ot do is to let us tell the men the truth. Sooner or later they will have to face the music and then we shall be able to state our case to the men."

Bevin stuck to his principle that agreements entered into by trade unions with employers had the sanctity of law. It was obviously an unpopular theory with his followers. But Bevin's persistence reflected his foresight. It was inevitable that without experienced leadership they would lose. They did. They went back after eight weeks, beaten and sullen.

Bevin found no consolation in his victory. Indeed, the whole business made Bevin's life more difficult because, knowing his men as he did, he knew that in order to keep their allegiance he would have to give some demonstration that he was not afraid of strife and turmoil.

He did not have long to wait. His chance came within eight months. Bevin demanded an increase of two shillings a half day for his dockers. The employers, realising that Bevin meant busi-ness this time, offered an immediate increase of one shilling and suggested that the other shilling should be argued in arbitration.

This was not good enough for Bevin. He declared that if any docker accepted the offer of an immediate shilling and went on working he would be "a Judas."

He went to see Lord Devonport. Lord Devonport listened to Bevin's argument and then curtly replied.

"Our answer is one shilling. Do what you will."

Bevin glared at him and with ominous calm, said, "We will." The strike was on.

Bevin subsequently told a court of inquiry that he would never negotiate with Lord Devonport again until Lord Devonport apologised for the implication that Bevin had been a party to defeating his own men the previous year.

"He inferred," said Mr. Bevin, "that I was a party to roguery. I am neither an actor nor a rogue. That was the greatest insult ever offered by an employer to a trade union leader."

Bevin was convinced that other port employers throughout the country were prepared to award his men the two shillings increase he was demanding. He was convinced that Lord Devonport was the one stumbling-block.

It was a short, sharp strike, but Bevin won.

Within a month, he was in another strike. This time London's transport services were paralysed. Now, this brought Bevin's power home to the vast mass of the people much more forcibly and intimately than the dockers' strike. Transport strikes always do. People started asking, "Who is this Bevin?" The newspapers attacked him bitterly for being a ruthless dictator. For nearly two weeks Londoners had to walk. Responsible journals like *The Nation* and *The Athenæum* recorded:

"We can recall no recent case in which a strike leader has assumed so truculent and irresponsible an attitude as Mr. Bevin. His assertion that 'We are not at war with the public' is nonsense.

"The whole object of this sudden extension of the strike is to cause such intolerable inconvenience to the public that it will insist on the employers being forced to accept his terms.

"The employers have gone a very long way to meet him; but he refuses to abate his demands by one penny, and actually uses the fact that the employers have offered so much to argue that it will be their fault if the strike goes on.

"The employers have come up now to figures representing within £130,000 (520,000 dollars) per annum of his full demand. Is it not monstrous, he suggests, that the public should be inconvenienced because they will not grant this further paltry sum? It is not as though the tramwaymen had such overwhelming grievances that no consideration for the public interests could be expected of them.

"It is true that, apart from the question of the financial capacity of the tramway undertakings, the merits of the men's demands were not seriously disputed. But the financial capacity of the industry is one of the governing factors in the wages problem, as agricultural labourers, miners, and many other sections of workpeople have bitter reason to know."

The Spectator observed.

"Whatever our opinions may be of the economic rights and wrongs of a strike, it is not tolerable that a series of sympathetic strikes, frequently directed for all practical purposes by a single man—in the present case, Mr. Bevin—should, in effect, place the public under a dictatorship."

Bevin was furious. He attacked the press and accused it of showing an abysmal ignorance of the cause of the dispute and the factors contributing to it.

"And this I attribute mainly," he continued, "to the fact that they never troubled about anything in these modern days of press production until it comes within the category of what they call 'interest' or it provides a 'sensation'."

Still, he won his strike and great benefit it gave him and his union, but the public and the press smarted.

At this time, Bevin was the most hated man in England. He was not too popular with the leaders of his own political party because of his statement that politics was still a game and the only faith the workers had was in direct action by their unions.

Within six months there was even another strike. Bevin was on holiday when the porters at Covent Garden, London's great fruit and vegetable centre, decided they had a good cause for striking. Bevin dashed back to London, and discovered that there was an important principle involved. This was the recognition of his union by the employers, a principle which Bevin had always held most dear. So he approved of the market porters' strike.

Bevin secured recognition but failed to increase the men's wages. The press and the public were jubilant. They gloated.

"One of the most remarkable features of the Covent Garden strike is the state of twilight in which it plunged the great Ernest Bevin, manipulator of more industrial disputes than any man of his generation. When Bevin strolled into the midst of the trouble, with threats of suspended food supplies and sympathetic action by transport workers as a whole, there was a general fear that the

local grievances in the market might develop into a national
catastrophe. This was largely due to the Bevin personality, but,
fortunately, the fears proved groundless and another reputation
crumpled. As a mediator, he proved his own worth; as an intimi-
dator he has done much to weaken his power.

"The eclipse of this man, coupled with his inability to create
great strikes out of small ones, is an interesting development. It
goes to prove that what the British working classes really want
is steady work, not manipulation of their interests to suit political
schemers or incipient revolutionaries."

All the same, the official record of Bevin's activities in those
days, both inside his own union and in his arguments before
industrial courts, showed that he was developing a constructive
sense which placed him far ahead of his fellows. It was, perhaps,
natural that Bevin should appear to the public to be truculent and
hostile, to have his more sober thoughts suppressed and his more
reflective announcements distorted. Very little development
inside his own union could be construed into evidence that Bevin
himself was trying to establish himself as a dictator.

The president of the union, Harry Gosling, had become the
Minister of Transport in the first Socialist Government, and so
it became necessary for him to resign his trade union presidency.

Promptly the newspapers announced that Bevin himself had
decided to assume the office of president while retaining his
general secretaryship. It was believed that this one man was
planning to assume all the major offices governing 400,000 members. Fanciful descriptions were published of secret meetings of
the union leaders in a Kensington office. It was reported that 84
officials of the union had gone on strike to appeal for the re-
appointment of Gosling as his union's president. It was further
reported that Bevin had two stalwart bodyguards. The irony of it
all was that Bevin was on holiday in the North when the whole of
this discussion, not much more than a routine affair, took place.

But the comments of those days are worth recording now
merely as a reflection of the attitude of the time towards Bevin.
They help, partly, to explain, too, why Bevin to this day has
retained considerable hostile mental reservations towards the
press, although he was a director of the *Daily Herald* for twenty
years. The presidency business, by the way, was settled by the
appointment of a "lay" member. That means that there is no

ERNEST BEVIN ADDRESSING THE ANNUAL CONFERENCE OF THE
TRADES UNION CONGRESS IN 1940
Shortly after he had become Minister of Labour

longer a full-time president of the union, and that the final
authority rests with the Executive Council of thirty members.

But Bevin was filling his life with activities which might have
had enormous consequences on the industrial life of Britain had
they succeeded. He was engaged with the leaders of the miners
and engineers in examining the creation of one vast union for all
those workers. Apparently, the difficulties in the way of this
gigantic industrial alliance were too great to be overcome, particularly as the miners, singly, the strongest trade union in the
country, were about to be involved in a struggle which shook the
country.

Bevin was very close to them in those days. The miners were
powerfully led by two fighting stalwarts. Their president was the
impressive Herbert Smith, of Yorkshire, the blunt, old man who,
with his cloth cap and highly-developed dialect, personified the
men he represented. Their secretary was Arthur Cook, the un-
yielding but volatile revolutionary whose incorruptibility was an
inspiration to his movement. He was young in years, less than
forty then, but old in campaigning. These two men were able to
convince Bevin and all other trade union leaders that the demands
for wage reductions which were made by the coal-owners in 1925
were merely a spearhead of an attack from all employers on the
wage standards of all organised workers in the country. Smith
and Cook turned their fight into a fight for all unions.

Bevin was the principal spokesman of all trade unions in the
crisis of 1925, which averted a general strike at the very last
minute. This is remarkable. Bevin had been appointed to the
General Council of the T.U.C. only in 1925. In point of seniority,
he was, therefore, the "baby" of this supreme policy-making
body of 32 members. Before and after 1925 it had been the
tradition of new members of the General Council to be seen and
not heard. Usually five or six years elapse before a member is put
up by the General Council to announce its policy. But Bevin had
always been a breaker of tradition. Just as fifteen years later he
was to step directly from outside Parliament to the front bench of
Ministers in the House of Commons, so now in 1925 he was
accepted on the stature he had already achieved for himself as a
natural leader of leaders.

Inside the General Council and in the annual conference of the
Trade Union Congress, Bevin showed remarkable skill in his

G

relations with the men whose reputations had been long established. The national leaders of the T.U.C. in those days were J. H. Thomas, the railwaymen's leader, J. R. Clynes, of the general workers, George Hicks, of the building workers, A. B. Swales, of the engineers, Alf. Purcell, of the furnishing trades, and Ben Tillett.

If there was a major discussion before the conference, these men were expected to join in. They were tremendously influential and uncannily accurate in gauging the mood of their followers.

Of all these, Jimmy Thomas was probably the most effective platform debater. His subsequent eclipse has tended to obscure this memory. Back in the middle twenties, however, Jimmy Thomas was the man whose voice commanded greatest attention. Bevin quite naturally, and without ostentation, joined this band of authoritative spokesmen and the greatest tribute to him is that the delegates to these conferences, as well as the members of the General Council, accepted all this as obvious.

Bevin was always suspicious of Jimmy Thomas, because of Jimmy's gregarious habit of intimate social contacts with the wealthy and the influential of the land. Jimmy's easy and affable acceptance of boiled shirts and ostentatious cigars was an affront in those days to Bevin's equally ostentatious austerity. But all this did not prevent Bevin's full appreciation of Jimmy Thomas's undoubted ability. It became inevitable, therefore, that when the real miners' crisis developed in 1926 with the final announcement, which pledged the whole of the organised workers to rallying to the support of the miners, it should be proposed by Jimmy Thomas and seconded by Ernest Bevin. Probably the most memorable and significant conference of trade union executives ever held in Britain was that held in the rather gloomy Memorial Hall, Farringdon Street, in the City of London, on the three days before the General Strike started. They were hectic days. While the executives sat patiently in one hall, whiling away their time by community singing, first of hymns and then of popular songs, the General Council of the T.U.C. continued seemingly endless and quite aimless discussions in another room of the building, while a small negotiating committee of the T.U.C. were at Downing Street, trying to persuade Mr. Baldwin, the Prime Minister, to influence the coal owners to withdraw the notices which they had posted at every pithead in Britain announcing new severely-cut wage rates.

The meetings dragged on for three days, and undoubtedly the greatest oratorical performance of that conference came from Ernest Bevin. He realised, however, how near a General Strike the country was. He realised, too, that there were grave misgivings among the trade union leaders and their followers that if a strike should come, the arrangements for conducting it were not complete. Bevin, with the General Council, were not going to begin wielding the big stick by announcing their detailed plans.

"But," he continued, "if it is wielded, I believe we will keep a stiff upper lip, cool heads and calm brains. We will accept, if forced to, a challenge unprecedented in the history of this or any other movement. It has been patent to everyone who has been looking at the mining industry, that it has to be completely recast, and it is not the only industry that has to be recast. It is false economy to expect a man to go down a mine and do his best and come up at the end of the week with not enough—not enough in thousands of cases—to feed himself, to say nothing of his wife and children who are dependent upon him. The nation cannot slide out of this responsibility."

"I am staggered," Bevin continued, "at the way this business is being carried on. Why does not the Labour Party in the House of Commons itself make a pronouncement on the question of the inadequacy of the miners' wages? Let them declare themselves on that floor, and their constituents will answer them, I believe, as to whether the country is prepared to see the wages of these men further driven down. If I interpret the feelings of this country aright, they want a solution to the mining problem, and I do not believe there is any class, unless it be the financiers, who want it at the expense of the miner, his wife and his children."

Bevin concluded, "You are moving towards an extraordinary position. In twenty-four hours from now you may have to cease being separate unions for this purpose. For this purpose, you will have to become one union with no autonomy. But, at the moment, we feel that to begin wielding any sort of threat in connection with the negotiations in the stage they are now in would be to place a weapon in the hands of our opponents."

That was on Thursday, April 29th, 1926. On Saturday afternoon, May 1st, most of the delegates had returned to their homes

in various parts of the country, believing that there was still a
faint hope of settlement.

But they did not leave London before taking a vote on the
proposal that if there was to be a strike the General Council of
the T.U.C. should take command. There was no doubt about the
mood of the conference. The vote for the General Council's
policy was 3,653,527. Against, only 49,911 votes were cast.

This virtually meant handing over the generalship of the
campaign to Ernest Bevin, because he, with Alf. Purcell, the
furniture operatives' leader, was made chief of the organisation.

Bevin went back to the new office of his union in Smith Square,
Westminster, and ironically occupied the room which years before
had been the library of Winston Churchill's town house.

Having completed the plan, Bevin moved over to Eccleston
Square, which was then the headquarters of the T.U.C., and it
was there he made his headquarters for the duration of the strike.

Bevin had planned to occupy himself in details. He could not
spare the time to serve on the delegations which were coming and
going between the T.U.C. headquarters and Downing Street, the
headquarters of Stanley Baldwin, the Prime Minister.

Bevin alone knew how the orders were to be dispatched to the
various sections of industry. He realised more than any one how
essential it was to keep such services as food distribution and
public utilities of water, gas and electricity going.

While other leaders were dismayed by the dramatic development of events on Sunday, May 2nd, Bevin was philosophical.
He knew the test would come. The whole issue boiled down at
that time to the request made by the trade union leaders to the
Prime Minister that he should intervene to persuade the coal
owners to withdraw their notices of wage reduction for two weeks
so that negotiations could be continued. If the Prime Minister
failed, the miners would refuse to work and if the miners were
"locked out" all other unions would cease work in sympathy,
believing that the attack on the miners was the attack on the wage
standards of all workers in the country.

The negotiating committee, consisting of three trade union
leaders and three representatives of the mine owners, were
actually in session in a room in the Prime Minister's residence on
the Sunday evening when Mr. Baldwin sent for the T.U.C. and
handed them a document. It announced that the Government

believed that no solution of the difficulties in the coal industry, which was both practicable and honourable to all concerned, could be reached except by sincere acceptance of the report of the Coal Commission. This meant an acceptance of lower wages by the miners, and this they refused to do.

Mr. Baldwin said that the Government would have been ready to continue negotiations and to continue the subsidy of the mining industry for two weeks if the miners were prepared to accept their cut.

"But," continued Mr. Baldwin, "it has come to the knowledge of the Government, not only that specific instructions have been sent by the executives of the trade unions directing their members in several of the most vital industries and services of the country to carry out a general strike on Tuesday next, but that overt acts have already taken place, including gross interference with the freedom of the press. Such action involves a challenge to the constitutional rights and freedom of the nation.

"His Majesty's Government, therefore, before it can continue negotiations, must require from the Trade Union Committee both a repudiation of the occasions referred to, that have already taken place, and an immediate and unconditional withdrawal of the instructions for a general strike."

This was delivered at midnight. The trade union leaders were in conference until 3-30 on the morning of Monday, May 3rd, and sent a letter to the Prime Minister bluntly declaring that he had put up these last-minute misgivings as an excuse for breaking off the peace discussions which were proceeding.

There was on both sides, trade union and government, a feeling that the clash had to come, although the trade unions have always insisted that the strike was not a direct challenge to constitutional authority.

It took the trade union chiefs in Downing Street some time to realise what Mr. Baldwin meant by his reference to "gross interference with the freedom of the press."

They had been sitting in with representative employers most of that Sunday evening. They knew nothing of the incident which had occurred in the offices of the *Daily Mail*. There the printers had refused to set a leader which they regarded as offensive and provocative to the trade unions.

For three years Bevin kept the secret of what had happened

inside Downing Street that night. He revealed to his tinplate
worker members in Swansea in April, 1929, that in his opinion,
Mr. Churchill, then one of the most influential members of Mr.
Baldwin's Government, was directly responsible for destroying
the peace moves which were developing between the trade union
leaders and the employers that night in Downing Street.

"If Mr. Churchill," Bevin declared, "had not come into the
Cabinet room on that Sunday night with the *Daily Mail* business,
the peace terms would have been in the hands of the Prime
Minister and there would have been no national strike."

He continued, "The two sides were in another room in
Downing Street, getting almost to the last clause for handing to
the Prime Minister, when Mr. Churchill saw red, walked in and
upset the Cabinet, and we had the ultimatum. That is a fact
which can be corroborated."

Bevin declared that Churchill had since admitted in private
that, had he foreseen what the National Strike was going to cost,
he would never have taken the line he did.

Bevin cried, "What sort of a statesman is that, who, when he
sees a few printers stop work, sees red? It will be the greatest
godsend to this country if Mr. Churchill is out of office for
evermore."

He explained, "It is not that Mr. Churchill is not a brilliant
man, but it is not safe to leave the destinies of millions of people
in the hands of a man with an unstable mind, a man who can fly
off at a tangent as he did in the war, with such terrible results for
millions of men."

That was an outspoken sample of the opinions most trade union
leaders held of Mr. Churchill in those days. Bevin, was, however,
one of the first of the trade union chiefs to realise the soundness
of Mr. Churchill's views on the menace of the Nazis and the
courage of his stand in the days of Munich and appeasement,
when Churchill was deliberately cold-shouldered from office by
the Conservatives. And later, when he served under Churchill, it
was Bevin who declared, "Winston Churchill is the expression of
the realism, the grimness, the resourcefulness, the strategic
conception and the determination of Britain to win this war."

But back in those days of internal strife it was Winston
Churchill whom the trade union chiefs regarded as their arch-
enemy among the Government Ministers. He was in command of

the fight on the Government side. The response to the strike leaders' call was overwhelming. More than 5,000,000 workers stopped work on that Tuesday morning. Bevin's instructions were that all members of the unions on strike should be calm and orderly. Mr. Churchill, however, put up a show of force in many industrial centres, particularly in the East End of London.

He organised parties of tanks and armoured cars, and, in most cases, they traversed empty streets. The working-class populace studiously kept indoors as the evidence of Britain's military might passed by.

Still, there were one or two clashes and prosecutions and imprisonment of local strike leaders ran into hundreds throughout the country.

Generally, however, the whole demonstration was remarkably well disciplined.

On the third day of the strike, it was reported to Bevin that the Government and employers' organisations were using thousands of London taxicabs as freight carriers. Within four hours Bevin stopped this "leak" in his side's organisation of the stoppage. Within four hours every taxicab driven by a trade union member had disappeared from the streets of London.

There was a little transport, it is true, for such vital services as food distribution. To secure a peaceful passage through the streets every one of these vehicles had to bear a prominently displayed label announcing "By permission of the T.U.C."

Hundreds of students and other citizens volunteered to drive railway trains and omnibuses in response to a Government call, but there was never more than a sketchy and slightly dangerous skeleton service in operation throughout the duration of the General Strike.

Both sides produced their own daily news-sheets. Winston Churchill was editor-in-chief of the Government's *British Gazette*, while Hamilton Fyfe, editor of the *Daily Herald*, and a team of assistants and censors, ran the *British Worker* on behalf of the T.U.C.

After the strike had been on a week and there seemed no sign of a break, Sir Herbert Samuel, the Liberal leader, who had been chairman of the Coal Commission, intervened. The non-acceptance of the Commission's report had led to the crisis. Sir Herbert Samuel (now Lord Samuel) made a private appeal to

Thomas added that there was bound to be a dislocation after such a tremendous upheaval, and that all parties would have to co-operate to "start things on the road again."

Thomas went on: "Your assistance in that is necessary; our assistance is necessary. We intend to give it and in doing that we believe that you can help. We trust your word as Prime Minister. We ask you to assist us in the way you only can assist us—by asking employers and all others to make the position as easy and smooth as possible, because the only thing we must not have is guerilla warfare."

Bevin, however, was not quite as conciliatory, and this was recognised by Cook and all others when the inevitable "inquest" came to be held. Bevin declared: "I want to urge this must not be regarded as an act of weakness, but rather one of strength. I am not talking of muscle and brawn, but rather that it took a little courage to take the line we have done. I want to ask you if you could tell us whether you are prepared to make a general request, as head of the Government, that ready facilities for reinstatement and that kind of thing shall be given forthwith.

"Employers no doubt have been active in carrying out the spirit of the Government during the fight, and they would no doubt respond to a statement of that character. I put it to you very strongly that it is one of the easiest ways of doing things. We have had a row and it does upset things, but we are quite willing to co-operate with our men to repair the damage just as much as the employers. But the employers are the people who can facilitate that kind of feeling, and I am sure they would respond to you if you issue that as a statement. It would be very helpful to us before we left the building if we could have some indication in that direction, because we shall have to send telegrams to unions whose headquarters are not in London, with whom we cannot converse, and coupling with it a declaration from yourself would, in a way, give the lead as to how the thing is to be approached.

"I would like you to give me an idea whether your proposal to call the parties together in order to effect a just settlement means that there is to be a resumption of the mining negotiations with us, or whether all the negotiations have to be carried on while the miners still remain out. I really feel in the event of our taking the lead in assuring you we were going to play the game and put our people back, that it was going to be free and unfettered negotia-

tions with the parties very speedily because thousands of our
people cannot go back if the colliers are still out, and if the colliers
are still out it is going to make it extremely difficult to get a
smooth running of the machine."

"Well, Mr. Bevin," Mr. Baldwin replied, "I cannot say more
here at this meeting now. I did not know what points you were
going to raise or that anything would be said beyond the statement of Mr. Pugh."

Baldwin admitted that he wanted to get the mines started as
soon as possible, but he insisted that he would have to see the
mine owners before it was possible to decide what could be done.

Bevin replied. "I am a little persistent. I do not want to take
up your time but we shall be meeting on these points soon?"

Baldwin gave no definite answer. All he would say was. "We
are going to consider right away what is best."

Unhappy weeks and months followed. There was mass victimisation in many trades. There was bitter recriminations from
many platforms. There was, particularly in the mining and heavy
industrial regions, the constant reminder that the struggle had not
ended with unqualified success because nearly a million miners
were trudging the streets workless. They showed incredible
solidarity behind Herbert Smith and Cook. They were out the
whole of the summer and throughout the autumn. Eventually,
they were beaten. When they returned to work two weeks before
Christmas they went back on the terms which they had resisted
from the start of the struggle.

Bevin, however, would have no part in regrets. He thundered:
"We are not going to join the party of whiners and apologists.
We believe the struggle was inevitable, that the challenge had to
be accepted. And whether it was conducted wisely or not, the
fact stands out in grand relief that the great bulk of the people
were loyal."

"Indeed," he declared, "many men who would not strike for
themselves have struck work and risked all on this occasion in
support of the miners." He was emphatic that the strike was not
a failure. "Even the governed class of this country, who in the end
know when to retreat for their own safety," Bevin went on,
"would be compelled by this great demonstration of unity to pay
greater regard to the consequences of their policies than hitherto.
It has produced a new alignment of forces. Politically, the effect

has been to break down barriers which existed within the working classes and united the workers on the industrial and political field more than anything else has done in the last century."

He continued, "Although there was no political object in the dispute, no one thought of upsetting the constitution, it is perfectly true that the Government was in the fight against us, but it was a case of coal owners plus Government, and in the background it was the coal owners who had taken the line all the time that they could withhold from the nation coal and industrial power at will and compel the nation to bend to their will as well as the people actually engaged in the industry. When members hear talk from politicians, including labour leaders, about the movement 'starving the nation into submission,' let them never forget that the one weapon that all the great employing interests have used to exercise their power and mastery, is the weapon of starvation, the ability to say to you, your wives and children, 'Starve until you are willing to bend to my will.' As to 'Never again,' let it not be forgotten," he concluded, "that nothing had ever occurred in the world that could not occur again in some form or other.

"While I am not an advocate of the general strike, or any other strike, unless it is absolutely inevitable in defence of our people, I am conscious always that there will be periods in the lives of nations and men which are great epoch-making events and bring about tremendous changes."

But the most remarkable thing about the aftermath of the General Strike was the recognition given to Bevin personally. The *Sunday Express*, for instance, wrote:

"The most forceful personality among the present trade union chiefs is Mr. Ernest Bevin. He was the only one whose reputation was enhanced by the general strike. But for his energetic grip on the situation during the last days of April there would in all probability have been no widespread stoppage.

"He alone took a comprehensive view. He made up his mind while others drifted. He acted while others talked—not for the first time.

"At the end of July, 1925, he had drawn up in masterly fashion the document which forced Mr. Baldwin to pay away twenty-three millions of the nation's money, to stave off the mining crisis for eight months.

"This document was the list of instructions to railwaymen and other transport workers as to what they should do in the event of the miners being locked out in the previous year. They were to refuse to touch any coal.

"The publication of these grim, laconic orders staggered the Prime Minister. It proved to him that he was up against trouble for which no preparation whatever had been made.

"There was in them none of the rhetoric usual in trade union manifestos, just a stark succinct statement of what was to happen at once.

"At once Mr. Baldwin backed down. The Cabinet decided that they must, at any cost (to the nation!) purchase delay. The subsidy was granted, and immediate measures were hurried on to put the Government in a position to defy the trade unions and carry on the everyday life of the country without them.

"So by the end of April all these measures had been taken. The Government were ready. What they expected was a repetition of the tactics of eight months before. But this time Bevin did not intend to let the transport workers and railwaymen go into the fight alone beside the miners. If there was to be a pitched battle in defence of the miners then the whole of the trade union forces must be thrown into it. No use asking one section to bear the burden of the attack."

Other newspapers recognised that at Downing Street, when the strike was declared off, he saw that the crucial point was "no victimisation," and he pleaded for it with great force though, unfortunately, in vain.

One of those remarkable paradoxes of English public life happened in August. The Government decided to send a strong mission to the United States to study their industrial problems and methods. Baldwin invited Bevin to be a member of this commission under the chairmanship of Sir William MacKenzie, who was later to become Lord Amulree.

Bevin jumped at the chance. He had been in America for a short personal visit four years earlier and, of course, his first overseas trip had been to the United States as the T.U.C. fraternal delegate in 1915. But he really knew very little about the American industrial set-up. When the Commission reached New York in the fall of 1926 MacKenzie decided to split up his delegation into working parties of three. In each party there was to be a Government official, a representative employer, and a trade union man. Bevin accompanied Mr. Michael Dewar, a leading industrialist, and Mr. (later Sir) Frederick Leggett, who was on the staff of the Ministry of Labour. The three set out and toured the industrial States from New Jersey to Ohio. It was a happy party, the three members took it in turn to introduce each other to the plant which they visited.

One day it would be Bevin's turn to seek out the president of a company, explain the object of the visit, and then bring in the other two members of his team. Then it would be Dewar's, and then Leggett's.

When they met Mr. Lichfield, president of the Goodyear Co., in Akron, in Ohio, it happened to be Michael Dewar's turn to present the delegation. First, he revealed his own identity to Mr. Lichfield and then presented Leggett as "leader of the Government side," and Bevin as "the leader of the general strike."

Mr. Lichfield was appalled. But he showed much more magnanimity and generosity to Bevin than one or two other American industrialists during the tour.

Indeed, at one plant in Youngstown, Ohio, Bevin was refused admission by the president of a leading steel concern. The steel president barked: "We want no agitators here," and showed Bevin the door. Bevin took it calmly, and "mooched" around Youngstown for the afternoon. Such a contingency had been discussed previously by the little group. It had been decided that if Bevin was refused admission anywhere, the other two would carry on and report their impressions to Bevin later that evening.

Generally, the tour was a tremendous success. They were given facilities to inspect plants, housing estates, and welfare arrangements.

There were occasions, it is true, on which Bevin showed a persistence in questions which was almost embarrassing. His investigation was thorough, but his conclusions were disturbing.

When he returned to New York to join up with all other parties on the Commission, he announced at a dinner, attended by American industrialists, that America would run into a crisis within three years. Bevin's prophecy proved gloomily correct, although the basis of his deduction was not subsequently accepted as correct by other authorities.

Bevin was shocked because he believed that in the United

States at that time employers were not interested in men over forty. He said it was a young man's country, but the stability of a nation depended on the contentment of middle-aged fathers of families.

Bevin was critical of the lack of state and federal social insurance schemes. He condemned the contrast between comparative affluence of men at work and the staggering plight of men out of work.

It is true to say that Bevin did not endear himself to many of the Americans whom he met during his 1926 visit. Many of them resented his candour, and attributed it to prejudice. His reputation in America was not enhanced when some months after his return to Britain he spoke to a British conference of works directors and managers at Balliol College, Oxford.

Bevin said: "Most of the talk about industrial relations in the United States is mere spoof—typical American spoof. I have found nothing miraculous in America, nothing due to any greater altruism or any better capacity than exists in Britain. The production of wealth in the United States since 1919 has increased by about 89 per cent., but so far as I can see the working people have not benefited more than six or seven per cent. by the intensification of production."

He continued: "There is a great deal of talk about relations between employers and employed, but in 90 per cent. of the so-called arrangements for industrial relations in the form of shop committees and councils, these are merely a subterfuge to prevent the genuine organisation of the working people, and a correct and fair representation of their views in dealing with the problems of the workshops.

"Efficiency of production ought not to mean slave driving, but I do not think hell could be worse than life in a certain works in America which I saw going at full speed.

"The City of London is much more up-to-date than New York, and I think that if this old country and Europe can get rid of their difficulties they have nothing to fear from the New World."

He forecast that in the next generation America would find it very difficult to obtain the type of labourer she needed for her mass-production factories.

The aim of all parents in America, he declared, was to get their children educated, and when they passed from school it was not into industry that they were going. They all made for what was called the "white collar jobs."

Most of the talk about the workers sharing in the increased prosperity of the country and in the control of industry was "bluff." He did not see the value of industry if it meant shortening the lives of the people who had to produce the wealth.

He concluded:

"Generally speaking, the best thing that we can learn from America is what to avoid rather than what to copy."

From the American point of view there is this to be said in favour of Bevin's outspokenness at that time. He said much of what he thought when he was in America and did not wait, as many other visitors have done, to return to his own country before expressing such criticisms.

All the same, it raises the question of Bevin's attitude generally to the United States. There is ample evidence of Bevin's tremendous admiration for many American political institutions.

"In the Western Hemisphere," he broadcast to the United States long before Pearl Harbour, "you have developed and had your being on the basis of democracy. So strong were these principles that you could have frontiers that were disarmed, you could keep your armed forces at an absolute minimum, almost limited, for many years, to a number just sufficient to preserve internal order. The separate Governments or peoples found a way to live together in peace. This may have been due to the fact that those who founded the United States and Canada were the men and women who had left the old countries and in those souls, even in those days, burned fiercely this love of freedom. Accordingly, every institution you devised worked as a check against possible domination, and at the same time allowed a great unity, based on liberty, to grow."

In many of his subsequent speeches he held up the United States as an example to copy.

But on the question which naturally interested him most until he became a Minister, he was put into a difficult position. He was put to the test of divided loyalties, and in order to avoid a charge of interfering in internal American affairs he has remained discreetly quiet.

For more than fifty years now the British Trades' Union Congress and the American Federation of Labour have exchanged fraternal delegates. No one urged the tightening of these bonds more than Bevin. After the days of Gompers, he became friendly with William Green, George Meany, John L. Lewis, who, when he last came to Britain, spent much time with Bevin, Robert Watt, and Dan Tobin.

But complications arose when the Congress of Industrial Organisations began to develop in the United States. Traditionally, Bevin, as an organiser of some of the lesser-skilled callings, felt a warm sympathy for the efforts of President Philip Murray, R. J. Thomas and Sidney Hillman to organise whole industries.

Bevin, like most British trade union leaders, kept hoping that the two great American organisations would get together voluntarily. That, they felt, would simplify relationships between the organised workers of the two countries enormously. But the most important thing of all is that the British labour leaders are eager to get closer than ever before to their opposite numbers in the United States. Of course, they have a philosophical basis for this desire. Their ultimate hope is that the future peace of the world can be achieved by some sort of world federation. And the first step towards it, they believe, is by understanding between the British Commonwealth and the United States.

If Bevin had not become a Minister there is little doubt that he would have been one of the leading lights from Britain in the formation of the World Trade Union Congress which came into being in 1945. In that the United States are represented by the C.I.O. This may drive the A.F.L. into greater isolation. It may even end the half-century of fraternal association between the British and the older-established American organisations. George Meany, the secretary-treasurer of the American Federation of Labour, came over to the T.U.C. specially in 1945 to emphasise that the A.F.L. wanted nothing to do with the Soviet trade unions. The British unions wanted friendship with those of both Russia and America. That is why they welcomed the offer of Sidney Hillman and the Congress of Industrial Organisations to participate in the work of the new world organisation. It retained a direct tie with the United States.

These are trade union affairs. As long as there is a Labour Government in Britain, the decisions and policies of the Trade Union Congress will have great influence on State policy.

H

This is particularly true as long as Ernest Bevin remains his country's Foreign Secretary. He became a national statesman late in life. He will never cease to be a trade union chief in principle—even after he formally retires from the position in March, 1946.

CHAPTER VI

LEADER OF LEADERS

THERE were at least three ironies in the way Bevin became a really nationally-established and acknowledged leader of all the trade unions. He had first emerged in Bristol in a time of distress and bitterness; now, sixteen years later, he was poised for his upward flight from a much more elevated level in a time of confusion and recrimination. The Conservative Government was taking its revenge for the general strike in repressive legislation designed to clip the wings of the unions and make a repetition of the great stoppage impossible. Employers were taking their revenge on their own workers with their own tools of victimisation and wage reductions. And inside the trade unions there was discouragement because thousands of members were giving up their cards and withholding their subscriptions and support. There was a sense of dismay and defeat among many of the union leaders because they could not see a clear way forward.

Bevin has always been introspective and quietly contemplative in such crises. When he mounts the rostrum in a great conference, when he starts speaking in a council chamber, or as he rises to address a public meeting no one knows what he is going to say. Except Bevin. He never shows his hand too soon. But he prepares it well in advance.

Subsequent developments were to show within two years how Bevin's mind had been working in the weeks before he travelled up to Edinburgh for the annual conference of the Trades Union Congress in September, 1927.

Obviously, he made up his mind to devote much of his time and nearly all his major pronouncements to the Trade Union Congress. But the question was the choice of field in which to specialise. Bevin had observed that four or five regular delegates to these annual conferences popped up to speak on any and every occasion. They dissipated their energies and in spite of their intrinsically able performances they had succeeded only in establishing for themselves a reputation for political windiness. He knew the irritation caused by speakers who, towards the end of their orations, confessed that they were expressing only their

own personal views and not the decisions of their unions. Few
things are more disliked by busy conferences. It was then that
Bevin made the decision to which he always stuck. He always
reflected the views of the majority of his own delegation, then
forty strong, representing 300,000 members.

There was great shrewdness here. His union by this time had
become the third largest in all the conference of more than 200
unions. Only the miners' and the railwaymens' unions were larger.
He quickly got the T.U.C. conference to accept him as the voice
of 300,000 even if the words and style were exclusively and
distinctively Bevin's own. And when Bevin spoke of "my people,"
as he did with a frequency never touched by any other leader,
some of his hearers winced because of the slightly arrogant and
possessive implications of the phrase, but they knew he could
justify it. Indeed, before he spread himself on the wider platforms
of the whole trade union movement he had built up for himself
a masterly situation of domination inside his own union. It was
highly departmentalised, as was inevitable in an amalgamation of
more than thirty separate unions. Each department had its own
experienced chief—men like Harold Clay, John Cliff, Ben Tillett,
Bill Devenay, Dan Hillman, Harry Gosling, and Stanley Hirst,
and, of course, May Forcey was maintaining her reputation for
orderliness and organisation. These men were given considerable
authority and autonomy in their own industries, but Bevin was the
general. He was always available for consultation and advice. He
had the right to intervene in any negotiations. While he guided the
executive council of lay members, the supreme policy-making
body of the union, he was scrupulous in carrying out their
decisions even if such decisions were against his advice. This was
rare. As far as the machinery of his union went, he had every
reason to be proud of it. Indeed, one of the great considerations of
that time before the general council of the Trades Union Congress
was how to scale down the number of unions which frequently
overlapped and dissipated their energies in fighting each other.
And Bevin's union was held up as a model of how to reconcile the
conflicting interests of many trades by bringing them together,
while at the same time allowing them considerable independence.
Yes, Bevin had good reason for feeling satisfied.

But the field was not wide enough for his restless insatiable
energies and interests.

The first irony was the companion he found for the first rungs of this upward climb. It was the new general secretary of the Trades Union Congress.

Walter Maclennan Citrine, ex-electrician from Merseyside, had been made general secretary only in 1926. Bevin had been made a member of the general council in 1925, when Citrine was assistant to Fred Bramley, who died the following year. Most of 1925 and 1926 had been eaten up by the abnormal circumstances of the threat and the event of the general strike.

It was really in 1927 that the two leaders were able to get down to the constructive phase of their co-operation. The irony of it all was not apparent for years. They seemed the perfect combination. They invariably reached the same conclusions on all major issues. True, their approach to and development of every problem, and their delivery and presentation of their arguments were strikingly dissimilar. They were the perfect contrasts. Citrine with his logical, meticulous, card-indexing mind and his carefully-phrased, impressively-mounting argument, delivered in a slightly metallic voice appealed mainly to reason. One of his invariable invitations to his audience was, "We must face this problem objectively, appreciating its implications, but dispelling from our minds all preconceived prejudice or bias."

Bevin, meaning the same thing, would command, "Face the facts. Let's see where they'll get us. Don't be hidebound by slogans." He spoke in the rich, slightly husky voice of a West-countryman. He spoke colloquially, but what impressed his audiences most was the breadth of his outlook. There were times when he seemed to suspect that some of his audience doubted his right to make profound declarations on such abstruse matters as foreign affairs or the intricacies of international finance. Here he would interpolate an odd phrase or two reminding his audience of how he had travelled overseas, or how he had served on this or that committee. That was his way of saying that he knew what he was talking about.

They were a great pair, these two. There were others on the general council and leading delegations who, at times, seemed to command equal attention and exert equal influence. Jimmy Thomas and Charles Cramp, the railwaymen's leaders, George Hicks, of the builders, Alf. Purcell, of the furniture makers, and Arthur Cook, of the miners, commanded great respect. Up to

that year, the major debates had been enlivened by W. J. Brown,
the civil service leader, who lost his right to attend after 1927 by
law. His union was not permitted to affiliate to the T.U.C. And
there was eloquent Harry Pollitt, the Communist delegate from
the boilermakers. Had these two continued to attend conferences
in later years they would have added much to their liveliness.
Both are great speakers, both have minds independent of influence by the general council, and both were critical of Bevin and
Citrine.

As the years went on it turned out that Bevin and Citrine were
critical of each other. Neither has made public reference to this
failure to get on. Each has tried, in the main with success, to
suppress these personal feelings in the interest of policy and
principles. But in the years that followed the tension between the
two leaders became embarrassing to other members of the general
council. Several members attempted to effect conciliation, but
they met with little success. Andrew Conley, the tailors' leader,
persuaded Sir Walter Citrine after a decade of this growing dislike
to invite Bevin to a meal to promote friendly relationships.
Citrine wrote this conciliatory letter in the interests of smoother
working inside the general council. He believed that Bevin had
been approached by another leader to accept the letter with
graciousness. Bevin, however, replied so coldly and formally that
the meal of peace was never eaten.

The second irony, which later events invest with a tremendous
significance, was the choice of subjects made by Bevin to impress
himself on that Edinburgh conference. His major contributions
were on foreign affairs.

Two years earlier, at Hull, the British trade unionists had
decided to form with the Soviet trade unions the Anglo-Russian
Joint Advisory Council. It had two main objectives. First to get a
better understanding between the organised workers of the two
countries. There was a great deal of sympathy in Britain to the
Soviet experiment, although the avowed Communists in Britain
were few and not influential. The second motion was to secure
the admission of the Russians to the International Federation of
Trade Unions.

For two years the two centres corresponded voluminously.
There were three meetings, one in Paris and the other two in
Berlin. But there was friction from the start. The British leaders

accused the Russians of trying to interfere in internal British affairs, and the Russian leaders accused the British of sabotage, opposition and procrastination. The Russians said the British leaders had "sold" their followers during the general strike. The British leaders, added the Russians, had done nothing when Britain severed diplomatic relations with Russia. Tomski, the Russian leader, had given a highly critical interview to the British Communist *Sunday Worker*. So the day of the great debate came at Edinburgh. It was one of those full-dress affairs when the normal standing orders of conference limiting speakers to five-minute contributions are suspended, and all the heavy guns of the movement are expected to take part.

The general council proposed to end the joint committee with the Russians. Citrine opened the debate, and Bevin wound it up. It was the traditional clash between the Right and the Left of the Trades Union Congress.

"There is something more than a mere question of injured dignity," Citrine declared, "that has compelled this general council to conclude that no good purpose can be served by continuing this joint council with the Russians while their present attitude is maintained. What separates us, we believe, is a very different conception as to the functions of that Anglo-Soviet Council. The experience of the Russian trade unions has been entirely different from the experience of unions in Europe as a whole, and right throughout their thinking there has emerged the conception that in some way Moscow is a stage upon which the revolutionary battle of the workers is being fought, and that the rest of the world's trade unionists are interested spectators in the auditorium. They have felt that unless the methods they have adopted and the principles they believe in are adopted by the other movements, that inevitably the revolutionary movement they have built up will be menaced and made of no effect. They cannot understand why other people hesitate to follow their example, and because of this they unfortunately discern enemies in people whose only desire is to be their sincere and warm friends. They feel it their duty not merely to prescribe a remedy that other nations and other centres must adopt, but they feel themselves compelled to insist on the adoption of their methods."

Citrine continued, "Another difference lies in the method of approaching each other. The Russians believe in declamation as distinct from calm considered statement. In fact, when Mr. Hicks and I were in Russia, we were told that such terms as "traitor" and "lickspittle" had become so common in the inner councils of the Russian movement that nobody took any notice of them, and they wondered we should be disturbed by it. We agreed on new safeguards in Berlin. Hardly was the ink dry on that agreement before Tomski was claiming the public right to violate them, and to use what criticisms he liked publicly and internationally. Tomski's claim was followed by a declaration by the official Russian Trade Union movement itself showing that what Tomski claimed as a personal right they regarded as a right on behalf of the official Trade Union movement. We have not bolted or barred the door. We say that so long as the present attitude is maintained we cannot go on. The next step lies with the Russian trade unions. We have exhibited patience and sub-mitted to abuse which would have made some of us refuse to sit in the same room with members of our own movement."

It was natural that there were many divided views on such a momentous proposal. They were not all Communists who opposed the general council. Bill Brown, the civil service chief, for instance, singing one of the swan songs he delivered that week, pleaded with the conference not to break off its Russian relation-ships. "It is not Tomski or Tomski's manners I am troubled about," he confessed, "but the need for the maintenance of unity between two great working classes. All the blame is not on the Russian side. The breaking of this connection is going to bring us nearer to war than we have been since 1918."

Percy Collick, the railway locomotive spokesman (now Parlia-mentary Secretary to the Ministry of Agriculture), followed his usual and lively role of being "agin the Government" by accusing the general council of not showing enough keenness and enthusi-asm to make the joint council a success. He demanded that the joint effort should be given another chance, but later in the debate it turned out that Collick, who had spent some time in Russia in 1921, was speaking for himself and not for his union.

Wise quiet old John R. Clynes, later to be Home Secretary, supported Citrine by advising that the best thing was for Russia to look after her own affairs, and leave Britain to mind her own business, but there was some surprise when Charles Cramp, the leader of the railwaymen, opposed the general council's proposal

mainly on the ground that to pass it would be to give moral
support to the hated Baldwin Conservative Government. Jimmy
Thomas, the other railwaymen's leader, revealed that there was a
split in the railmen's ranks because he was supporting the general
council, of which he was a member, in spite of the majority
decision of his own delegation. Arthur Cook, the fiery, sincere
leader of the miners, wanted the whole matter deferred.

So, when Bevin got up to speak and end the debate the conclusion was in some doubt because of the attitude of the two most
powerful unions, the miners and the railwaymen.

Bevin looked pale and grim, as he always did in major debates,
when he got up to speak. His "line" was known because the
decision of the general council had been unanimous. But his
treatment was unknown. That was the reason for the invariable
attention Bevin commanded. Calmly he pointed out that no one
had attempted to justify the attitude of the Russians to the
general council. He declared, "You have to appreciate that
running through these things there are two distinct moral
standards. One is the moral standard accepted by the British
movement; to differ but to hammer out their differences, and
when a decision is arrived at, to loyally and honourably abide by
it. That is the British standard. The Russian standard, as I see it,
is that the end justifies the means. That has been our experience
on the general council."

"Now these two moral standards," Bevin continued, "cannot
be reconciled in the promotion of a unified movement. If you
turn down this resolution it means that the general council would
be expected to meet the Russians on the Joint Committee. How
would we meet them? If you had been called a traitor, a twister,
a liar, and everything else that can be thought of, and you had to
meet the man who called you that, would you meet him as a
friend or as an antagonist? That does not promote international
unity; that is the wrong way to assemble for a conference. Already
I have, with one or two others in this Congress, done all we could.
I attended the first meeting with the German, Belgian, French
and others that followed the war. We went over to Amsterdam
with all the bitter antagonisms of the war in January, 1919, and
united the transport trades, and we set out to build our international. If we had gone into those meetings calling the men who
had their feelings embittered during the agony of four years, liars

and traitors, there would have been no international of the transport workers of the world. That is not the right method of making
it. I sincerely hope there will be no differences of opinion. Give us
the consensus of opinion of this Congress. Are we not entitled to
it? Is it fair after the silence of the general council, after sitting
down week after week, month after month, after circulars have
been sent to our own branches that attempt to decry us and belie
us we have kept silent in the interests of international unity?"
The Citrine-Bevin proposal was accepted by 2,551,000 to 620,000.

That was an example of Bevin batting for his side, contributing
to the debates as a member of a team.

But within an hour the conference was to have an example of
Bevin as the initiator of an idea that astounded the conference by
its breadth of outlook. It was the first example of the Bevin technique of forcing these annual conferences to consider wider
aspects of their interests than the "bread-and-butter" questions
of wages and working conditions, which he considered more
suitable matters for individual unions. He got up and boldly
announced support for the idea of a United States of Europe.

He met plenty of opposition to this new-fangled idea. But he
carried his resolution convincingly. It said, "Notwithstanding the
political divisions of Europe, this Congress instructs the general
council to further, through the international organisations, a
policy having for its object the creation of a European public
opinion in favour of Europe becoming an economic entity."

He pointed out that national aspirations and political divisions
were bound to be great handicaps to world economic development for a long time, perhaps longer than all of them then in
Synod Hall, Edinburgh, would be on earth. Then, to explain his
interest in such unfamiliar matters, he recalled, "I have recently
been to the Continent of America. I was asked to go out to
investigate some of the reasons for American prosperity. I did not
find that the American capitalist was any more beneficent than
the British capitalist. I did not find that there was any greater
genius for organisation in America. I did not find all the wonder-
ful things that have been said in the newspapers about the United
States, but what I did find was this, that I went there from a little
island, and I was asked to compare its possibilities with a continent. I found that there were 130,000,000 people within one
economic entity, with no tariffs, with a mobility among the

people to move about without the boundary handicaps that apply
in Europe. I found a frontier 3,000 miles long without a gun, with
commerce passing to and fro pretty freely, and I came to the
conclusion that if we are to deal with the problems of Europe we
have got to try and teach the people of Europe that their economic
interests, their economic development have to transcend merely
national boundaries. I am a little bit of a dreamer; I think it is
necessary."

He talked about the Danubian basin. He talked about Bismarck.
And then he used the phrase that arrested the attention of his
audience, and incidentally, provided a criticism of him three
years later when world circumstances changed and forced him to
give more support to the idea of promoting a community of
interests inside the British Empire.

"The Labour movement," he continued, "should carry on a
great educational work in the way of promoting the development
of all forms of national culture, even to the extent of political
divisions, and yet trying at the same time, to inculcate the spirit
of a United States of Europe—at least on an economic basis, even
if we cannot on a totally political basis. Cast your eye over Europe
with its millions of underfed, with its millions of people with a
wretchedly low standard of living. We can have mass production,
we can have intensified production, and we must direct the
consuming power in order to absorb that mass production to the
millions of people in Europe whose standard of living is not far
removed from the animal, and whose standards are capable of
being raised at least 1,000 per cent. by bringing together their
productive capacity in return for the craftsmanship of our own
Western Europe."

Bevin did not have to wait long for opposition. Up jumped
J. B. Figgins, an able railwayman, to retort, "I agree Bevin is a
dreamer, but he is no thinker." It took a bold man to say that
then. It has not been said in recent years.

Figgins declared that the creation of a United States of Europe
for increased mass production would merely intensify competition
with the United States of America. There can be no economic
unity in Europe, Figgins went on. The only thing worth working
for was world economic unity.

Arthur Cook, of the miners, was soon on his feet to shout:
"This cuts right across our whole idealism, built up in the early

days of forming an all-embracing international. We have given
lip service to the formation of a world-wide international and now
we are going to confine ourselves to Europe. One could think our
interests could be confined there, but they cannot, and any
student of economic development can quite see that we have to
look away from Europe rather than at Europe to create new
associations if we are to deal practically with the absorption of
men who cannot be employed here in industries like mining.
This is absolutely absurd, impracticable, idealism. It is an
abstraction."

The only supporter Bevin found was Jack Jones, of the General
and Municipal Workers, who welcomed the proposal as one holding out hope for the unemployed. He was followed by the extreme
Left Winger, Tomkins, of the furnishing trades, who called the
Bevin idea a reactionary bolster to the capitalist system.

Bevin was angry, He said he would not have intervened but for
"the thoughtless kind of discussion" that had been introduced.
He declared that he was urging this proposal because he was an
internationalist. He pointed out how the big employers were
developing cartels. He claimed that the only hope was to get an
indivisible nation spreading across from the borders of Russia to
the extreme tip of France, with the uplifting of working-class
standards in the most backward countries of Europe. Higher
standards meant more demand for consumer goods, and more
employment for all. It was noticeable that Bevin did not include
Russia in his idea of a United States of Europe.

In spite of Bevin's torrential, and rather ragged, eloquence, the
lining up of miners and railwaymen together was always a menace
to any proposal.

Bevin was obviously relieved, and pleased, when the result of
the card vote was announced. He had won by 2,258,000 to
1,464,000.

The third irony was created by the fact that while Bevin was
establishing his ascendancy over the conference on international
affairs, circumstances were developing which forced him to
concentrate on major domestic issues. The result was that when,
years later, Britain and the world was surprised by his appointment to the office of Foreign Secretary even regular delegates to
the Trade Union Congress forgot that his major debut as a leader
of the movement had been in these fields.

True, Bevin had made a powerful intervention in that 1927 conference on the major domestic issue of the day. He replied to Prime Minister Baldwin's appeal for industrial peace by declaring that while no section of the community was more desirous of industrial peace than the workers, there could be no industrial peace as long as the Government showed their class bias by attacks on the wages standards and the introduction of the oppressive Trades Disputes Act.

Bevin accused Baldwin of deliberately conveying that the trade unions had always been warlike, and had been against negotiations. "The softer Baldwin's words, the more repressive his acts," said Bevin, "and the only way he can prove his sincerity is to resign and have a general election."

That was a true reflection of the trade unions' mood at that time towards Baldwin and his Government. Remember, the trade unions were sore because of their diminished authority and membership. They were incensed, too, by falling employment and the victimisation which still went on although the general strike had been over more than seventeen months. Many thousands of workers had spent the whole of that time tramping the streets looking for work, living on meagre allowances grudgingly given by the relief authorities.

Solemnly, the thirty-two leaders, members of the general council of the trade union movement, met in their London offices soon after they had left the Edinburgh conference to consider the policy they should adopt.

They knew as well as any group in the country that the economic dislocation which had followed the war had left Britain's industrial position in a calamitous state. They blamed Government inaction. They argued that the general strike of the preceding year had been a symptom of the depression and not a contributory cause. They got to the stage when they had to consider the policy they would recommend to their followers.

Bearded Ben Turner, the textile workers' leader, was that year's chairman of the general council. He had little part, however, in drafting the lines of discussion which the general council were to pursue.

This draft bears the unmistakable stamp of Citrine and Bevin. They decided that there were three avenues of approach to this depressing problem. The first was to say frankly that the unions would do everything possible to bring the industrial machine to a standstill, to ensure by all possible means the breakdown of the entire system, in the hope of creating a revolutionary situation on the assumption that this might be turned to the advantage of the workers and to the abolition of capitalism.

That was Red Revolution. It was turned down as futile, certain to fail, and sure to lead to bloodshed and misery. It is, however, interesting to record that this possibility appears on the official records of the Trades Union Congress.

The second line was one of standing aside and telling the employers to get on with their own job, while the unions would pursue a policy of fighting sectionally for improvements. The objections to this course were that it was entirely inconsistent with the modern demand for a completely altered status of the workers in industry, and that it was a futile policy, a confession of failure, for unions to say that they were going to take no hand in the momentous changes that were taking place in the life of the nation.

The third was for the trade union movement to say boldly that not only was it concerned with the prosperity of industry, but that it was going to have a voice in the way industry was carried on, so that it could influence the new developments that were taking place. The ultimate policy of the movement could find more use for an efficient industry than for a derelict one. The unions could use their power to promote and guide the scientific reorganisation of industry as well as obtain material advantages from that reorganisation.

It was the third course that the general council took. They agreed that it was the only one if the trade union movement was to endure as a living constructive force. They were not entirely unanimous. One or two members had the feeling that if ever the revolution was to come this seemed the best time. But these were in a tiny majority. There is no doubt about the weight of opinion in favour of this policy. But it was one thing to decide on a line of policy and quite another to have the opportunity of putting it into practice, especially in the political circumstances with a powerful Conservative majority in office, and public opinion still slightly ruffled from the inconvenience caused in the previous year by the general strike.

Towards the end of November a letter was received by Mr.

Citrine. It was signed by Sir Alfred Mond, the great chemical chief, and twenty other prominent industrialists, including Sir Herbert Austin, the motor car manufacturer, Sir Arthur Dorman, Sir Robert Hadfield, and Sir Frederick Mills, the steel leaders, Lord Aberconway, Lord Colwyn, Lord Londonderry, and Mr. David Davies, the coal millionaires, Sir Hugo Hirst, the electrical magnate, Mr. Kenneth Lee and Sir Peter Rylands, the textile manufacturers, Sir Josiah Stamp, the railway chief, Lord Weir, the contractor, and Sir David Milne-Watson, public utilities leader, and, later, Lord Ashfield, head of London transport, and Mr. Samuel Courtauld, the rayon pioneer.

These men had household names in Britain. They dominated their respective spheres of industry. Citrine made a characteristic gesture in having all their associations looked up, and their standing verified. He found that the signatories to this letter held directorships in 189 companies. They included 98 chairmanships between them, and many of them had been presidents of such important bodies as the Federation of British Industries and the Confederation of British Employers. There was no doubt that they represented the cream of big business in Britain.

They invited the general council to a conference to discuss questions relating to the whole field of industrial reorganisation and industrial relations.

Now, although this invitation came at a crucial time, and conformed to the desire of the general council, the trade union leaders indulged in no unseemly rush to accept it. They knew the implications of such a move. It was Bevin who suggested that they think it over for a month. They chose seven of their leaders, including Ben Turner, the chairman, Citrine, Bevin and Jimmy Thomas, to study procedure. This sub-committee recommended that before the two sides got down to business, four conditions would have to be observed. First, the powers and authority of the respective parties should be settled, secondly, no discussions should trespass on the functions of existing organisations, thirdly, that all discussions should be "without prejudice," and, fourthly, that the object should be the review of general principles connected with the economic situation and with matters common to industry generally.

There was need to move cautiously. The leaders of the influential Amalgamated Engineering Union had got wind of the talks and had demanded an explanation from Citrine of the powers under which the general council were acting in accepting such invitations.

The 56 leaders, 32 from the general council and 24 of the employers, met in the Royal Society's Apartments in Burlington House, London, on January 12th, 1928, and Sir Alfred Mond, who presided, quickly explained that the industrialists had acted in their private capacity. They had, he said, wished to assist and not destroy the trade union movement. By discussing matters as individuals they felt themselves free from traditional procedure and controversies.

Mond (who became Lord Melchett the following year) had obviously come fully prepared because he submitted eight or nine topics for discussion at further meetings. They included such controversial matters as rationalisation and amalgamation, security and status of workers, works councils, financial partici- pation by the workers in industry, and investigation into the causes of disputes.

Leaders from both sides joined in the discussion. Both sides were obviously feeling their way. Some of the questions were pointed and topical. Bevin wanted a quick end to victimisation. He wanted reinstatement of all men who had been refused their jobs because of their part in the strike of 1926. He wanted all questions of finance and management brought within the dis- cussions. In those days this was a sensational request because, only six years previously, there had been a national strike of engineers over this very question of managerial function. But the employers agreed.

In fact, there was a generally conciliatory atmosphere about that first meeting. There was one exception. Arthur Cook, of the miners, serving his first year on the general council, would not enter into the spirit of the conference. "There are present," he barked, "men who have spent their lives trying to destroy the unions. I cannot commit the miners, neither could any other members of the general council commit anyone, nor have you employers any power. This conference can do no good and it is a waste of time."

Mond admitted that the mining industry needed more change than any, but he insisted the conference could do some good. Cook never acquiesced in these proceedings. He was the solitary opponent at the birth of this movement, which came to be known either as "the Mond-Turner talks," or "Mondism."

It led to one of the classic debates in the history of the Trades Union Congress. The discussion on this question of continuing such collaboration established an approach to industrial problems which was maintained, with only slight variations, right up to the start of the second world war. It clearly emphasised the cleavages within the ranks of the trade union movement. But it also established that British trade unionism is evolutionary and not revolutionary.

Some indication of the determination of the general council to prepare their armoury for the conference fight was shown by a small incident which occurred in May, four months before the conference opened in Swansea.

Sir Alfred Mond was travelling in Rome early in May. He gave a newspaper interview in which it was alleged he praised the Fascist regime. The general council could not face a conference accusation that they were associating with a self-confessed admirer of the Fascists. So Citrine sent Mond a letter asking for an explanation.

Mond declared that the interview was given in English to an Italian journalist. It appeared in Italian, and the retranslation of a "summarised and incorrect" version had been telegraphed to London. Mond insisted that the English version bore no resemblance to his interview. "My opinions, publications and actions," Mond protested, "should by this time have convinced all sincere persons of my belief in constitutional freedom, industrial progress and co-operation."

His explanation was accepted, otherwise the talks would have been concluded by the trade unionists immediately. That was the sensitive atmosphere which prevailed throughout that summer.

The discussion at the T.U.C. in Swansea continued throughout the whole of the day. Ben Turner was the conference president, and the "star team" was put on by the general council. Citrine opened, Clynes and Thomas intervened during the debate, and the winding up was left to Bevin.

It is on a division of deep principle that the Trade Union conferences are at their best. There are rarely interruptions of speakers, unless they are palpably garrulous or reveal that they are acting as spokesmen for outside interests, by which most

I

delegates mean the Communist Party. It should be explained that Communists are not banned from attending the Trade Union Congress as delegates or trade union officials. Indeed, one Communist, Bert Papworth, the London busman, has become a member of the general council in the last two years, and he was nominated by Bevin's old union. But to this day, obvious Communist propaganda causes many protests.

Citrine confessed that for months members of the general council had been victims of scurrilous and exaggerated attacks which had distorted the work of the general council. He declared that no existing employers' organisation was prepared to open talks with the trade union leaders on the scope accepted by the Mond group.

"None of us," he asserted, "can be satisfied with the position of the workers at the present time. None of us can be complacent about it, none of us can feel aloof from it. Every one of us must be daily looking round for some means to try to advance and improve the condition of those whom we represent. The position of the workers and the long-continued depression have created something which, in the view of eminent economists, may be compared with the industrial revolution in the last part of the eighteenth century. We may be even now in the throes of a revolution such as that. We are too near events to calculate fully their significance."

He went through a history of the trade union movement. He claimed that at last the general council had emerged as real leaders. Unless they accepted the Mond invitation they would have to wait until another organised body of employers was prepared to open discussions. He denied that any pact had been entered into with the Mond group. He repudiated the charge of collaboration. Citrine's performance followed a pattern which he was then developing, but which he has now mastered. He opened on the defensive, by anticipating the lines of attack from the critics and then passed on to the offensive, by stressing the advantages of his own policy. He concluded, "We cannot await the advent of the breakdown of capitalism before we start marching towards control. If control is one of our specific objects we are most likely to give effect to it by seeing a body of employers and trying to get them to admit our claim—a body of men who have said they will exclude nothing and are willing to discuss anything —and with them to try and come to some arrangement. I say emphatically the council has taken a wise and courageous step."

It was J. T. Brownlie, one of the ablest leaders the British engineers have had this century, who opened the attack. He challenged the constitutional right of the general council to enter into any talks with individual and unrepresentative employers, and proposed that the record of the talks should be received as information only. No further talks should take place until all unions had an opportunity to consider the implications of "such a grave departure from the historical policy of Congress."

A.B. (Lons) Swales, another engineers' leader, who was a member of the general council of the Trades Union Congress, confessed that he had been against the Mond talks all the way through. He thought the general council had assumed too much authority to itself, and scored a neat point in saying that when in previous years the general council had tried to increase its authority it had been turned down by speeches from Bevin and one or two others—before they joined the general council.

George Hicks, another member of the general council, supported the engineers by demanding greater consultations with individual trade unions, and with more representative employers' organisations. Hicks, one of the most famous raconteurs among the trade union leaders, lost some of his effectiveness on this day by being so long in describing the horrors of rationalised industry in the United States—"the joyless, expressionless faces of those who work in rationalised factories"—that a delegate jumped up to plead with President Turner to protect the conference from "such irrelevancies."

J. R. Clynes, the leader of the general workers, commanded a hearing throughout his life by his quiet sincerity. In his mild manner he, a member of the general council but not of the little group of leaders who had conducted negotiations with the Mond group, made an effective contribution by asserting that the trade union leaders had gained important concessions which many employers' organisations would resent as excessive concessions to trade union views.

It was Arthur Cook, the miners' leader, who brought the fireworks into the debate. Every word of his vehement, excited sentences contained an implied attack on his colleagues on the general council. "You cannot hope," he cried, "to safeguard the workers under the capitalist system. Antagonism has grown. That cannot be denied. There is irreconcilable antagonism which is bound to lead to irreconcilable antagonists."

There were moments when Cook was scarcely coherent. He shouted with his face deeply, dangerously flushed. Obviously, he was on the verge of a breakdown. His fire was consuming him. "Do you think," he shouted, "that any employer will give up the weapon of victimisation? Never. There has been no change since these negotiations have taken place in the policy of the employers. They are pursuing the same policy of reducing wages. Everybody is agreed that rationalisation does not start on a certain day or at a certain time. It is with us now. You will notice that Mond is developing it in the chemical industry."

Cook paused for a moment to wipe the perspiration from his brow. Then he roared, "Do not have alliances with the enemy. They say, 'Your leaders are sitting down with us and they agree you must face the facts of industry.' Yes, face the facts. The facts of the workers' home, the facts of the worker's life. Let us dare to insist upon the need of the worker and not make the worker the slave of industry. Comrades, this is a vital principle, and one that is going to affect the political and industrial movement; one that is going to bind us with shackles to capitalism, which is the thing we want to break. I ask you in the interests of the workers, let us build up our own organisation, our own intelligence department, our own forces that will win for the workers, not more unemployment, but the right to regular and adequately paid work."

He staggered from the platform, and collapsed in the annexe to the hall. He lost consciousness and was carried into a small room. After a few minutes of first aid attention he revived and struggled to his feet. He threw back the friends who tried to restrain him. Tears ran down his livid cheeks. "Have I beaten them? Have I beaten them?" he cried. A doctor came and ordered Cook to his hotel to rest and restore his nerves. It was Cook who reflected the misgivings and crushed hopes of the militant extremists in the conference. Cook, the miners' hero, the incorruptible and the implacable who died prematurely only three years later.

But while Cook had collapsed, his own president, sturdy, pugnacious Herbert Smith, the Yorkshire miner, had mounted the rostrum to announce, "Why am I following the miners' secretary? Because I am here to tell you what the decision of the Miners' Federation is—not what Mr. Cook's decision is, or what my decision is, but what the Miners' Federation decision is. It is that the general council did right in accepting that invitation and they find no fault with them. The members of the general council have not lowered their value by going to these discussions. On the contrary, they have raised their value by defending their cause."

A. G. Tomkins, the furnishing trades' leader, declared he was bringing a "breeze" from the workshops. Tomkins is another delegate who receives a good-natured ovation year after year, mainly because he is traditionally against the trade union authorities. "You have either to choose to fight in the interests of the working class, or you have to collaborate with the capitalist class, as the general council have acted."

J. H. Thomas, whose great influence in the Congress throughout the nineteen-twenties has been forgotten since he suffered political eclipse in the mid-1930's, was the big shot who defended the general council's attitude in the middle of the debate. He did it with his usual confidence and skill. Thomas analysed and disposed of the arguments of most of the opposition speakers, and quite unblushingly revealed inconsistencies on the part of some of his fellow-members on the general council, notably George Hicks. Thomas ended by announcing blandly, "We are going to meet the other side. Never believe that the other side are cleverer than we are. Why should we admit that? It is a most contemptible admission, and I do not admit it. I am never going into a conference believing that the other people are cleverer than I am, for the simple reason that I have proved the reverse."

"You have not been a victim," shouted a delegate from the side of the hall.

Jimmy Thomas put on his most injured look. "Just fancy," he appealed to the whole conference, "here is a man attending Congress, I believe, for the first time who says to me I have not been victimised."

Thomas was speechless with indignation, but his next sentence was, "But the issue is bigger than this personal issue. Your general council are elected by you for good or for ill; they are the chosen people to conduct your affairs. If they cannot be trusted, shift them, but while you elect them and return them, and whilst they are charged with responsibility, they would be cowards if they shirked action because of the abuse, the misrepresentation, the wilful lies of people. After all, in this Congress we have to face the facts. We have not today to meet the charges and lies and libel that have been made. You will observe that all the opponents dare not come to the rostrum at this Congress and repeat what they have said. Instead of lying, instead of abusing, and instead of misrepresenting us, here inside this Congress is the place to meet the facts, and the commonsense and honesty of our delegates will give the ultimate judgment."

McTaggart, one of the woodworkers, was frequently interrupted because, in his unfamiliarity with handling Congress audiences, he committed the lapse of declaring that the principle that was being instilled into the breast of every trade unionist was that he was organised not to pay trade union officials huge salaries because in many cases these officials had forgotten all about the working-class . . . . then McTaggart was drawn into a back-chat act with one or two irate officials. He had to be "rescued" by Ben Turner, the president, who demanded a courteous hearing for McTaggart. McTaggart had, however, lost the sympathy of his audience, so in one second he scrambled through the speech he had intended to make originally, which was that the most effective way of making progress was to organise the millions of non-unionists in the country.

As Bevin lumbered up to the rostrum to speak there was one of those rare eve-of-big-moment silences, when the rustling of a sheet of paper on the president's desk could have been heard at the far end of the hall.

Bevin spoke for half an hour, and although he threw out some challenging observations, he was not interrupted because the points he made were thought-provoking. Bevin has mastered the art of knowing a trade union audience.

"We have had some long lectures on economics this afternoon," he drawled. "Well, friends, I always say the difference between a politician and an industrial leader is this; our political party is working for change, but the industrial leader has every day of his life to deal with facts as they are. You have built up a political party because there are certain changes that have got to be effected, and they cannot be effected across the negotiating table or in relations with employers at all. But with regard to the trade union officer—and this is where you people criticise us ignorantly—what are the factors? A challenge is being made by our movement for more power. The fight went on right throughout the post-war period, one side trying to drive us back to conditions worse than 1914. I have claimed from the beginning, and I have never apologised for it, that the general strike was a culminating point to that conflict for power which had been going on. In view of this invitation and subsequent development—if it was not all that we desired—it proved that we had not lost the fight after all."

He went on to say that with the Mond group they had carried the principle of trade union recognition in terms further than most unions had achieved.

He squared his shoulders as he said, "I am going to claim this, too. It is all very well for people to talk as if the working-class of Great Britain are cracking their skins for a fight and a revolution, and we are holding them back. Are they? There are not many of them as fast as we are ourselves. That is the position."

He declared that the Mond conferences had acted as the greatest check on company union growth in Britain. The Mond employers had also agreed, against Prime Minister Baldwin, that the trade unions were not responsible for 1926. "The employers," Bevin continued, "have agreed that whoever was responsible for 1926 it was not the workman who was loyal to the call of his union." In his own union, he revealed, he had used this Mond conference document to have victimised workers restored to their former jobs.

He believed a survey of unemployment was needed. "With whom can you discuss it? he asked, "Government departments, who do nothing? No, I would rather sit down with some considered policy on a problem of that character facing the capitalists themselves across the table—not in alliance with them, for I am not more in alliance with them than I am in alliance with the dock owners or anybody else whom I have to fight every day. Is the strike the only way to fight? Cannot we fight by discussion as well as starvation? Cannot we fight by intelligence?

"On rationalisation," he continued, "we have faced the employers across the table. It is said," he explained, "that what we did wrong was in welcoming it. I do welcome rationalisation, and I make no apology for so doing. This hybrid state of the small employer and the combine fighting each other over a long period and fighting against the threatened bondage of bankruptcy is causing penury and trouble among the whole of our people. I would rather see a real organised attempt at effective organisation by rationalisation than I would see a long-drawn out weary road from the small employer to the big."

Now all along in these proposals, Bevin was steamrolling ideas that would have created tremendous controversy had they been introduced away from the context of his speech. He was thinking aloud, and throwing his ideas at the conference with a detachment which stunned his hearers.

There is another part of that speech which is worth recalling today because of what happened a dozen or so years later. Said Bevin of the Mond conferences, "Directly the idea of compulsory arbitration, compulsory investigation, and the interference of the State by legislation arose, we rejected it out of hand, and the employers agreed with the rejection." When Bevin became Minister of Labour he insisted on all these things, justifying them by the national needs.

Bevin declared, "I look forward to the time when the general council will be coming and laying down before this great parliament of its own creation annual reports on the discussions of great economic problems, trying to attract your attention on lines of analyses, lines of investigation, not mere debating points blown by the wind. Thus and thus only will the movement be really intelligently dealing with the real economic problems of our times."

That again was prophetic. These surveys of industrial and economic trends are now accepted features of the annual activities of the general council.

Then, they were novel and resented as an attempt by the general council to assume excessive powers and encroach upon the rights of individual unions.

Bevin's outspoken declaration was the climax of the justification for continuing the Mond talks. The conference approved by 3,075,000 votes to 566,000—an overwhelming triumph.

But once again circumstances killed the movement, though not the trend it started.

Throughout the winter of 1928 and the spring of 1929 the talks between the trade union leaders and the big industrialists went on.

They were mainly concerned with unemployment, the most disturbing feature of the day in British internal affairs. By March, 1929, they produced a remarkable interim joint report on unemployment. It was remarkable not only for its proposals but for its reflection of the degree of unanimity which both sides managed to reach after a tradition of hostility which had gone on unchecked since the start of the Industrial Revolution more than a century earlier. The lion and the lamb were snuggling down contentedly together, though each kept one eye open.

There were some distinctive recommendations in this joint report. One was a proposal that the Government should float a loan to buy up a tract of Canada for settlement by thousands of British families for whom no living could be found in their native land. This scheme, it was suggested, should be operated by a joint committee of employers and workers under a Special Minister. It crystallised that trinity idea of State, employers and employed, which was the cardinal principle of the philosophy held independently by Bevin and Citrine, and applied so effectively by the former when he became Minister of Labour and National Service.

Another proposal was that trade relations should be resumed with Russia. Bevin observed rather cynically a year or two after this that Russia's business with Britain seemed to be 90 per cent. propaganda and 10 per cent. orders for goods'

Then there was the suggestion that all firms and industries should, as soon as circumstances permitted, set up their own "labour reserve funds" to make grants to men of 65 to augment their State pensions if they retired from work.

School-leaving age should be raised from 14 to 15. The principle behind these two proposals was clear. Britain had too many workers then, as she was to have too few a decade later, and the idea was to stop the flow of entry into industry by youth and expedite the departure of oldsters.

But the most significant agreement of all was on rationalisation, although the trade union chiefs were fully aware that by streamlining industries into efficiency and closing down many obsolete plants and mines, unemployment might actually be increased temporarily. But all these schemes were to go forward in consultation with the trade unions.

That, to the trade union chiefs, was the great justification of these employer-worker relationships. Still, it had to be admitted that the two sides, influential though they were in their own spheres, were still unrepresentative. They were committing no

one but themselves. This had some advantage because the talks
went on in greater freedom than if constituent bodies had to be
consulted at every step. All the same the talks were commanding
a great deal of attention. What the parties said jointly was being
widely read and discussed, even if little positive action seemed to
be developing from these proposals. They went on working
steadily for a joint National Industrial Council—a sort of supreme
court or Parliament for industry.

Suddenly there was a movement. A very tentative invitation to
joint talks was received by the trade union chiefs from the two
great employers' organisations, the Federation of British Industries and the National Confederation of Employers' Organisations.
It was very qualified, very halting. Indeed, though asking the
trade union chiefs to come to talk, the invitation added, "At this
conference they" (the two employers' organisations) "could
explain the difficulties which stand in the way of consultation
with your council through a National Industrial Council."

It was subsequently explained that the Confederation dealt
only with labour questions. The Federation, on the other hand,
was interested only in commercial and economic questions. Each
was jealous of its own province, yet both had come together to
issue this joint invitation to a conference with the Trades Union
Congress. That in itself was historic.

When the conference met in the Hotel Metropole in London
on April 23rd, 1929, Lord Gainford, the coal owner, president of
the Federation of British Industries, took the chair and politely
hoped that the prosperity of industry as well as better relations
between the two sides would result from the meeting. But it was
obvious from the brevity of his comment and the punctiliousness
of his words that he personally saw little hope of a permanent
development.

Sir Ralph Wedgwood, chairman of the National Confederation
and one of Britain's greatest railroad administrators, offered however to meet the trade union leaders from time to time for
consultations on "current aspects of agreed questions." And Mr.
(afterwards Sir) Lennox Lee, the textile magnate, who was
president-elect of the Federation of British Industries, added
that he "wished to establish co-operation and consultation with the
T.U.C. on matters of commercial and economic interest." Mr.
Lee added that such consultations on an *ad hoc* basis would be

more effective, if more elastic, than a more formal and rigid National Industrial Council.

There seemed little doubt that while the leaders of the two powerful employers' organisations were not prepared to admit the trade unions as equal partners on policy discussions, they recognised that the trade unions had become too powerful to be ignored.

Bevin asked the industrial chiefs to be more explicit in defining the demarcation between "labour" and economic questions. "How can they be separated?" he demanded. He believed that divisions of these fields were both impracticable and an academic quibble.

Only one member of that company felt any elation at the timorous, hesitant opening of these parleys. He was the incorrigible revolutionary miner, Arthur Cook, who could not keep the note of self-gratification and justification out of his voice as he cried, "I always told my colleagues that you organised employers would not accept the proposals we made with the Mond group." Cook went on to taunt the employers, "If the speeches you have made today represent the mind of organised capital, no co-operation is possible. If your system is wrong be big enough to face it."

In spite of this discordant note which was as embarrassing to some of the trade union leaders like Jimmy Thomas as it was galling to some of the employers, the two sides appointed six leaders each to work out plans for further joint conferences. Inevitably, Bevin and Citrine were among the six chosen by the trade union side.

Thus was born a relationship between the trade unions and the organised employers which has been maintained to this day with the exchange of views on all major current problems, and in the gravest crises, in the preparation of joint submissions to the Government. In open public discussions the two sides meet only at the annual conferences of the International Labour Office, where invariably they display to the world that "agreement to differ" which the British hug to their breasts as a mark of their difference from most other peoples.

Bevin still had to meet the annual hurdle of opposition at the annual conference of the Trades Union Congress. Tomkins, the furniture makers' leader, demanded the ending of all talks with any group of employers as they, he insisted, were "a serious

menace to the interests of the working-class movement." Brownlie, the principal leader of the engineers, went the same way. He
was confident that capitalism was coming to an end, anyway, and
that Mond, "a class-conscious capitalist," had started these talks
only to delay the inevitable end of his creed. Percy Collick, the
locomotive engineer, wanted the unions to organise to give the
death-blow to capitalism.

Bevin retorted, "Rationalisation is coming in spite of us, and
the question is, are we going to be inside the movement taking
part in what is going on and taking our place in it? I object to the
suggestion of inferiority complex on our part. I object to the view
that a trade union leader entering into conference with a Mond is
inferior to a Mond in brain capacity or anything else."

Now this was the sort of interpolation which made many of
his critics think that Bevin was becoming self-satisfied. Only a few
months previously, during a 3,000-mile speaking tour in the
general election which resulted in Ramsay MacDonald becoming
Prime Minister of a British Labour Government, Bevin had
declared to an audience of North Wales quarrymen, "I am not
given to boasting, but if I were asked to take on any job which
Mr. Baldwin" (then Prime Minister) "has handled, I would do it
with perfect confidence."

And here in this speech at the T.U.C. conference in Belfast,
with MacDonald barely four months in office, he was telling the
conference delegates, but for the benefit of the Government,
"If trade unionism confines its work to the mere discussion of
wages, and nothing else, then we are not performing the functions
that the needs of the times call upon us to perform in relation to
the organisation of the industrial system, and, through the
function of Parliament, to translate into law what we accomplish
on the industrial side. Parliament will never lead the industrial
system. Parliament will follow the industrial system."

But Bevin was not in search of personal glory. He could have
had it. Arthur Henderson, who was then Foreign Secretary,
wanted Prime Minister MacDonald to make Bevin and Citrine
peers to strengthen their Party in the House of Lords. MacDonald
agreed—but Bevin and Citrine would not accept. Both of them,
quite independently, as was their wont in the consideration of any
personal problems, refused the invitation. Each believed in the

superior effectiveness and continuity of the industrial, rather than the political, wing of the movement.

Bevin soon felt he was called upon to rebuke the Government he had helped to power. He accused them of not showing enough readiness to consult the trade union chiefs in the preliminary stages of projected legislation of especial interest to them. The relationships between the trade unions and the Labour Government of MacDonald was complicated by the determination of the Ministers to demonstrate beyond dubiety their impartiality to all. They accepted the view that they were in office to govern for the benefit of the whole nation and not for the particular interest of any section. They felt they could not show "favouritism" to the trade unions.

The Government decided its policy on unemployment, for instance, before consulting the trade unions. The "offender" on this occasion was Miss Margaret Bondfield, the Minister of Labour. Bevin, having issued a list of further expected legislation to remind the Government not to repeat Miss Bondfield's error of no-consultation, solemnly warned, "The attitude of trade unionists throughout the country is that anybody who seeks to bring down this Government or to undermine it in a fractious or egotistical manner before these problems have been dealt with will receive short shrift from the trade unionists. Indeed, they have subscribed their money for the purpose of building up the political party in order that such problems may be dealt with. We do not want the Government undermined. We want it strengthened. On the other hand, it is essential that the Government should pay strict attention to, and consult with, the great movement from which it draws its strength and power."

It was, however, as much by his deeds as by his words that he increased his hold upon the respect and loyalty of his members.

He worked for five years to get the International Labour Office conference to adopt a draft convention on dockers' accidents. He succeeded in Geneva in that summer of 1929.

His scheme was virtually a new international law for the regulation and provision of safety conditions for dockers in all the ports of the world.

This convention was not conceived merely in general terms and short articles as was usually the case.

It went to the length of naming much of the gear, machinery

and apparatus used in the loading and unloading of ships, and definitely laid down the minimum provisions, such as the height of fencing, and details of ladders, gangways, chains and first aid provisions needed to reduce the accident rates among dock workers.

During that session at Geneva there was a curious incident. A distinguished and famous representative of the British Government was entertaining a group of international delegates in the corner of a salon during one of those social receptions which are such a useful feature of these world conferences.

This British raconteur was a clever, if somewhat cruel, mimic. Bevin was convinced that he was disparagingly imitating Miss Bondfield, the Minister of Labour, who was not attending the conference but was well known to all present.

Bevin strode across the room, and got down at once to a roaring denunciation of the Government delegate. Bevin cared nothing for the obvious embarrassment of the Britishers present, nor for the discomfiture of the foreign representatives. His censure was scathing, his invective scalding. His justification was the defence of a woman he continued to respect even if he had had differences from her. He has an easily-roused sense of chivalry. On this occasion it was fortified by shared political convictions. Bevin was never reconciled to that official.

During these Geneva days Bevin was heavily preoccupied with extending his own vast union. It was running smoothly, and Bevin was so impressed by the success of his amalgamating efforts that he saw no reason to set a bound to them. Constantly, talks were going on with leaders of other unions. There were some major successes, like the affiliation of the old Workers' Union, that same organisation which had planned to organise the unhappy workers of Bristol twenty years before.

But the most ambitious new development was Bevin's decision to organise the seamen. There had been trouble with the National Union of Seamen because of the activities of its dominating and domineering chief, Havelock Wilson. He had decided that trade unions had no business to dabble in politics. He entered into mutual arrangements with the shipowners to make every ship a "closed shop." No seaman could get a job without a union ticket. That was bad enough. There was deep suspicion that in return for this monopoly Wilson had entered into a pact not to demand higher wages and better conditions. But the suspicions against Wilson did not flare up into open hostility until Wilson offered £10,000 to a group of miners in Nottinghamshire to form their own breakaway, non-political union entering into close relationships with the coalowners and defying the established miners' federation.

The general council of the Trades Union Congress, having received appeals for help from Herbert Smith and Arthur Cook, the national chiefs of the miners, stepped in and demanded explanations from Havelock Wilson. He was defiant. He admitted the facts but refused to enter into any discussions, so the general council expelled him and his union from the Trades Union Congress.

Then Bevin took a hand. He opened a marine section for sailors and firemen, and a catering department for ships' cooks. So long as Wilson and his union were affiliated to Congress, Bevin explained, he took no steps to print card, book or bill. He added virtuously that his union had never "poached" on the preserves of others and had always been loyal to Congress. But now Havelock Wilson was trying to split the trade union movement.

Bevin alleged, "Large sums of money were subscribed to the breakaway movement inaugurated by shipowners, bankers and other capitalists with a view, we presume, to undermining the labour movement. Surely the task it had of dealing with maritime problems affecting the seamen was sufficient without endeavouring to create a fissure in the side of the great miners' organisation. We are credibly informed that the so-called Industrial Peace Movement, which openly showed itself during the miners' dispute, was already conceived and discussed in readiness for a previously threatened engineering dispute which did not develop."

If Havelock Wilson wanted a fight, Bevin was the man to accept the challenge. And Bevin was shrewd enough to establish his own basis for his counter-attack. He said, "The employers will never finally succeed in keeping the men out of the union of their choice, and a union cannot be kept in being by sheer force of employers' organisations alone. A union is only secure when it rests upon the loyalty of a very large majority of the members, and all our evidence goes to show that there are not 10 per cent. of the men of the sea today who, in their hearts, are loyal to this

disaffiliated union, and time will prove this. Further, a union can
only live by rendering real and effective service, and, in a study
of the conditions of the men of the sea. we are convinced that if
there was ever a section of men needing both efficient industrial
and political protection it is the seamen. They have the highest
death-rate of any section of workers in the country."

Bevin sent his organisers into the ports. It was a hard and
costly business. But the struggle never reached a climax. Within
three months of the opening of the fight Havelock Wilson was
dead. His death was recorded with some graciousness in the
official records of the Trade Union Congress. This notice recalled,
"He was regarded as one of the foremost fighting trade union
leaders from 1888 onwards, and was hated by the shipowners in
consequence. The fact that in later years he maintained an attitude contrary to that of the general trade union movement does
not lessen regard for and recognition of his earlier activities."
Within a year his union, under the leadership of genial Bob
Spence, was back in the fold, its policy reverting to trade union
orthodoxy.

But the whole incident served to arouse speculation on Bevin's
ambition. Into the conference of 1930 in Nottingham he led
nearly 390,000 members, more than a tenth of the whole trade
union membership of the country. He was second in strength to
the miners. By today his union has well over a million members,
and covers one-sixth of the whole field.

Bevin, however, established his ascendancy over the Congress
by the breadth of the proposals he sponsored. Throughout the
year he had "lived" in the higher realms of economic discussions,
on the T.U.C's Economic Committee, on the Prime Minister's
Economic Council, and on the Macmillan Committee on Finance
and Industry.

Bevin and his colleagues on the T.U.C. Economic Committee
spent much of their time deciding the attitude of their movement
towards economic groups and the Imperial Conference, which
was to be held late in the year in London. Their approach was
hampered by the realisation that trade unionists in Britain were,
in the main, free traders, although no formal declarations had
been made on this issue for a generation.

Bevin, Arthur Pugh and Milne-Bailey, the most active constructive minds on the committee, decided to approach the whole

complex problem with open minds, discarding all traditional prejudices. They quickly concluded that Britain could be isolationist no longer. And they decided that their ultimate ideal of world economic unity was far from practical realisation. So they divided the possibilities into three groups.

There was the European bloc. The factors in its favour were that the countries of Western Europe are closely allied geographically, that they shared a common plight due to the war, and a common apprehension of America's economic power. They might be powerful enough to ensure the peace of the world. Further, the experience of the League of Nations and other international bodies encouraged the hope that once the bloc was formed, the creation of machinery for international adjudication and administration would inevitably follow, and this would in time evolve into an organ of genuine international government.

The factors against were the racial and language difficulties; the fact that all were, or soon would be, predominantly manufacturing countries, and therefore very far from being self-contained; and that largely, because of this fact, their economic interests tended to clash rather than coincide. This last consideration was a very strong one. It was difficult to believe that the nations of Western Europe would continue long in agreement in the absence of a world settlement, especially in view of the nationalistic aims and policies of many of these countries. Hitler was not to achieve power for nearly three years but his creed, even then, was being screamed hysterically across the Continent.

Then came the British Commonwealth. The factors in its favour were that the block already existed in a tentative kind of way. There were undoubtedly ties of sentiment that counted still in the economic sphere. Supplies of raw materials and of manufactured goods could be balanced, the group being rich in raw materials, and, in fact, almost self-contained. There was, to a large extent, a common language. There was an abundant opportunity for movements of population within the group.

There was, too, already to some extent a tariff bond within the Commonwealth in the form of preferences and other commercial discriminations, applying to both the Dominions and the Colonies.

The factors urged against were the geographical separation between the different parts of the group, a defect which was

K

rapidly becoming much less serious owing to the great development in communications and transport, and the burden of defence in view of the scattered nature of the group and the economic position of some of the component parts.

Thirdly, there was the Anglo-American bloc. The committee presumed that this grouping would include the British Commonwealth and would be, in effect, an English-speaking bloc. The factors in favour of such a bloc were that such a group would be self-contained and would be quite powerful enough to ensure the peace of the world, and there was, to a large extent, a common language and race.

The factors against were that at the time the economic interests of the United States tended to clash rather than coincide; that the distance between the components tended to make common policy difficult and that, to many Americans, at any rate, the United States could manage quite well without any such alliance. American ideas, in fact, the committee believed, ran rather to a Pan-American Union, which existed already, though some of the South American and Central American States were by no means in love with it, owing to their fear of United States domination. And some Americans were asking what incentive there was for the United States to join with Britain, and what gain it would be to them.

Bevin and his colleagues, perhaps not surprisingly, in spite of Bevin's earlier advocacy of a United States of Europe, decided to urge support for closer agreements among the nations of the British Commonwealth.

Such a policy, they argued, would not in any way affect detrimentally their support, and participation in the work of the League of Nations. Rather the contrary. They should be in a better position, they said, to strengthen the scope and authority of the League. Similarly, they went on, this policy would not in the least affect detrimentally their relations with the International Federation of Trade Unions, or the International Labour Movement generally, but would strengthen them inside these movements. "Naturally," they added, "we should not be prevented by this policy from concluding European or other international agreements on the marketing of coal, steel and other commodities. The difference would be that we should bargain as a Commonwealth group instead of as Great Britain, and in many cases this would be a decided advantage."

But the trouble was that Lord Beaverbrook and his newspapers were at that time at the top of their campaign for Empire Free Trade. And this really was a trouble to Bevin. He was violently anti-Beaverbrook long before he had ever met the object first of his dislike and then of his hatred. Beaverbrook's success in many fields, notably in newspaper production, had been distasteful to Bevin, whose directorship of the *Daily Herald* made him technically a newspaper proprietor.

So, when Bevin rose to propose the new Empire policy to the Congress he promptly avowed that it had nothing to do with the Beaverbrook campaign. "I should have thought," he said with a touch of injured pride, "that the trade union movement, and the nation as well, would welcome the fact that the Trades Union Congress was not content to leave great problems of this character to our opponents, but that as each subject arose we should at least make up our minds on the matter and pronounce our views irrespective of any other Party or Press. While being guided by our general socialist philosophy we can come to a conclusion irrespective of even our other wing." (He meant the Labour Party.)

Bevin explained that he wanted the Governments of the British Commonwealth to set up an investigating organisation. Are we not entitled through the Dominion and Colonial Governments, he asked, to say that we will not leave the economic exploitation of raw materials in colonial territories to the tender mercies of company promoters and the rest? Are we not entitled to have a real economic survey, a geological survey, a mineralogical survey, a biological survey? Are we not entitled through the Colonial Governments to stipulate that the development of those raw materials shall be in an ordered manner? Are we not entitled to know what the conditions of health are?

Then, he went on, when all British governments understood the size and nature of their supplies and distribution problems, they could all go to a World Economic Conference, and when they found that one country had oil, another cotton, and another rubber, it would not be the case of armies and navies settling the business, but the British nations could say to the others, "Here are the resources at our disposal, resources which will be open to you, there being no restriction of raw material for your needs, but in return there must be no restriction of supplies imposed on us, so that we too may have the raw materials that we need without the fighting and the financial struggles that have gone on hitherto."

There was considerable opposition. A. V. Hermon, an earnest young electrician recently returned from Russia, taunted that the new proposals were being submitted to divert attention from the failure of Mondism, and "to cover up the betrayal of the actual struggle of the workers." Hermon, who was reading a long typewritten statement, so irritated the delegates that he was not permitted to finish his speech. Bevin alleged later that it had been written in Moscow. Jimmy Rowan, the leader of the electrical workers, disowned Hermon, who was, Rowan revealed, speaking for himself and not his union.

The traditional way of refusing to accept a report was its "reference back" to the general council, and Herbert Elvin, leader of the clerks and a member of the general council, moved this. Tom Naylor, of the London Society of Compositors, seconded. They were obviously free traders. More time for consideration was demanded by such powerful representatives as Charles Dukes, of the general workers, S. O. Davies, of the miners, and Percy Collick, of the locomotive engineers. Every time one of these spokesmen of the "big battalions" got up, the prospects for Bevin's plan seemed a little gloomier. And one of the most piquant criticisms of all came from sturdy Tom Scoulding, one of Bevin's most experienced lieutenants. He did not like the new plan at all. "The British Empire means so little to me," declared Tom, "that if I were unemployed and had the money all right, I would be leaving for the United States of America tomorrow."

Tom went on in his rich Cockney way, "I want to say that this economic bloc within the British Empire which is proposed by the general council will no doubt carry on the competitive system against the United States of America and bring about another bloody holocaust. As a matter of fact, I regard it as the illegitimate offspring, brought into the world by 'Nurse Bevin,' of that most horrible union, the Turner-Mond Union."

Bevin had plenty of criticisms to deal with in his reply. He mentioned all other debaters than Tom Scoulding by name. But he answered part of Tom's comments, by retorting, "I am prepared to defend the Mond-Turner report. If the Labour Party in the House of Commons will stand up to the principles of the Mond report as a contribution to the unemployment problem they will deal with more thousands of men than in all the schemes they have produced up to now."

Bevin insisted that Britain had to organise itself. He needed all his skill to avoid defeat. When the vote was taken on the reference back of his report, 1,401,000 voted for and 1,878,000 against. The majority of 477,000 for Bevin was, for him, a narrow victory.

The next day, Mr. Bevin had to return to some of the effects of rationalisation to which he had agreed in principle during the Mond-Turner talks. He admitted there were grave dangers of rationalisation being carried out in uneconomic forms. He secured conference agreement to his proposals that the general council should be given powers to promote legislation to prevent workers' conditions being worsened, and that individual unions should be urged to negotiate for shorter working hours to limit labour displacements.

When the political crisis hit Britain in August, 1931, Bevin felt that he had been placed in a personally invidious position by the defection of the Labour Government.

He had served a year earlier on the Macmillan Committee and had favoured devaluation rather than a return to pre-1925 standards. It was in 1925 that Mr. Baldwin had made the American debt settlement, which Bevin believed to be the most disastrous step ever taken by a British statesman. And throughout 1930-31 he had served on the Economic Council of Prime Minister MacDonald.

When the collapse came in August Bevin felt he should have known weeks earlier the trend that economic events were taking. He was convinced that MacDonald, Snowden and J. H. Thomas had been withholding vital information from their advisers for long before the crash came.

When MacDonald and Snowden met the trade union leaders on the afternoon of August 20th, 1931, the latter had decided that they would consider whatever statement was made to them by the Ministers before reaching any conclusions. They went into that conference "on guard."

MacDonald infuriated them. It was Citrine who reported to

the annual Congress two weeks later, "We were addressed by the Prime Minister, and much as I regret to say it, never have I heard a body of responsible intelligent men addressed in the manner in which we were addressed that day. We heard a general statement devoid of any specific reference of any kind. We heard a general statement which told us about the financial difficulties, but which told us nothing so intimately as we had already seen in the Press. We heard a statement about the necessity for balancing the budget, the danger that might arise if that course was not followed, and we were finally told that the Budget could only be balanced by a combination of two methods. On the one side there must be economies. A hint was thrown out that new taxation of some kind would be necessary, and the vague phrase 'equality of sacrifice' was used. And then, after addressing us in this way and telling us exactly nothing, the Prime Minister sat down."

MacDonald thought that was enough, but the trade union chiefs thought differently. They insisted on more details, so Philip Snowden, who only a year previously had been proudly called the "Iron Chancellor," got up to say that the Cabinet had been considering a series of proposals, but none of them had been accepted. It was probable, he added, that workers, employers and the State would have to contribute more to the unemployment insurance fund though benefits would not be cut for 26 weeks. Economies would have to be effected in salary and wage cuts in Government service, among school teachers, in the fighting services, and among the police. Even Cabinet Ministers would have to suffer a 20 per cent. reduction. Snowden steadfastly refused to tell the trade union men how he proposed to apply "equality of sacrifice." They went back to their headquarters to consider their attitude.

There is little doubt that they were desperately unhappy. They had fought for years to put a Labour Government in power. But they had also fought for years to resist wage cuts. And the only sure thing emerging from the Government's proposals was a wholesale slash in wages.

They felt that for years, since 1925, they had all been operating on a policy of contraction, contraction, contraction. They felt that if it was carried to its logical conclusion it would lead to economic disaster.

They had four hours in which to make up their minds how they would react to the Government proposals and to decide what alternative contructive policy they could put up to the Cabinet, which was meeting at 10 o'clock that night.

They gave four reasons why MacDonald and Snowden should not go on with their plans. There were four other ways of meeting the crisis, suggested the trade union leaders. There should be a levy on all sections of the community to avoid the whole burden falling on the workers. There should be a temporary suspension of the Sinking Fund from which interest on long-contracted debts is paid. There should be a tax on all fixed interest-bearing securities. And the Government should be asked whether they were considering the introduction of a revenue tariff.

Now the general council, notably Bevin, took a curious line on this last proposal. They debated whether they should propose a revenue tariff themselves. After a debate which took up most of their session they decided that they would not run the risk of dividing Congress and creating discord in their own ranks.

That night, at 9-30, the trade union chiefs went to the Cabinet offices and told Snowden they would be compelled to oppose his wage-cut proposals. Snowden replied sadly, "You do not know how serious the problem is. We believe firmly that if sterling collapses, if the £ suddenly depreciates, you will have chaos and ruin in this country. You will have unemployment rising, not merely to 5,000,000 but to 10,000,000. You will have nothing but chaos and the workers will suffer most of all."

Bevin, Citrine and some of the other leaders were convinced that Snowden, MacDonald and one or two other Ministers had already made up their minds on the course they intended to follow, and that nothing suggested by the trade unionists would make any difference.

Bevin and other members of the Economic Committee were told by the general council to stand by that week-end to consider any contingency that might arise. They heard nothing until the following Monday, August 24th. Then they were told that a "National Government" was being formed with MacDonald, the Socialist, as Prime Minister, and Baldwin, the Conservative leader, as second-in-command.

Four days later, Arthur Henderson, who had been Foreign Secretary in the Labour Government, and was easily the outstanding politician who did not "cross over" with MacDonald, was elected leader of the Party.

Within a week Bevin had secured the agreement of the annual conference of the Trades Union Congress to his scheme for setting up an investigation into planned industry in Britain. He was still convinced that he had been right four years earlier in advocating the Mond-Turner talks, but now he felt that circumstances were compelling the examination of some change from unrestricted capitalism. "I think," he said, "we are just at the parting of the ways. When we use the term 'breakdown of capitalism' it becomes a phrase very often without our trying to appreciate exactly what it is that is breaking down. The task is given to industry of adjusting itself to something that it has no control over, or anything to do with. In other words, we have a system of individualistic production, as between nation and nation in exchange, over which they have had control in the past. It was known as the 'Bank Rate' method. That is no longer operated by one country. London was the sole operating point. Control is now divided between New York, Amsterdam, Paris, Brussels and London, and entering into the control of the system now are the semi-financial political influences which, whatever may have been said for the old control, even prevents that from functioning adequately. But there is another great factor. The old system, to work, must be able to revolve with the globe. In other words, it must be really international and the cycles of exchange must be restored with it. And cutting right across world economy today is the new development in Russia. Russia has introduced, whatever may be said about it, a new motive for industry—a motive which is not profit. That new economy involves planning, and the attack on the Russian planning does not arise because of the way Russian labour might be treated. It arises because it is planning against the old world economy of scramble and individualism and profit."

Bevin made it quite clear that he had not become a convert to the Russian system. He urged, however, that Congress would have to agree to an examination of planning to get out of the rut of being merely "hewers of wood and drawers of water." In fact, what the conference did that day was to confirm a policy of economic investigation which Bevin had introduced only a year or two earlier, and which has now become an integral part of the organisation, operated largely by thoughtful, sincere, unassuming and self-effacing leaders of the type of Jóseph Hallsworth, George Chester, George Thomson, and John Brown. They did not go in for the spectacular, but their influence on major policy decisions is great.

The political split naturally caused considerable perturbation and readjustments in the ranks of the Labour Party. Arthur Henderson, the new leader, wanted help. He persuaded Bevin to fight in the general election of October, 1931. It took some doing. Bevin was still much more interested in the industrial than in the political side. He was offered Gateshead, which was regarded as a safe Labour seat, but the consideration which induced him to accept was not so much the safety of the seat as the fact that he was fighting in the same county as Ramsay MacDonald, who was offering himself for re-election in the Seaham Division of County Durham.

As it turned out the landslide against Labour was such that Bevin lost his "safe" seat by a convincing margin, while MacDonald was returned to Parliament.

But the campaign itself was to Bevin's liking. There was plenty of hard-hitting from Bevin, there were new experiences of meeting many types of North-eastern workers with whom Bevin, who had concentrated in London and the West, had previously made little intimate contact.

Bevin went into the centre of MacDonald's division at Seaham and roared at the electorate, "If any of you vote for MacDonald next week go afterwards to the Employment Exchange and apologise to the workless men there because they are going to lose 2s. 9d. (55 cents) a week. Apologise to them and their wives. Yours is the responsibility. MacDonald cannot cut your money without your help."

But it made little difference. He was a stranger in those parts, although his reputation was becoming international. The mood of the nation was against him. It was scared. In its misery it concluded that, whatever the hardships involved, its destinies in a time of crisis were safer in the hands of a group of leaders of all parties than in the rump of a Party which was being denigrated by former members like MacDonald, Snowden and Thomas. And most electors saw immediate benefits in tariffs.

Mr. Bevin was inclined after his election defeat to concentrate

on industrial affairs to the exclusion of politics. It was not pique
which prompted such an attitude, although he had serious differences of opinion on principle with such prominent political
leaders as Mr. Herbert Morrison. The two men have much in
common. They are both energetic and resourceful. They are both
men of decision. Each believes in the major importance of his
wing of the movement. Bevin regarded the trade union as the
initiator of reforms and the Labour Party as not much more than
the instrument for pushing some of these reforms through.
Morrison, on the other hand, while mindful of the financial help
given to the Party by the trade unions, felt strongly that the
Party was a fully responsible body entitled to considerable freedom in coming to its decisions. The two men could acknowledge
some respect for each other, but no affection. But the big clash
came on principle.

Bevin with his ideas of planning and controlling basic industries and services believed that the boards at the top should
contain representatives of organised employers and trade unions.
Morrison was for placing the control in the hands of independent
and impartial executives, chosen for their ability and detachment
and not for their past associations. Bevin's retort to that line was
that men who had grown up in an industry or service must have
more knowledge of and insight into its needs than any trained
"bureaucrat" of whom he had a horror. Still, in the years that
followed, Bevin came more and more to emphasise the value of
specially trained business executives, and he did as much as any
man in Britain to make provisions for such training.

Bevin showed some of his impatience with politicians by
producing, in 1933, his own plan for curing unemployment. It
was the greatest curse on his nation at the time, as, indeed, it was
on the United States and other major industrial nations.

He proved to his own satisfaction that his plan could absorb
2,000,000 workless. It was not costly to the State—not more than
£30,000,000 a year, but the value of substituting work and hope
for misery and despair for millions of the nation's able-bodied
men was beyond price. His main proposals were that increased
old-age pensions of £1 (4 dollars) a week for an individual, and
£1 15s. (7 dollars) a week for man and wife, irrespective of the
wife's age, should be paid to men at 65 only on retirement from
industry. Optional pensions should be available at 60 on the same

condition of retirement. The school-leaving-age should be raised to 16. Working hours should be reduced to about 40 a week.

There was much discussion in all quarters on his proposals. But no action. Curiously enough, some of his own workers were not too enthusiastic about the proposal to reduce working hours. They feared the result of being deprived of overtime, which yielded the best returns. Incidentally, all these proposals have now been accepted by Britain, and are in process of being applied.

In his internal industrial affairs Mr. Bevin was, however, unable to escape politics. There was a wave of activity by the Communists. There were lightning and unauthorised strikes in some of the most important sections of his union, notably the bus-men and groups of dockers on London River. Bevin discovered a "Communist plot" to undermine his authority inside his own union. Years later, when he was a Minister of the Crown, he was tolerant and benevolent in his reminiscences of these Communist activities. He asserted that many Communists were only men with eager minds who had to find some outlet for their energies. His solution, he stated in retrospect, was to make them officials of his union and, he added, they invariably mellowed with responsibility.

But in the tense struggle which went on in the hungry, bitter early thirties there was subtle venom from the Communists, and outraged anger from Bevin.

When the London busmen decided to strike in September, 1932, Bevin needed all his experience to avert the strike. He short-circuited normal channels. He saw Lord Ashfield and negotiated improved terms which were accepted by a delegate conference of London busmen the evening before the strike was to start. He was accused by the *Daily Worker*, the Communist organ, of treachery to his men. He brought an action for libel and was awarded damages of £7,000. Bevin's case was overwhelming. The hearing showed clearly how much he was hated by the Communists.

The Communist campaign was general at that time. Their influence grew to such an extent that by 1935 the general council of the Trades Union Congress issued a circular to all their affiliated unions requesting them to re-examine their rules with a

view to banning Communists from holding offices. This was
christened "the Black Circular" by the Communists.

It was issued over the signature of Sir Walter Citrine, who had
recently been knighted, although it transpired at the annual
conference that he was in the United States when the circular was
drafted and despatched from headquarters.

When the discussion took place at the annual conference at
Margate it was obvious that many unions—and some of them
were powerful—resented the circular as an intrusion into their
own autonomy. The general council's case was that if the Communists were not crushed out of the trade union movement in
Britain then the trade unions would risk disintegration or suppression. The debate went on for three hours, and all the time the
cheerful, cynical features of Mr. Harry Pollitt, the ablest and the
most attractive of all the Communist leaders, looked down on the
seething floor from the public gallery. As usual, Bevin was the
great hammer of the Reds. He recounted how hundreds of local
trades councils had appealed to the general council for protection.
Local unions selected Communists as delegates to these trade
councils, and, reported officials of the councils, they came to the
meetings with their spoiling tactics all prepared. In hundreds of
meetings it was reported that no business was done because the
Communists insisted on moving the reference back of every clause
in the minutes of the previous meeting. Bevin cried, "There is an
organism at work. If you had my job in the last five years you
would say there is an organism. But the Communists are not
going to get us down. I had admissions at my own executive at
their last meeting that money was handed over to representatives
of my union to get me and certain other officials in my union
down. Part of the policy was to carry on the vilification through
trades councils and bodies of that character. Vote for the reference back and you give the stamp of approval to the most nefari-
ous practices this movement has ever had to face."

It was a narrow majority of approval which Bevin secured for
the general council—1,869,000 for and 1,427,000 against, mainly
because the miners, the engineers and the printers were against
the circular. Some of their spokesmen had suggested that Communists are a lively leavening to any meeting, and therefore should
not be banned from making their provocative contributions to

discussions. But they were banned, like a famous bridegroom, for seven years.

Bevin's most statesmanlike contribution to that Margate conference, however, dealt with the international situation of the day. Mussolini was on the warpath against Abyssinia. Hitler was sabre-rattling.

Bevin declared that it was not enough to pass resolutions condemning the dictators. And he recognised that, watchful and on the defensive though Britain was, she was not prepared to go to war. Bevin hated the dictators, and he loathed their creed.

But he called on the British Government to urge the League of Nations to summon a World Economic Conference "and to place on its agenda the international control of the sources and supply of raw materials, with the application of the principle of economic equality of opportunity for all nations in the undeveloped regions of the earth."

The sources of international relationship, he declared, had been poisoned by the speculation associated with the development of mining and the production of raw materials in the various parts of the world.

He continued, "No more striking illustration could have been brought out than we have seen during the past few days—the disposal of an oil concession to an American company in Abyssinia. Prior to this crisis, it may have been that a company going into a part of the world like that, where there is no democratic system and where there is a good deal of ignorance of the Western World and its tactics—could secure concessions and then troops would have to be sent to defend the theft that the company had committed."

He went, "When you look at the raw materials required for war, whose movement sanctions would have to prohibit, you find that they number about 25 basic materials from which spring nearly all the metals and power required both for industry and war. If these materials were internationally controlled, produced according to world requirements and could be obtained by every industrial nation by purchase and not by conquest, 90 per cent. of the world causes of war would be entirely removed. You cannot hold a monopoly of world trade. The development of steam wiped that out, and that had been succeeded by the growth of electricity and other forms of power." Bevin was then speaking in the tenth year before the Atomic Age.

He declared, "This is a direct challenge to the narrow economic nationalism that has grown up. You have got to face it. You cannot put nations in cages and expect them to remain at peace. The growth of population need not mean war if the people are allowed to move into undeveloped territory. The proof of that is to be found in the United States. The United States took 1,250,000 people as emigrants every ten years prior to the last war. One recognises cases in that particular territory where they had to put on a restriction because of the rapid growth. But no one could pass through the United States today without realising that it is a great country, representing the gathering together of the peoples of the world and moulding them into a new culture and a new development."

Mr. Bevin recalled that when the League of Nations was established it was primarily a political organisation, the bringing together of the diplomatic powers. It created an International Labour Office. He added, "What we on the general council would like Geneva to recognise is this: Just as in the light of day at Geneva you can discuss international labour problems, you ought in a similar manner in open conference to be able to discuss economic matters. We intend to press upon the movement that it is against the old imperialist policy because it does not solve anything. Suppose we are faced presently with the question of handing back the German Colonies? The handing back of a piece of territory from one country to another does not give to that country the total supply of raw materials that it needs. These raw materials are scattered all over the world, and none of Germany's problems would be solved by any such process."

And then he made a statement which appears to be in direct contradiction to his views five years earlier. "During the last few months," he reported, "there has been a plea that we should have a Customs Union within our Empire. Do it, my friends, and the rest of the world is bound to challenge you immediately. It is the end of any British Commonwealth of Nations immediately you attempt it. During the regime of the Labour Government, unknown to this country or to the public, there was all the danger of a serious conflict with the United States over copper, over rubber, over tin. I think that will be admitted by those who were in the Cabinet at the time. Happily, it was settled, and I believe it was settled because we happened to have a Labour Government at the time."

He concluded, "As representatives of a movement that, ere long, I am convinced, will have the responsibility of the Government of this great empire, we offer to the world an alternative. We say to the world, we recognise that from the day we trod the imperial path, there has been a great change in world requirements, world demands and the seeking of opportunities for the people of the world. We have been left a heritage and the responsibility of an Empire, and we will not break it up. We will not destroy it. It is at least a third of the world linked together in various forms. Instead of breaking it up we will carry it a stage further forward by using an economic organisation that we can create through the League. From Empire organisation we will pass into the stage of world organisation."

Naturally, such a statement delivered with the forcefulness which Bevin had developed, created a great impression and won great support. But there were many delegates in that conference who marvelled at the length of the road which had been travelled from the early days of the century when the Trades Union Congress was concerned almost exclusively with working conditions in their own land. There were some who felt that Bevin had been inconsistent in the last eight years. But the majority held that his views had developed realistically with the dizzily changing circumstances of the times.

While that speech was undoubtedly his greatest contribution to British political thought in that year, the one which caused the greatest and most painful sensation was made a month later, at the annual conference of the Labour Party at Brighton.

The issue before the conference was profoundly important. On the one hand, it was for the application of sanctions against Mussolini and possible war in defence against the counter-attack of the dictators; on the other, pacifism and isolationism.

The weight of opinion seemed to be for sanctions, with all they implied, but revered old George Lansbury, who had been leader of the Labour Party since the death of Arthur Henderson, three years earlier, was a sincere and life-long Pacifist. His most influential supporter was Sir Stafford Cripps, who had resigned from the Party executive the previous week in protest against the proposal to support sanctions against Italy.

When Lansbury rose to speak against the policy of sanctions which his executive had adopted, the great audience rose and sang, "For He's a Jolly Good Fellow." There was no doubt about his popularity. The old man, with his kindly face and his blameless personal Christian life, inspired deep affection.

There was deep silence as Lansbury, obviously filled with emotion, said very quietly, "It is bitter and difficult for me to stand here today and publicly repudiate a big fundamental piece of policy. I have never been more convinced that I am right and that the movement is making a terrible mistake. Next Tuesday we are meeting in London, that part of the movement which elects the Parliamentary leader, and together we shall discuss this matter, and I hope we shall arrive at a satisfactory solution."

Lansbury went on, "I cannot see the difference between mass murder organised by the League of Nations and mass murder organised between individual nations. To me it is exactly the same. If I had the power to go to Geneva, backed by the people, I would say we would be willing that the whole of the resources under our control should be pooled for the service of all mankind."

He almost broke down as he said, "It may be that I shall not meet you on this platform ever any more." The delegates shouted their dissent from the idea.

"Wait a minute," added Lansbury, "There are things coming to life that make changes inevitable. It may very well be that in the carrying out of your policy I shall be in your way. But one thing I want to do—and that is the only thing worth while today —is at least to warn the young of the dangers of force and compulsion. God intended us to live peaceably and quietly with one another, and if some people do not allow us to do so I am ready to stand as the early Christians stood and say, 'This is our faith. This is where we stand, and, if necessary, this is where we die'."

The old man's simple statement of faith was profoundly moving. Many delegates, especially the women, were frankly and openly wiping the tears from their eyes. As the old man walked with his head erect from the rostrum down the central aisle of the conference hall to stand at the back of the delegates he was given

[Photo: Keystone Press Agency, Ltd.

JACOB EPSTEIN WITH HIS SCULPTURE OF THE HEAD OF ERNEST BEVIN

a tremendous ovation even from those who differed from him. They were all so palpably seeing the end of a political career. More, the belief of Lansbury reminded hundreds of them of the atmosphere in which they had been brought up.

It was in this emotional, nostalgic and conscience-questing atmosphere that Bevin climbed to the rostrum.

His voice was harsh as he said, "I hope that the conference will not be influenced by sentiment or personal attachment."

And then with the suddenness and the sting of a whip-lash across the face, Bevin roared his contempt for those who "hawked their consciences around on their sleeves."

The whole conference was shocked. Here was a cold detachment and a vicious reality which was alien to the traditions of a movement often influenced by sentiment. There were murmurs of disapproval but no roar of protest. Many of the delegates felt that Bevin was putting into harsh words their own secret thoughts.

Bevin promptly moved to the offensive. He accused Lansbury of having approached the press on the previous Sunday to emphasise his own personal views. Bevin declared, "That was very cutting for colleagues who have to sit on a committee in conditions of that character. Loyalty to a decision gets less publicity than disloyalty. I think that all of us representing responsible trade unions have a serious ground for complaint."

He revealed that when the leaders of the Labour Party met Sir Samuel Hoare, the Foreign Secretary, Lansbury had pledged his Party to support sanctions.

Then Bevin turned on Sir Stafford Cripps, who, he added, "has stabbed us in the back by resigning and not going through with collective decision."

Bevin continued, "Every one of us on the general council of the Trades Union Congress feels he has been let down. Our predecessors formed this party. It was not Keir Hardie. The Labour Party grew out of the bowels of the T.U.C. The great crime of Ramsay MacDonald was that he never called his party together. The crime of these people is that they have gone out and sown discord at a moment when our candidates want unity to face an election." So completely had Bevin swung the conference round that when Lansbury rose to make a personal explanation he could get no hearing.

The following Tuesday the Parliamentary Labour Party

elected a new leader. They meant the appointment to be temporary until the two fairly equally balanced forces behind the chief contenders for the position, Herbert Morrison and Arthur Greenwood, could develop a more obvious numerical disparity.

The man they chose, Clement Richard Attlee, has stayed for ten years and is now the Prime Minister of Great Britain.

Technically, Bevin reached the height of his fame as a trade union leader in 1937 when he was elected chairman of the Trades Union Congress and president of its annual conference.

But for him the year was one of maddening contrasts. He called 26,000 London busmen out on strike on April 30th, 1927, to secure for them a $7\frac{1}{2}$ hour working day. It turned out to be the last major official strike he led. But it went wrong. Bevin and his executive council decided to place the direction of the strike in the hands of the Central Bus Committee, appointed by the busmen themselves. He hoped that the strike would be over before the Coronation of the King in the third week in May. It was not. The tempers of all parties became frayed—not least those of the populace of and visitors to London for the Coronation celebrations. Acrimony developed between Bevin and the Central Bus Committee to such a degree that Bevin secured the permission of his executive council to transfer the direction of the strike back from the Central Bus Committee to himself. Bevin secured a settlement of the strike after it had lasted 27 days. He described the settlement as honourable, mainly because he secured the reinstatement of all who had taken part in it and he strengthened future negotiating arrangements between his union and the Transport Board. But the men did not secure a reduction in their working hours.

The end of the strike did not mean the end of skirmishing between Bevin and those who had led the strike in its earlier stages. Some of them formed a breakaway union, which never flourished. Others were disciplined by the union executive. Bevin himself temporarily broke off relationships with the Press by excluding them from the biennial conference of his union which took place in August.

It was in this mood of aloof and injured dignity that he opened the sixty-ninth annual conference at Norwich on September 6th, 1937.

Many delegates were shocked by his appearance. The strain of the past year had obviously affected his health. There was a tell-tale twitching of his facial muscles as he spoke. But his presidential address was distinctively personal and forcefully delivered. Internally there was some cause for rejoicing because for the first time for ten years the membership of the T.U.C. had passed the 4,000,000 mark. But the conference was disturbed by the international situation. There was war in the Far East and war in Spain.

In retrospect, however, the most significant sentences of his presidential address dealt with his misgivings about what would happen in Britain when the armament programme neared completion. He outlined a programme for the creation of an internal development fund, the provision of greater trading facilities, and the introduction of a world economic survey. Obviously, he thought at that time that a war would be averted.

"One of the most regrettable things," he observed, "is that we only seem to be in full work either when there is a war or when we are preparing for war. When the arms programme ends, the view gains ground that a slump is inevitable. It will be if we leave things to drift on. But if the nation can organise a great defence programme against war it can do so against other great enemies—unemployment, poverty, malnutrition and disease. Preparations must, however, be got under way forthwith."

Mr. Bevin's own personal position if war came was in no doubt. He had told the members of the Foreign Press Association in London months earlier, "If there is a resort to war for dominance do not take the Labour Party too cheaply. We would defend our own country."

For the first time for more than twenty years Bevin, as president, took no part in the conference debates.

As it happened he was to make his swan-song as a trade union leader at that conference. True, he spoke at wartime conferences, but his appearances then were the results of invitations to a distinguished Ministerial visitor.

He did not take part in the 1938 and 1939 conferences because he was on a world tour, partly for the benefit of his health and partly as a member of the British delegation, led by Lord Lothian, to the British Commonwealth Relations conference, which met in Sydney, Australia, in September, 1938.

When he returned from his world tour in the winter of 1938 he was anxious that Parliament should set up a powerful Select Committee to investigate the administration of the whole Colonial Empire.

He contrasted the efficient way in which the Americans were developing Honolulu with the comparative neglect by Britain of the Fiji Islands. This, he said, was typical.

"In my view," Bevin said, "too much of the Colonial Empire has been kept for purely strategic purposes and not sufficient attention has been paid to development."

He pointed out that Parliament in Britain was responsible for 66,000,000 voteless people living in such territory—"under the dictatorship of the Colonial Office"—and the matter called for far more informed attention than Parliament could then give it. He added, "Unless the present attitude to the Colonies is revised it might develop sooner or later into a very serious world trouble."

He advocated a Commonwealth Labour Conference with a proper agenda to examine such problems as defence, migration, trade relationship to the world and the attitude to the Colonies.

In Canada, Mr. Bevin observed, it was difficult to know whether she was in the Commonwealth or outside. She had, he went on, the American Navy at the back door and the British at the front, and the talk there about war was non-committal. The ordinary Canadian of British stock, he thought, would take the same attitude as on previous occasions when Britain was in trouble. Some Canadians, however, he said, did not seem to realise that if they declared neutrality they could only do so by ceasing to be part of the Commonwealth and would lose various trading privileges. In the development of better relations between Britain and the United States, Canada could play a very big part.

Australia, he believed, would be prepared to shoulder heavy liabilities for defence. He was greatly impressed by the efficient administration of the Government in New Zealand and in some Australian States.

There was, he reported, one reason for some disaffection towards the United Kingdom in the Dominions. This was the "crabbing" attitude taken up in Britain by the powers-that-be to social developments in those dominions. Bevin alleged that when a country like New Zealand and certain States in Australia got busy "with a good forward policy" it seemed to be resented in

Britain and a whispering propaganda was set going by financiers and others.

Bevin obviously benefited enormously from his world tour. He was "years younger" than when he left that conference in Norwich in 1937. He was more cheerful in his outlook, too.

I have kept to the end of this summary of his major performances during the decade of his prime as a trade union leader that final speech he made at Norwich—for one reason. It was one of the most revealing and introspective speeches he ever made.

Kindly old Allan Findlay, the patternmaker, who was vice-president of the Congress, in moving the vote of thanks to Bevin for his chairmanship, had referred to Bevin as "one of the outstanding men of the movement." Findlay continued, "The Church suffered a great loss and this movement experienced a great gain when the earliest aspirations of Mr. Bevin came in conflict with his intellectual honesty. We have never had a better president of Congress, and no better is likely to follow him."

Bevin replied, "There has been a kind of propaganda for many years on the part of a section in this country to try to depict me as a kind of dictator and over-riding person. Well, it has been my lot since 1918 to bring together into one union 37 unions, and anybody who has had experience of amalgamations knows that unless those who are handling them can exercise tolerance, such a thing cannot be brought to a success. It has been a feature of certain sections of the Press and others to refer to 'This boss Bevin business'."

I must confess that when he mentioned this I blushed, and could have sworn that at that moment he had his unfriendly eye on me sitting two yards beneath him at the Press table. Later all my colleagues averred that they had undergone a precisely similar experience.

Bevin went on, "I do not think I need contradict it. It is not true. It is not true as my own colleagues on the general council know. It is not true as my own union know. My colleagues on the general council know that what one tries to do is to collect and compose the differences of everybody in order to try and shape a policy for this great movement. I have been very proud to be President of Congress. I tried to help in its inception." Here he was obviously referring not to Congress, which had been in existence then for 70 years, but to the general council which had been reformed from the old Parliamentary Committee in 1921. It was Bevin himself who drafted the preliminary constitution for the general council and the methods of voting for its 32 members.

He continued, "I like constructive work better than advocacy and more than platform work. My colleagues on the general council will agree that if there is an abstruse problem they have never appealed to me in vain to try to solve it. I like to create things. The reason I have got into trouble with a good many people in the Labour movement is this. I hold strongly the view that once a decision has been arrived at nobody had the right to go outside and undermine what has been done. Never once have I challenged a decision of Congress. I might, if I thought it was wrong, try to alter it legitimately, but I never challenged it."

Bevin might have made an explanation here. In the preceding ten years not once had he been in a minority on a major issue. In other words, Congress had always agreed with his views, partly because of his force in submitting them, and partly because of his instinct in reaching conclusions which he knew to be in accord with the mood of the movement.

"I am proud of this great movement," he declared, "proud of the work it has done nationally and internationally. The honour that has been bestowed upon me I value more than any other honour. I would not change the loyalty of the 600,000 members of my union for all the pelf and place that Society can give. It is the greatest pride of one's life to know that in the homes of thousands of one's own mates, in the branches from as far as Malta in the East to Galway in the West, there is a belief in you; that they trusted you and respected your integrity, and when you did me the honour of electing me to the chair of this Congress I felt it very deeply, because, I believe, however controversial I have had to be at times, people have always given me credit for sincerity. But this great work has meant being away from home a great deal, travelling about the country and long hours at the office. The price has to be paid, and it is paid for in domestic life, in the isolation of one's own people, and the time they have to spend on their own. Therefore, I take this as a tribute not only to myself, but also to Mrs. Bevin and my family."

Bevin had delivered his own epitaph on his trade union leadership, and he had given it with a candour, a detachment and an un-self-consciousness peculiar to him.

This characteristic remains with him. He still talks about "my people" when he refers not only to members of his own union, but to all who work. He has been accused of arrogance and conceit when all he means to convey is his pride in his associations.

He was telling the House of Commons years later—in 1944— how he and Prime Minister Winston Churchill were watching the troops moving off to the invasion of Europe, when one of the soldiers shouted, "See they don't let us down when we come back this time, Ernie." "Ernie?" queried a scandalised, orthodox Conservative. Bevin explained simply, "Yes, Ernie, that's what my people call me."

But his reference in his final speech to "this boss Bevin business" had one result. It led many qualified newspapermen and trade union officials to analyse many of the circumstances behind the outburst.

We were six or seven in that railway compartment travelling back from Norwich to London that evening. Conference had ended, and naturally the talk turned pretty quickly to Bevin's speech. We were not to know then that it was his last as a trade union chief.

We were agreed on one thing. Bevin had been described frequently as "the big boss" by political and industrial newspaper commentators attached to the big-circulation groups. More, he had come to be accepted as such by most of the British public and indeed by many trade union officials who realised that, technically, the description was unjustified.

Mark that word technically. Those on the inside of the trade unions, particularly in his own union, knew how scrupulous Bevin had always been in deferring to the decisions of his executive council, which was composed entirely of lay members. Lay members are men still engaged in their normal callings as dockers, busmen, flour mill operatives, clerks, chemical workers, and in a score of other trades covered by the vast organisation. They also knew of course that Bevin's influence on his executive was greater than that of any other leader in any other union with the possible exception of Bill Brown in the civil service association.

Bevin's apparent resentment was partly influenced by the times. In 1937 there was terrific hatred of anything to do with the idea of dictators and dictatorships. It was the negation of the democratic idea. Bevin was pleased enough to be known as "the Dockers' K.C." in the very early twenties before the first of the European dictators got into the saddle. So his objection was not against a label, as such.

It was partly based, too, on his conviction that the motive for describing him as "Boss Bevin" was malice. He was not altogether justified here. Bevin knows a lot about newspapers and newspapermen, but there is one canon of theirs he has never accepted. They believe that people are more interested in other people than in principles and generalities. There is plenty of evidence to confirm them in this. It is the secret of the success of the newspapers which emphasise this principle.

Bevin argued that the organisation was greater than any individual in it. That did not prevent him making frequent use of the personal pronoun, nor was he loathe to remind his hearers of his individual contributions to the organisations with which he was associated.

But his view was, and is, shared by many other trade union leaders. It is reflected in their announcements and in their own publications. The result is that most of these trade union journals are insufferably dull. They are produced for "the converted," for members whose keenness in trade union affairs is great enough to stifle any regrets they may have that these reports and pamphlets are so impersonal.

Inevitably this attitude of Bevin's led to the stifling of any sense of organised public relations within his union. The men his union employ to produce their own journal do a first-rate job within the limitations imposed on them by the theory that while it is important to put across decisions it is undignified to name the members or officials who have helped to form such policies.

The result was that to thousands of members the great union became an impersonal sort of machine. Ironically, the effect of this development did not become obvious to the public until long after Bevin had ceased to be in active control of his union. It was in the Autumn of 1945 that the union's discipline over its own members showed the first serious signs of cracking. First, the dockers and then the London busmen acted unconstitutionally and in defiance of the union leadership. Mr. Arthur Deakin, who had been second in command to Bevin since 1935 and who carried on when Bevin became a Minister had to contradict John Donovan, the dockers' section chief, publicly.

Donovan had stated that the union would negotiate only for those dockers who gave up their strike and returned to work. Deakin declared that the union would act for all its members. There was another significant piece of evidence to show the union's indifference to public relations. More than 40,000 dockers in all the major ports of Britain had come out on strike, and had been idle four days, before the union revealed that the claims for improved wages and conditions which the dockers were demanding had actually been submitted to the port employers nearly two weeks before. It was too late then. The dockers were out, and they were in no mood to listen to their official leaders. They stayed out another ten days and Britain witnessed the humiliation of seeing 10,000 soldiers unloading, on soldiers' pay, foodships to prevent the nation starving.

Some day every major trade union in Britain will have an effective public relations officer not only to tell their members what is happening and who is doing things inside the union but also to inform us whose job it is to tell the public. Trade unions have become an integral part of British public life. They have become accepted as such very largely because of the work of specialist industrial writers employed by every newspaper. The sneers of some trade union leaders that the only time the public hears of them is when there is strife and trouble are becoming hollow.

Bevin set the pace in most things. His one blind spot was in this business of public relations. But for that he would never have been called "Boss Bevin" in the first place. In spite of it, his deeds and the work of his union became known to the nation and to the world. Bevin never went out of his way to acknowledge this. He seemed to accept it as natural.

CHAPTER VII

MAN WHO MOBILISED HIS COUNTRY

BEVIN did not wait to become a Minister before starting his war duties. As the head of the most diverse trade union in Britain he was immediately involved in mobilisation and transition problems. His members on the docks, on road transport and in the fishing trawler fleets found their peace-time jobs converted into war stations almost automatically.

But there were many other sections whose peace-time jobs were on the production and distribution of luxury goods and who were obviously going to lose their livelihood quickly.

Bevin's main interest, however, was in the stabilisation of prices and wages. There were many proposals and counter-proposals being exchanged by all types of organisations immediately after the war started in September, 1939. The most insistent was that all workers should agree to have a stop put on their wages. Wages should be frozen, it was suggested, in order to avoid inflation and industrial disturbances. The idea was not put forward officially by the Government, but it was being repeated by so many prominent industrialists that there was every likelihood that the Treasury would adopt the proposal.

So, to put the point of view of the trade unions beyond any dubiety Mr. Bevin considered it necessary to issue a warning to the Government and the Chancellor of the Exchequer, Sir Kingsley Wood.

The Chancellor was believed to favour the idea that working people should not have wage advances commensurate with the increased cost of living.

Bevin declared, "Millions of our people are working at an unprecedented strain. Some of them are in our factories seven days a week and some from 8 to 12 hours a day. True, they are getting overtime. But, on the other hand, they are taking out of themselves years of their lives to give the country the output essential at this moment."

"I cannot find," he observed, "in any price-fixing that is going on, or in any other arrangements, that the capitalists of the country are making any sacrifices. They pay income tax, but every penny of this is calculated in cost before their selling figure is fixed. If there is to be taxation let it be honest. The old way of taxing so that folks know not what they pay—by increasing the cost of living, manipulating the currency and in other ways—is going to undermine the strength of the nation in prosecuting this war to a successful conclusion.

Bevin revealed that he and the other trade union leaders had already proposed a policy to the Government. It was that the Government should keep prices at the level obtaining at the outbreak of war, and not allow increases, "Or," he added, "if increases have to be met they should be met from the Exchequer. This will reduce to a minimum the problem of wage difficulties during the war."

That is the policy which Britain adopted, but a public discussion of it, with implied criticisms against the Government at such an early stage of the war revealed that Britain was far from being politically united at the start of the war. The Prime Minister was Mr. Neville Chamberlain. He was suspect because of his appeasement policy in the Munich days the previous year. On the eve of the war it was Mr. Arthur Greenwood, Deputy-leader of the Labour Opposition, who, responding to shouts of "Speak for England" even from the Conservative back-benchers, made the speech which led to the declaration of war next morning. There was a feeling that Mr. Chamberlain was always having to be pushed to stand up to Hitler.

But that was not the especial reason which made Bevin hostile to him. Bevin, Citrine and four or five other leaders had visited Chamberlain in the earliest days of the war to ask him to alter on the Statute Book the one piece of legislation which infuriated the trade union leaders. That was the Trades Disputes Act which had been introduced to hamper the unions in the repressive mood which followed the general strike of 1926. The union leaders felt that if they were going to be treated as partners in this greatest and most perilous national adventure of all, the most positive evidence of good faith on the part of the Conservative Government would be the amendment of some clauses in the Act they hated so much. They were not asking for its complete repeal.

Chamberlain treated them tactlessly. He told them in effect that if their conduct during the war warranted it, he had little doubt that at the end of the war his Party would take such good conduct into consideration. The trade union leaders considered that Chamberlain was treating them like children. Bevin got so angry that he lost his temper, and bellowed at the Prime Minister.

Bevin was convinced that, in spite of the war and in spite of some of his speeches appealing for unity, Chamberlain was still playing the party game.

Bevin himself was whole-heartedly in favour of the war. He realised, as he told the Convocation of the Teachers' College of New York less than a month before the start of the war, in a noble speech on the future of democracy, that Hitler's victory would mean the end of all free institutions in the West. He, therefore, regarded the war as a Holy Crusade. And he was prepared to make his own constructive contributions to victory.

It was Bevin, within five weeks of the start of the war, who issued an official appeal to his own members to join his dockers' "flying column." These columns were made up of dockers who could be moved from one port to another to ensure the speedy delivery of food for the whole population and munitions and raw materials for war industries. He worked out his plan in co-operation with Mr. Ernest Brown whom he was to supplant as Minister of Labour within eight months.

Dockers taken away from their homes were to be guaranteed at least 15 shillings (three dollars) a day by the State, and as this included a daily lodging allowance of five shillings (one dollar), Bevin was not attempting any profiteering in wage rates.

Bevin said in his appeal to his members, "We will not transfer a mobile column to a dock unless it is proved that there are not enough men at that dock to do all the loading and unloading needed expeditiously. Another advantage is that we expect to avoid the confusion which arose after the last war. Take the London docks as an example. Normally, they employed about 36,000 dockers. Yet in 1919, because of men who had rushed to the docks to find sheltered jobs, we took a register and immediately registered 65,000 men. There'll be none of that this time." At last, after nearly 20 years, Bevin had found an opportunity to put one of his pet schemes of dock registration into effect. And his statement shows that even then he had his eye on post-war settlement.

The immediate result of his appeal was unexpected. It came within four days from, of all people, Dr. Goebbels, the Nazi propaganda chief, who blared over the radio to Britain, that this new mobile corps was "a brigade of strike breakers and blacklegs on the American model."

Bevin retorted, "This shows how dispirited Goebbels must be. Happily, there must be thousands of people of the old German Transport Workers' Union who know the British unions and myself well enough to know that we would not indulge in any blackleg arrangements. Would not the German workers themselves welcome the freedom the British workers have in negotiating their agreements? How happy they would be to return to their old system of free trade unionism, instead of the suppression they have suffered under Hitler." And that reply was broadcast all over the German air by the British authorities.

There was one other Minister with whom Bevin worked closely. That was Mr. Winston Churchill, who was then First Lord of the Admiralty. Bevin and Winston Churchill had become good friends because each realised the other was determined to do and sacrifice everything for the defeat of the Nazis. They met in those early months of the war to re-arrange Britain's fishing fleets. Some trawlers were converted into minesweeping and minelaying auxiliaries of the Royal Navy. Others were returned from war duties to augment sections of the fishing fleets which had been over-raided. They worked together unostentatiously but effectively. It was an association which few people knew of. This ignorance was largely responsible for the surprise Mr. Churchill sprang on the nation in May, 1940, when he called Bevin to Ministerial office.

It happened that in those evenings of the first winter of the war I saw Bevin fairly frequently in the purlieus of Transport House, his union headquarters. Bevin, by the way, not only refused to allow his headquarters to be evacuated from London to the probable greater safety of the provinces, but caused some discomfiture to other trade union leaders who had left the capital by advising them publicly to return to London.

But in those days Bevin was at his most mellow, and was most attractive as a companion. He was at a curious stage in his own life. His illness of two years previously had given him the idea that he might exercise his option of retiring voluntarily from his union at the age of 60. That would be in 1941. He never accumulated wealth. His top salary with his union was £1,250 (5,000 dollars) a year. But he planned a quiet retirement to his own West Country, and the pension he would receive from his union would more than suffice for his modest intentions. He could live on the £700 (2,800 dollars) annual pension he had earned from his organisation.

Sometimes he would laugh a little ruefully, and observe, "It looks as if Hitler has spoiled my little plan—unless we beat him quickly." Bevin was determined that, if his health held out, he would not "pack up" during the war.

But at that time Bevin was more concerned by the evidence he accumulated that Britain was not likely to win the war then—or ever, unless there were drastic changes. Bevin was in a good position to know. But he was not in a good position to effect changes. There were good security reasons why the national shortcomings should not be revealed openly on the floor of the House of Commons. Bevin knew, though, that the continuation of unemployment in the country was having a disastrous psychological effect on the whole war effort. As it happened, Bevin's concern probably turned out to be a good thing for the nation. There is no doubt at all that it was during the first six months of the war that he worked out most of the plans that he administered during its last five years. Bevin, with his colleagues on the general council of the Trades Union Congress, were constantly going on deputations to this Minister and that, but there was little evidence that their suggestions were heeded, or even welcomed. From time to time there were whispers that some of the trade union men thought they could do the job better than those in charge, and it was probable that they would welcome an opportunity in office. But that could never be as long as Neville Chamberlain was the Prime Minister of Britain.

The change came from the military disasters on the Continent. The breakthrough of the Nazis in the West meant the end of the Chamberlain administration in London.

It happened in the early days of May, 1940. It was the week before the British Labour Party were meeting for their annual conference in Bournemouth, the fashionable South Coast holiday resort. Indeed, Mr. Churchill's formation of his new Government was not complete when the Labour Party delegates were assembling in Bournemouth two days before the start of the conference. Next to Downing Street itself, the busiest political centre in the world in those days was the cliff-top hotel in Bournemouth which the Labour Party executive had made its headquarters. It was because of the seriousness and portentousness of the political situation that the general council of the Trades Union Congress was also summoned to meet in Bournemouth that weekend.

Incidentally, the relationship of these two controlling bodies, the executive of the Labour Party and the general council of the Trades Union Congress, to each other is little understood even in Britain. Each body is completely autonomous and independent. The general council is concerned mainly with industrial affairs, the executive with political. Although their monthly meetings are held on the same day in the same building in London, they meet in separate rooms and hold joint meetings only on extraordinary occasions. They have a link in the National Council of Labour, on which a small team of representatives from the two sides and from the Parliamentary Labour Party, meet to co-ordinate policy. The chairmen of the three bodies preside in rotation over the delibera- tions of the National Council of Labour. Naturally, there is a fair amount of overlapping between the general council and the national executive, and occasionally some jealousy, but to the outer world they present a united front.

The political crisis of May, 1940, was obviously a major occasion demanding the joint meeting of the two full bodies. The general council of the Trades Union Congress held its own session before being joined by the political leaders.

There was an air of tension and a suggestion of drama in the meeting of the general council. It was known that Winston Churchill was forming his National Government. It was felt by members of the general council that he would probably invite one of their number to join his Government, if only as a compliment to the organised workers of the country.

I travelled down to Bournemouth with some of the trade union leaders. They were full of speculation. But it was obvious that they were unaware of actual developments. As we sped through the lovely county of Hampshire on that beautiful May day, the members of the general council in the company were virtually tossing up as to whether Churchill would ask Citrine or Bevin to join the Government. It is significant that no other name was mentioned. It is equally significant that, technically and tradi- tionally, neither Citrine nor Bevin was entitled to an invitation to become a Minister, because for generations Prime Ministers had reserved ministerial appointments for experienced members of Parliament. Neither of the two trade union chiefs had ever been a Member of Parliament.

The discussion on the relative merits of the two leaders was revealing but inconclusive. Bevin, it was felt, had the drive and the force, Citrine the patient and painstaking sense of administration. One of the party suggested, "Perhaps Winston will ask them both?" The members of the general council were shocked. One of them blurted out, "My God, we couldn't lose both of them at once. What would happen to the general council?" It was a bit unfair on some other members of the general council, but it is true that during the past 15 years Bevin and Citrine have stood head and shoulders above all their colleagues in public appeal.

The general council assembled that evening in Bournemouth. As usual, Citrine and his competent lieutenant, Vincent Tewson, were first in the room. One of the general councillors shouted jovially as he entered to Citrine, "Come on, Walter, don't hold out on us any more. What has Churchill offered you?" Citrine, with a slightly wintry smile, replied, a little primly, "I would not accept any office without the formal permission of the general council." And the genial councillor called back, "Quite right, Walter, trust you to observe the rules."

Then most of the others filed in, singly and in little groups. Citrine reported the general position, and reminded the general council that they would be joined shortly by the executive of the Labour Party for the formulation of a joint statement to submit to the annual conference of the Party two days hence.

Then Bevin asked permission to make a statement. He disclosed that two days earlier he had been invited by Mr. Churchill to join the Government. As he paused, one of his neighbours demanded, "What did you say, Ernie?" Bevin, who had not heard Citrine's earlier observation, quietly answered, "I told Churchill I was prepared to accept, if it was the wish of the general council that I should do so."

There was no hesitation on the part of the general council. Quite rightly, they construed the invitation as a compliment to the whole trade union movement. But their next reaction was interesting. They urged Bevin to accept the Ministry of Supply. Not only did they regard the post as commensurate with their importance and with Bevin's ability, but they recalled the prestige which its predecessor, the Ministry of Munitions, had achieved in the last war.

Bevin shook his head, and smiled a trifle mysteriously. "Well, what have you taken, Ernie?" demanded his neighbour. "Labour," Bevin replied tersely.

They thought it was one of his massive leg-pulls. The Ministry of Labour had never been regarded as a first-class department. Its reputation had been tarnished by its intimate association with depression and unemployment. It was a post which had finished many politicians. In fact, no politician had ever made a success of it. And here was Bevin, backed by the reasonable claim that he was supported by the nation's 6,000,000 organised workers, calmly accepting what his colleagues regarded as a minor post.

Then Bevin corrected himself to give his office its new title, "Labour and National Service." That caused some raising of the eyebrows. Quickly they realised that Bevin had been satisfied by the enhanced status of the Ministry. He gave an explanation, more or less in an aside, to an official sitting beside him, "I take no job that ends with the war. I take a Ministry whose value will be permanent to our people."

This was significant. It meant that Bevin had decided to start a new career at the age of 59. He was not going to be satisfied with a stop-gap job, however arduous and important. He obviously had constructive, long-term ideas which he proposed to introduce.

The country did not have to wait long to discover how true this was. During the week of the Bournemouth conference, which enthusiastically and with some emotion gave its leaders full approval of "its whole support to the new Government in its effort to secure a swift victory and a just peace," the military situation in the Continent of Europe deteriorated rapidly.

The Nazi hordes seemed irresistible. They were everywhere. Britain was within two weeks of the tragedy of Dunkirk. The situation had not appeared so grave to the inhabitants of Britain since the Spanish Armada blew up the Channel nearly four centuries ago. But the extraordinary fact was that throughout the land there was an undefinable spirit of elation at the test that was to come, rather than any sense of defeatism from the disastrous news coming hourly from the other side of the Channel.

Mr. Churchill and his Government had grave faces and heavy

M

hearts. The Prime Minister warned his colleagues that Britain would be lucky if she managed to evacuate 20 per cent. of her forces from the Continent. To the public they kept a bold front, giving a true warning of the gravity of the hour. The announcement of Mr. Churchill's new team had a tremendously exhilarating effect on the nation.

But there were many who had grave misgivings about Mr. Bevin. To considerable and influential sections of the British public he was remembered as the man who was always either leading a strike or threatening to call one. They were oblivious of his constructive work.

Their fears were instinctive. They had not long to wait before grounds for their feelings were provided—by Bevin himself.

He showed little sign of nervousness as he walked alone to the rather gloomy portals of Montague House, his new headquarters in Whitehall, to take up his post. He intended to make his entry with exaggerated modesty by asking the doorkeeper for an interview with Sir Thomas Phillips, the experienced Permanent Secretary of the department.

Bevin likes these dramatic touches. A correspondent in a Left-wing weekly newspaper suggested recently that Bevin is of Welsh descent and that his surname is really an Anglicised version of "Ap Evan" (the Son of Evan). As far as Bevin himself knows, his forbears have lived for generations on the borders of Somerset and Devon. Still, his subsequent achievements in the Ministry of Labour showed more of the dramatic and imaginative qualities of the Celt than the phlegmatic casualness of the West Country.

Bevin's intended casual entry was thwarted by the doorkeeper, who turned out to be a keen trade unionist, and who, as he pointed out to Bevin, remembered the face of his new Minister from many previous visits on deputations to predecessors. So Bevin was ushered with appropriate ceremony into the rooms of his new chief lieutenants. Lovely, spacious rooms they are in spite of the drabness induced by the uniformity of Government departments, because this Montague House was formerly the town house of the Dukes of Buccleuch. In fact, a room at the top of the building was formerly the town nursery of the present Queen of England. Now it is used as a filing room for unemployment cards.

Bevin, of course, was well known to the permanent officials. One of the senior men in the department, Sir Frederick Leggett, who had established a great reputation as an industrial peace-maker, had been his companion on the mission to the United States in 1926. Meeting old acquaintances suited Bevin better than having to get used to new men, because he was in a hurry. He had hardly taken his hat off in his own room, before he produced from his pocket a folded sheet of foolscap paper. He said to Sir Thomas Phillips, "Here is the man-power plan on which we are going to win the war."

British civil servants are trained to hide their feelings. Bevin gave them their biggest test. They had never had such a previous experience from a new Minister. The custom had been for the permanent officials to "nurse" their new political chiefs into familiarity with the department.

Suavely, they asked Bevin if his plan had received the approval of the War Cabinet. Bevin replied that he would see to that. In the meantime they could be studying it. That was another shock. Here was a new Minister referring to the august and supreme War Cabinet as if, one of them confessed later, "he was referring to a sub-committee of the Transport Workers' Union."

The next day Bevin unfolded his plan to the War Cabinet. It gave them a shock. It demanded nothing less than the total mobilisation of the nation's manpower, and, what was even more startling and disturbing, such a stringent control of working conditions that employers were to be refused the right to choose their own workers.

He got his powers, because he was so sure of two things. He knew how little progress had been made in the eight months of the war in the scientific organisation of the country's resources. There were 1,300,000 unemployed in Britain when the war started. There were still more than 700,000 for whom no jobs could be found.

Secondly, he realised that to win the war there would be more jobs than workers and, indeed, the country was already running into a shortage of skilled craftsmen.

More, he knew the mood of the people. He knew that most of them were merely waiting to be told what their war stations were. He knew that as long as there were great cohorts of men without jobs, those who were in work would find it impossible to realise that there was urgency in what they were doing.

He said bluntly to the Government, "You cannot, in the middle of a war with the enemy at your gates be too nice as to the methods you have to adopt, or sit down and work out with meticulous and mathematical precision exactly how you are going to do this or that. But I feel it would be unfair and unwise and psychologically wrong to ask me to appeal to the workmen to give a bigger output unless at the same time you agree immediately to the policy that no other citizen can profit as a result of that increased output."

There is no doubt that Bevin was feared by the employers. But for his earnestness in getting on with the job, the fact would have given him some sardonic pleasure.

He realised very quickly that if his job was to be a smooth success he would have to have the full co-operation of five groups simultaneously—a difficult job for a man who had been compelled by his choice of calling to spend much of his life in controversy and dispute.

There were five different reasons why he succeeded.

Firstly, the Government was immensely relieved that a man so full of energy, ideas and confidence had been found to tackle a job which had always been difficult. This question of handling manpower had failed largely because no previous Minister of Labour had demanded such wide powers with such force and reason. Members of the Cabinet realised quickly that there was a certain ruthlessness about Bevin which suited the mood and plight of the nation.

He found some unexpected allies. They were Lord Halifax and Sir John Anderson, both of whom by tradition and background might have been expected to demur at Bevin's impulsiveness. Both of them were administrators of long experience. Both were orthodox, and both were fully appreciative of the implications of some of Bevin's proposals.

There was, however, a curious coldness and aloofness in the attitude of some of the Labour Party Ministers towards Bevin. At least, he thought so, because he commented upon it to some of his most intimate friends at the time.

After all, he was completely devoid of Ministerial and Parliamentary experience, and would have welcomed some hints from colleagues of experience. It may have been that he was unduly sensitive or expectant. Some of these colleagues were unaware for some time of Bevin's feeling of disappointment. One of them, when told about it, promptly approached Bevin and explained that the most probable explanation was that each of the Labour Ministers was as fully pre-occupied in his post as Bevin. Another point to remember was that not one of the Labour Ministers had been in office for at least nine years, and certainly none had ever served in such harassing circumstances.

However, the atmosphere of chilliness was soon dissipated. Bevin commanded attention and forced appreciation by his own performances. At the end of five years, Bevin's personal prestige was among the greatest contributions to the success of the Labour Party in the general election of 1945.

Bevin's relations with Churchill were cordial and mutually-respectful from the very start. And, towards the end of the National Government a close and constant sense of consultation developed between Anthony Eden and Bevin, when the possibility of Bevin becoming Eden's successor seemed remote.

There was one Ministerial association which never developed into friendship. That was with Lord Beaverbrook, who along with Bevin, later became a member of the War Cabinet. I know that both men tried desperately hard to get to like each other. On balance Beaverbrook tried the harder. There were points of similarity—their loyalty to Churchill, their aggressive energy, and their determination to prosecute the war to the end. But the contrasts were greater. Beaverbrook hated committees and regarded them as time-wasting and obstructive. Bevin regarded committees, especially of representative employers and trade union leaders, as valuable and constructive. Beaverbrook regarded his job of producing the aircraft for the Battle of Britain and the subsequent air offensive as being of such supreme importance at the time that it should be given unquestioned priority in men and materials and not subjected to any scrutiny or comparison with any other demand. Bevin, on the other hand, insisted on the creation of a National Production Council to examine all demands with detachment in order that the whole production field could be developed by strict schedule. Bevin subsequently complained that Beaverbrook "practically wrecked" this Council, but Beaverbrook's defence was that the goods were produced anyway.

And, perhaps the most important of all, there was the startling opposition of their personal and political views. Beaverbrook believed in unfettered, unrestricted freedom from State interference. He was prepared to accept some restraint during the war, but on condition that all restrictive ordinances should be removed as soon as the war ended.

Bevin, with his passion for orderliness, became the arch-advocate of controls. Controls of all kinds, during and after the war. The clash between Bevin and Beaverbrook was one of the classic personal disagreements of the war, yet both Ministers achieved greater successes than any of their colleagues, save Churchill.

Generally, however, in those early days Bevin's impact on his Ministerial colleagues was overwhelming.

Secondly, he won the civil servants in his department. On recovering from the effects of Bevin's first whirlwind invasion of their orderly but cumbersome routine, the senior men got down to it and within three days produced drafts of orders which were revolutionary. These experienced administrators were responding to something that had always been missing. That was Decision. There was plenty of decision about Bevin. What was more important was that his decisions had purpose and were practical. But for that there might have been a revolt. The administrative and executive classes of the British civil service are well organised, and they have plenty of protection from precedent if they refuse to obey an order which is palpably against the public interest. Bevin would have crushed the revolt by arranging for wholesale transfers of the recalcitrant members of his staff to other departments.

All the same the business would have been unpleasant and hampering. Instead, there was complete co-operation. Indeed, an enthusiasm developed which became the envy of all other departments throughout the war.

Bevin, having secured the help of his headquarters men, then started a tour of all his regions. So thorough was it that it took more than a year to complete.

There are 1,200 local Employment Offices throughout Britain. Each has a manager, and most of these managers had spent a lifetime in a routine associated with depression and misery. Bevin was quick to observe that in the exchanges he visited he saw plenty of facilities for registering and recording the details of men out of work, but little provision for finding work. The machine had developed into an apathetic, negative sort of monster.

Bevin permitted me during the early days of the war to "sit in" at some of these regional conferences of his.

Into a regional centre would be invited all the managers of the employment offices of the area. Usually there would be about 60 present. Bevin would open the discussion by outlining his immediate programme. His peroration never varied in substance.

He would end, "I cannot issue regulations which will cover all the contingencies you are likely to meet in the course of your day to day work. You must use your own initiative. If you make a mistake I will stand by you. One thing I will not forgive. That is inaction."

This was a clever move on Bevin's part. It gave every local official a sense of playing a part in the national policy of his department.

Local men felt at ease with their Minister. There was an air of informality about these conferences. Bevin handed his cigarettes around to those on the platform with him, and they usually included such worthies in the service as the oldest local office manager. Men from offices in little-known moorland towns, or sleepy country market places got up to discuss their problems with their chief. Occasionally, he would interrupt them to ask them if they had thought of doing this or that, and the local men, who knew their regulations fairly thoroughly, though there was to come a time when these regulations were issued in such a torrent that they might have been forgiven for being a bit behind-hand in their reading, would explain why Bevin's suggestion was not immediately practicable. So Bevin would make a note, and see that the regulations were amended to cut through formalities.

Within six months Bevin not only raised his department to the status of a first-class Ministry because of the impact of his orders on the whole community, but what is more remarkable, he made every official in it conscious of the importance of his own work.

Thirdly, he had to win the confidence of the nation's organised employers. He was, after all, proposing to curb their freedom more directly and more spectacularly than that of any other class. That was merely because they had always had more freedom and scope for their own initiative than those whom they employed.

But the real difficulty here was that those at the head of the great organisations, like the Federation of British Industries, the Confederation of British Employers' Organisations, the Mining Association, and the Engineering Employers' Federation, were the very men who had parleyed with Bevin in those first tentative approaches towards co-operation ten and eleven years before. They thought they knew Bevin.

In the last decade they were the men who had consulted with Bevin and his colleagues from time to time on issues of mutual interest, but there had always been one reservation. The employers had always stuck to the sanctity of "managerial function." They had always preserved the right to manage their own businesses in their own way. And in this right was freedom to hire and freedom to fire. They knew some of Bevin's ultimate ideals of triple control of major industries by the State, the employers and the employed. They were suspicious of his intentions to use the dislocation of war as a cloak for the introduction of his own philosophies.

But Bevin could not do without them. Since the start of the war there had been a National Joint Advisory Council, consisting of the general council of the Trades Union Congress and the representatives of the British Employers' Confederation, but it was an unwieldy body of between 50 and 60 members. It met rarely, and settled little. So Bevin proposed that each side should pick seven of their ablest men to form a joint consultative committee. Bevin undertook to consult this committee before introducing any major orders which affected industry. He kept his promise. There were occasions when some members of his consultative committee even from his own side like Sir Walter Citrine were highly critical of some of his proposals. They even induced him to make last-minute amendments. But the offer of such consultation on such conditions was one which the organised employers could not refuse.

It was one thing making a settlement with the national representatives of the employers in London; quite another to secure the unqualified approval of the highly-organised independent and influential local employers.

So he decided to go and see them in their own centres. One of the most important of these regional meetings took place in Glasgow on a Sunday morning. Here he met the leaders of Scotland's great engineering and shipbuilding industries. They prided themselves on their toughness and gloried in their independence of London.

One speaker after another got up to recite chapter after chapter of complaints and shortcomings. Bevin had two members of his department with him. One nudged the other and whispered, "The Old Man will explode any time now."

Bevin did nothing of the sort. He listened politely for nearly two hours. He told these dour Scots the plain highly confidential story of Britain's plight. They were appalled. But they were impressed by Bevin's sincerity and by the knowledge he showed of their difficulties. He admitted that some of his plans cut across their ideas, but also showed how his ideas of "rationing labour" would help them. At the end of his forty-minute recital they got up and permitted themselves the rare luxury of applause.

From that moment onwards the Clyde was with Bevin. This was great news for Winston Churchill and those other members of his Government who remembered the Clyde troubles of the last war.

Fourthly, he got the aid of all the trade unions by taking them into his confidence.

On the face of it, with Bevin's past record on the general council of the Trades Union Congress, this might appear to have been an easy job. No one appreciated more than Bevin what the handicaps were. He knew that getting to the top in the trade union world, as in any other, was bound to be accompanied by the creation of jealousies and criticisms, although there is a good comradeship between most of the trade union leaders.

Even more important was the professional jealousy of the craft unions, and their resentment of any interference with the privileges and rights they had won over many years of hard bargaining and intensive organisation. As it happened, it was to the craft unions that Bevin had to make his greatest appeals, because the shortage of trained men, caused because youngsters had not taken up apprenticeships in the depression of ten years earlier, made inevitable the dilution of their trades and this meant the introduction of unskilled and semi-skilled men and women to do the work of trained men.

So, on May 25th, 1940, within two weeks of his appointment to office, he addressed a great conference in London of all the executives of all the unions. He took nearly 2,000 men into his confidence, and it was kept. True, the secret was known to the nation very shortly afterwards in the form of orders and regulations, but the background of his appeal was preserved in the minds of the men to whom he spoke because it would, undoubtedly have been of great cheer to the enemy in those days.

"The end has come to the 'phoney war' period," he declared, "when Government departments have been conducting a private war of their own to secure priorities."

Bevin thundered, "There must be a Production Council, and that council must be in possession of the strategy of war. We can't have departments like the Army and the Air Force ordering this and ordering that and ordering something else, and expect me to supply labour to the whim of every command and the idiosyncrasy of every general, whether there are materials or not. The War Cabinet has agreed that this Production Council shall be established, and it will be its duty to survey consistently the war materials of the country, the most urgent production and the swinging of production from one form to another, according to the vagaries of the war. I ask our people in the workshops to accept our decisions as to which is the most urgent job—even when we cannot always tell them 'why' at the time."

He announced that he was setting up a Labour Supply Board of four. They were four very dissimilar personalities. There were two representing employers, and two had trade union experience. It was odd that Bevin did not ask the trade unions to choose their representatives. He picked his own.

Major-General Kenelm Appleyard, who had developed very successfully a trading estate of many diverse factories in the north-east of England, and helped to kill the depression in that badly-hit area, was one of the employers. The other was A. P. Young, a brilliant organiser, and executive head of a great electrical concern in the Midlands. One trade union leader was bushy-eyebrowed, dogmatic Richard Coppock, the leader of the building trade workers. Coppock, a slightly smaller edition of John L. Lewis, but with a close resemblance to the American miners' leader, was able to stay the course only five months because his own union demanded his personal supervision of the complicated problems the war was to bring to their industry.

And the fourth was John Carruthers Little, who had been president of the Amalgamated Engineering Union until five days after the start of the war. Then his union's rules, the tightest, most religiously-observed of any in the land, compelled his retirement under the age limit of 65. Jack Little had welcomed his own retirement. He had gone to a little cottage on the coast of Northumberland to indulge his passion of the study of the stars. He had been a skilful amateur astronomer most of his life. Now he planned to become a full-time one, with a telescope given him as a farewell gift by the men he had led for years. Bevin sent Jack a telegram. That was the end of star-gazing for Jack for five years. He stayed the course longest of all. He was with Bevin until the latter's last day as Minister of Labour.

But how effective he was in the job of seeing that all firms used skilled labour sparingly and efficiently. He was the key link between the Ministry and the craft unions. Years later, when the war reached its greatest intensity, I heard Jack Little's successor, the popular Jack Tanner, tell his union that all young skilled men had to be prepared to teach women their jobs, and then go off to the wars and mend tanks, jeeps and lorries.

Fifthly, the public responded to Bevin's most drastic orders, which reflected their realisation that they were alone in all the world, with their sister nations of the British Commonwealth, against the all-conquering Nazis. France and the whole of western Europe had crumbled.

There is tremendous significance in this. If Bevin or any other Minister had introduced his new rules, say, six months earlier, or if the Allied forces had been registering wholesale victories in Europe and the Mediterranean zones it is doubtful whether they would have been accepted with equanimity. As it was, they were welcomed with alacrity because they showed the sense of stern reality which gave comfort to the bewildered masses.

For the first act of the Government in the crisis was to amend and extend the Emergency Powers Act which had been introduced at the start of the war.

This new order required "all persons to place themselves, their services and their property at the disposal of His Majesty so far as might appear to be necessary or expedient for securing the public safety, the defence of the realm, the maintenance of public order, or the efficient prosecution of the war, or for maintaining supplies or services essential to the life of the community."

At the same time other regulations under the Act, "vested in the Minister of Labour and National Service the control and use of all labour by giving him power to direct any person in Great Britain to perform such services as may be specified by directions issued by the Minister to require persons of any class or description to register particulars about themselves, and power to enter and inspect premises, and to require employers to keep and produce such books, documents and records as might be necessary."

The regulation added, "Any directions of the Minister might, in accordance with his instructions, be given on his behalf by duly authorised persons called 'National Service Officers.' The Minister is also given power to make orders for regulating the engagement of workers by employers and the duration of their employment."

This was total mobilisation with a vengeance. There was a startling completeness about the authority given to Bevin because his right to issue orders meant that he could do so without having every step of his programme debated by Parliament. He was given authority which no man had assumed in England since the days of Cromwell.

Some of his permanent officials were startled by the powers given to their department. Bevin sensed this. He called his chief officials together and gave them what was virtually a lecture on the English people. He assured them it would be rarely necessary to invoke the penal sanctions which his orders contained. There would be few cases of individuals refusing to obey. There would be few prosecutions. There would be few fines of £100 or sentences of imprisonment of three months on people who would not accept the instructions of these national service officers. He was right. There were few cases of refusal for at least a year. Even then the proportion of people who refused orders never reached 1 per cent. of those who obeyed.

But Bevin also realised that more than tossing out a stream of orders was needed.

He developed a remarkable series of welfare activities. They took many forms. Folks uprooted from their homes had to be looked after, so he developed a system of billeting schemes. Every man and woman sent away from home to work was escorted on the trains by Ministry officials, was met by another official, was given a warm cup of tea and a meal and was taken to a new home and introduced to a landlady, whose standards were kept up to specified levels.

There was entertainment in the factories. Bevin himself went down to Woolwich Arsenal with Sir Seymour Hicks, the comedian, to see and hear Will Fyfe the Scots comedian, and Joan Cross the opera singer in the first of 500,000 of these wartime factory concerts.

And soon every factory employing more than 250 workers was compelled to install a full canteen providing hot meals at low rates for all workers. Bevin may have been ahead of his people here because in thousands of cases workers did not avail themselves immediately of these facilities.

In charge of these welfare arrangements was an athletic civil servant named Godfrey Ince. Bevin had known him for many years. In fact Ince had barely doffed his officer's uniform after the last war before being made secretary of the Shaw Commission of Inquiry into dock conditions in 1920. So Ince had observed Bevin when the latter achieved his first national triumph. And Bevin had been aware of Ince. A year was to pass before Bevin promoted Ince to the specially-created post of Director General of Manpower.

In the meantime two things happened. Bevin got on with the detailed job of mobilising the nation and Ince survived the greatest test of his welfare arrangements.

This came from Scotland. For some time an agitation had been developing in Scotland against the transfer of Scots lassies to war jobs in England. There were two grounds for this outcry. Local authorities and employers in Scotland wanted more war jobs in their areas and they argued that by keeping their labour there they would have an added inducement to persuade the supply authorities to give contracts their way. Then there was the deeper outcry from the parents who feared for the morals of daughters brought up in the strict Sabbatarianism of Scottish homes.

So Bevin, after consulting Ince, invited the folk of Scotland to send a commission into the Midlands of England to see for themselves how their daughters were faring. It was a strong Commission. On it were representatives of the Church, of industry and of the trade unions. They were given ample facilities to inspect the factories where the girls worked, the private billets and the great communal hostels where they lived, and the dance halls and cinemas where they spent their evenings. Some of the Commission even popped into the public houses of the great Midlands centres to see how Scottish and other "imported" girls conducted themselves. The Commission interviewed nearly 3,000 of the girls from Scotland. Only five of these girls wanted to return to their homes.

Much of this result was due to a psychological rebellion on the part of the girls against the strictness of home life in Scotland. The girls who had come South were earning better money than their fathers had ever earned in Scotland. They were given much more personal freedom. There was none of this business of having to be home at fixed hours every evening. But the result was also a great triumph for the thoroughness with which Ince's department had done its job.

Bevin's first detailed job after getting the whole country to adapt itself to individual registration, was to tackle the startling shortage of skilled men. In the Midlands of England a regular trade in "poaching" skilled craftsmen had grown up. Firms actually employed "touts" or agents to tour neighbouring areas to tempt skilled men to leave their present jobs for higher wages and extravagant promises of good prospects. Workers were given bribes for a list of the private addresses of the men who worked in the tool rooms of their factories. Every evening the touts would visit these skilled men in their homes in the back streets of the Midland centres to induce them to change jobs. The touts themselves received as much as £2 (eight dollars) for every skilled man they signed on.

The result was that the wealthier and more selfish firms were threatening to "corner" the inadequate supply of skilled craftsmen. Once a firm was able to assure one of the supply ministries that it was adequately staffed to cope with rush orders, government contracts flowed in. Some firms had contracts assuring them full work for three years ahead, while others were in danger of being denuded of their skilled men completely, and of being unable to fulfil important war jobs.

Bevin stopped all this by issuing an order which compelled all employers in the vital industries to hire all their men through the local employment exchange. No employer could hire his own men.

This was the sort of action which assured the public that Bevin was administering his authority with impartiality. The response from the workshops was tremendous. Indeed, it became alarming. Men and women were working 70 and 80 hours a week. Bevin decided this could not go on. He felt that production would suffer long before the winter because of excessive fatigue among workers. So he gave instructions that working hours were to be curtailed nearer normal—to about 50 to 54 hours a week.

Among the first to object were the workers themselves. True, they had been working long hours and they were tired. But they had been earning high wages, and the curtailment of hours meant a reduction in wages. Bevin got over that objection by inducing both sides in industry to extend systems of payment by results. Workers soon found that by working at top pressure for 54 hours they were able to earn as much as they had received for working 70 hours.

Bevin introduced this variation in the nick of time. Within two weeks the Luftwaffe raids started over Britain, first by day and then by night. At times the dislocation of transport and the damage to factories was extensive. It was as well that the workers were adapting themselves to working intensely in shorter spells.

Bevin himself, like most other Ministers at that time, was breaking his own rules. He was working above the 70 hours a week, and was sharing the bombing experiences of all others. At that time he was living in a suite on the fifth floor of a popular hotel in the Strand, London, chosen for him because of its proximity to his office. On one night four fire bombs fell on the roof of this hotel. Bevin took his stand on the roof with the firewatchers and fighters.

He was working at a disturbing pace, though he showed few signs of flagging because of his enthusiasm.

He spent many of his weekends in the great provincial industrial centres. On one of these visits his attendants determined to draw up for him a programme which would give him at least one morning free from formal engagements.

Soon after breakfast Bevin realised that within two miles of the hotel in which he was staying there was a modern office of his union which he had opened formally just before the start of the war. His two associates groaned. They wanted a rest, too. They persuaded Bevin to relax and examine some official papers in his despatch case. By mid-morning the old hankering to see this

union office returned to him. There was some delay in getting his
motor car around to the hotel, because his chauffeur had been
advised that the Minister was unlikely to need his services during
the morning.

At last they set off. Bevin enthusiastic, his two officials a little
glum. There was a curious air of calm about the offices. This did
not disturb Bevin at all. He knew his own way around.

He bounced out of his car, his officials at his heels. He took
them up to the top floor and immediately started to act as a guide.
"Here," he announced proudly, opening a strong oaken door, "is
the regional board room. You see how compact everything is, and
what a fine vista you have from those windows." The two officials
looked politely through the windows to acres and acres of smoking
chimneys and ugly factories.

Then Bevin took them to the lower floors, on each explaining
the functions of every office. Bevin was enthralled. He was showing them the most modern example of the growth of his beloved
union. Then, they reached the ground floor. This, Bevin explained as they neared the bottom of the stairs, is the general
office.

Then, with the flourish of an impresario, Bevin pushed the
door open. Before them sat two girls, an office boy and a junior
clerk, contentedly munching sandwiches from paper bags. On the
table there were two bottles of milk on a newspaper. Bevin looked
distastefully at the sight. His officials peered over his shoulders.
"Bah," snorted Bevin, "you can't even rise to a tablecloth." And
he slammed the door, and strode out to his automobile.

Back in the hotel, Bevin retired to his room. One official
explained to the other, "It isn't that he's got above them. He's
just mad they haven't risen with him."

Throughout this period women were volunteering for their
war jobs. They were being registered in age groups with men, but
the women could decide for themselves whether they preferred
to join the auxiliary uniformed services or go into the factories.
There was an unusual, but convenient, division of preferences.
Throughout this voluntary phase one-third chose the uniformed
services, one-third industry, and one-third said they did not mind
which branch of national service they were drafted into.

The result was that from the indifferent third Bevin's officials were able to satisfy the most immediate demands, first of the services and then of industry.

Incidentally, there was at that time a curious reluctance for service in the Auxiliary Territorial Service, the women's branch of the Army. There were more applicants for service in Women's Royal Naval Service and in the Women's Auxiliary Air Force.

This intrigued Bevin. He came to the conclusion that the snag was stockings. In the W.R.N.S. the stockings, though black, had a sheen which suggested elegance. The light khaki stockings issued to girls in the Army service were dull, utilitarian and un-romantic. Bevin toyed with the idea of persuading the Army authorities to issue artificial silk stockings to the girls. One thing held him back. He was biding his time to introduce conscription.

He knew with sureness that the idea of introducing compulsory service would fail unless the public demand for such an innovation grew. He also knew that it was growing. In fact, it started with the women who had volunteered. They became restive about the women who were doing no kind of national service. The women who had responded to the call for volunteers became Bevin's unconscious recruiting agents. They wanted to know why so many women were doing nothing. Their parents became querulous. Members of Parliament started asking questions, and some sections of the press started mild campaigns accusing Bevin of being too soft-hearted. They started to demand more action from him.

This suited him. By January of 1941 he was able to introduce his regulations to conscript women with little public opposition. There was plenty behind the scenes. This move brought the war home with a vengeance to every household in the country. Many of the wealthier were convinced that Bevin was proposing to dragoon their daughters as an act of personal spite against their class. The most interesting feature of this quite influential secret campaign was that it was conducted solely by parents. Nearly all the daughters were on the side of compulsion, thus suggesting that they had been held back from volunteering earlier by their parents.

His machine was ready to cope with compulsion. In every town a Women's Advisory Panel was set up to consider any cases of hardship which might arise from women being regarded as "mobile," and therefore liable to be directed away from their homes. Mothers of young children were exempted from these regulations.

There had not been such administrative preparedness when Bevin first called for volunteers. It happened in an hotel room in Newcastle-on-Tyne on a Sunday morning. A little group of us had accompanied Bevin up to the North-east, and on the Saturday evening he told us with a glint of mischievousness in his eyes that if we wanted to see him next day it would have to be very early in the morning, as he proposed to spend most of the day with the dockers on the Tyne and addressing public meetings later in the day. So we agreed, with considerable reluctance on our part, to meet him in his hotel at 9 o'clock in the morning. We said, with the easy affability which then existed between Bevin and the newspapermen, that he had better be good to warrant a conference at such an unseemly hour. His officials were dubious later that evening, because they could not think of any new scheme then in Bevin's mind.

But on the Sunday morning, after sympathising with us for having to be astir so early, he calmly announced his call for volunteers from the women of Britain. Next day every London newspaper blazoned, "Bevin wants 100,000 women." He roared delightedly at its ambiguity.

All the same, the combined efforts of volunteering and conscription of men and women did not satisfy the national needs.

Bevin once more proved an accurate diagnostician. The trouble was that there was too great a labour turnover in all industries. Employers were impatiently firing workers who took too long to learn their jobs. And workers got discouraged and threw up their jobs.

So, on March 5th, 1941, Bevin introduced the first of his Essential Work Orders.

There were many revolutionary features in these orders. No employer could hire or fire any of his staff without the permission of the National Service Officer. No permission was given unless a worker had been guilty of grievous misconduct. No worker could leave his or her job without the permission of the National Service Officer.

On the other hand, there were definite advantages in factories being scheduled under the Order. If a factory was scheduled it was given its supply of the available labour. But no worker was directed to such a factory unless the wages and working conditions were up to the standard of the industry. Thus firms operating "sweated trade" conditions could get no workers.

There was a general levelling-up of wage rates. The unions had agreed to give up the strike weapon, and their grievances were settled by submission of their claims to the National Arbitration Tribunal.

Even now Bevin was not satisfied. In May, 1941, he told Godfrey Ince that the nation's "hand-to-mouth" reliance on labour supplies had to end. He gave Ince the incredibly difficult task of budgeting the national manpower needs for at least a year ahead. Ince achieved it by calling on all Service departments and the supply ministries to provide him with their following year's anticipated manpower requirements. Ince thus knew how many men and women his department was expected to supply. Against this he formed an accurate estimate of how many youngsters would be forthcoming from the call-up at 18 for boys and 19 for girls, and how many men and women could further be "squeezed out" of the less-essential trades and services. And what fresh regulations would be needed to bridge any gap.

It was because of this survey that, late in 1941, Bevin and Ince decided to change the whole system of deferment which had operated since the start of the war. Back in 1939, Sir William Beveridge, and his assistants, Nicholson and S. G. Holloway, had devised an ingenious schedule of every industry in the country. In the most important, no man above 18 could be called to the Forces, in others, no man above 21, 23, 25 and 27, and in the least important, no man above 35 or 40. In these last industries and services this meant that practically all men could be called up to the Forces. This system was known as "block deferments."

Thus, the test of a man's war job had been his age and not his ability. It had worked very well in the early stages of the war, but now a finer mesh was needed.

So Bevin and Ince introduced a new system of individual deferment. It was a colossal task. It meant that every single man who had been kept in industry hitherto because of his age had to have his case re-examined to see whether he was fulfilling his highest contribution to national needs in his factory.

All employers and every man had to prove that the job each of them was doing was of greater national importance than shoulder-ing a rifle, or driving a tank, or piloting an aeroplane.

Forty-four manpower boards were set up throughout the country. Each board had five members. And all of them were made temporary civil servants. They dealt with more than 5,000,000 cases.

The chairmen of each of these boards were drawn from widely different types of experience. Two of the ablest were a university professor (who has since become a Minister of the Crown), and the transport officer of a cider factory.

They commanded a team of experts who had authority to enter every factory. This factory probe had two objects. The first was to see whether a man could be spared from an industry to enter the forces. The second whether he was too skilled for the work he was doing. It frequently happened, therefore, that a highly-skilled man was transferred not to the Forces but to a more important job in his own factory or even to another factory on more important production.

Bevin, therefore, came to command a machine which decided every man's post. It ended any recriminations between those who fought in uniform and those who remained in industry. It was the nearest any democratic nation got to the practice of dictatorship, and it was made possible by the will of the people.

There were other problems dealt with by Bevin. He devised a special system for docks, for example, which completely de-casualised them and made them the direct employees, not of their old bosses in the ports, but of a State-sponsored National Dock Labour Corporation.

There was the great and complex problem of manpower for the coal mines, a problem, incidentally, which has remained unsolved to this day and which robs Britain of a flying start to recapture its lost export markets.

Bevin has had critics who accuse him of being partly responsi-ble for this drainage of manpower away from the coal mines. The trouble started in the month after France fell. The end of France, Britain's most valuable overseas coal market, meant that thous-ands of miners became unemployed in South Wales. They were a sore temptation to Bevin. A temptation he could not resist. He wanted men desperately in other industries. He encouraged these unwanted miners to go into other war industries. Miners' leaders claim that they warned Bevin that the day would soon come when there would be a shortage of miners to produce the coal needed by the nation's munitions programme. Bevin advised Will Lawther, Ebby Edwards, Arthur Horner and the other miners' leaders to consider working longer hours because, he suggested, if too many miners were brought back to the mines there might come a time when the mining areas would again become distressed areas.

Within three years Bevin was to devise his ballot scheme for young miners. He had given men called up to the Forces the option of being directed into the mines instead of going into uniform, but few had accepted this chance of remaining in civilian life. So he was forced to introduce compulsion to the mines. Every youth in Britain had registered for military service on reaching the age of 17 years and nine months. Each had been given a number, ending with a digit from 0 to 9.

Bevin arranged for ten slips of paper, each bearing a single number, to be placed into a hat. Then he called one of his secretaries in to extract one of these bits of paper. Every boy whose registration number ended with the extracted digit had to go into the mines, unless he had already been accepted for service as an artificer in a submarine or for flying duties in the Royal Air Force.

It was an arbitrary device which showed no respect for social distinctions. It mattered not which school the boy had attended. It was the most spectacular illustration of Bevin's claim that the war had levelled all in Britain to a single class.

He seems to have realised that this move would not be too popular. The whole proceedings were surrounded in secrecy. The name of the secretary who extracted that first ballot paper was suppressed, as some of the Ministry officials confessed, lest she should be molested by mothers of boys who were sent to the coal mines. Bevin himself regretted the necessity for such a procedure. It is ironic that these boys should be known universally as "Bevin boys," although Bevin himself always refers to them as "ballotees."

Bevin's major war job finished by mid-1943. By that time he had perfected an organisation which resulted in Britain's armed forces being increased from 477,000 in mid-1939 to 5,086,000 in the month he left office in mid-1945; in the civil defence services being increased from 80,000 to 384,000; in the munitions

industries going up from 3,106,000 to 5,233,000; and in total
mobilisation of men and women in all forms of service from
18,480,000 in mid-1939 to 22,265,000 by September, 1943.

The most spectacular rise of all was among the women. When
the war started there were 4,837,000 employed in all forms of jobs
in Britain. By September, 1943, there were 7,265,000, and thousands of them were women who had never needed to work in
their lives.

Many prophesied in those war years that when the war ended
this would be remembered against Bevin. It was forecast that he
would suffer politically for having disintegrated homes, and
separated families. Bevin himself was told of this many times. He
never shared such forebodings. I remember him saying one
evening, when this point was brought up to him, "Not on your
life. I am not imposing dictation from above on an unwilling
people. All I am doing is putting the form to what people want.
We are all in this war and the people who know it best of all are
those who are now being directed to jobs all over the place."

Bevin had no intention of resting on his laurels. There was
nothing more he could do to extend mobilisation after 1943.
Ince's year's forecast made allowances for all wastages and intakes
up to the end of 1944. There was even an estimate of battle casu-
alities in these secret returns. Although both the United States
and Soviet Russia were now making their mighty contributions
to the cause of the United Nations there was no "let-up" on
Britain's part. If anything the restrictions on labour supplies to
less-essential industries and services were even more rigidly
applied.

But Bevin's speeches showed that his mind was turning towards
inculcating into an oft-ignored group a greater sense of their
importance and a greater acknowledgement of their value to the
nation than they had ever had. This was the managerial and
working executive class. Although they were fairly well organised
in some industries they had no political influence and little public
recognition. It had been customary to regard industry as being
divided into two groups only; the employers and the employed.

There was little political motive in Bevin's tribute to them. It
sprang from real gratitude for the part they had played in Britain's
war effort. Established firms had created "shadow factories" in
the heart of the countryside for greater safety from bombing;

medium-sized and smaller firms had extended beyond recognition in the early years of the war; and great plants where no woman had been employed previously now employed more women than men. Now all these things called for quick adaptation on the part of executives, particularly personnel managers. Bevin introduced a whole range of training schemes for executive grades. It is probable that these will become a permanent feature of industrial life in Britain.

And there was another class to which Bevin turned his attention at this time. This was the vast army employed in catering establishments of all types and sizes, from the small roadside, mobile tea stands, by way of public houses, cafes, restaurants, seaside boarding houses, night clubs, and railway buffets to the biggest and most luxurious hotels in London.

There was a terrific howl from the trade, whose leaders alleged that Bevin was interfering in their affairs only because, as a trade union leader, he had failed to organise such workers before he came to office. Bevin ignored that allegation. But the political opposition that was set up by the catering trade he was unable to ignore. The political opposition was based on the agreement made at the time of the formation of the national government that no controversial domestic legislation would be introduced during the war, and there was plenty of controversy about this. Bevin blandly replied that all he was doing was to set up a series of commissions of inquiries into conditions in each section of the trade. He argued that if such committees found that conditions were adequate no recommendations would be made. On the other hand, if conditions were proved to be bad, surely no one could object to their improvement, and the elimination of all sweated labour conditions from the land.

One afternoon, Bevin was sitting in his office in his new headquarters in St. James's Square, London, when two of his administrative officials came in to tell him that they had found twenty reasons why objections might be raised to his catering proposals. Bevin, without waiting for further amplification, calmly replied, "Good, now go back and work out twenty reasons for overcoming the objections." That was the end of that interview.

Bevin convinced himself and many of his critics that his catering commission could lead to the establishment of a really efficient and contented industry, which would be of enormous value in increasing Britain's wealth by attracting overseas visitors. He calculated that the industry could be developed to support more than 1,000,000 well-paid workers. He got the Bill he introduced into Parliament sponsored by some of his most influential Conservative colleagues in the Cabinet. It was carried by a comfortable majority, but 119 Conservative members voted against the Bill. It was the biggest vote of the whole war period against the Government.

Bevin had his first holiday of the war in the late summer of 1943. He took Mrs. Bevin to the North of Scotland. He went away contented because he had been able to report to Mr. Churchill that the whole of the mobilisation plan had been completed. It could now run under its own impetus.

While he was away, Mr. Churchill decided that a start should be made on preparations for demobilisation. Mr. Bevin's department, through his genial Parliamentary Secretary, George Tomlinson, was already working on the training and rehabilitation of the disabled servicemen. But the problem of the release of the fit men had yet to be investigated. Churchill decided that after his arduous job on mobilisation, Bevin should be relieved as much as possible of the details of the reverse programme.

With Cabinet approval, Prime Minister Churchill handed the job on to a committee of Parliamentary Secretaries, or junior Ministers. They were working on the job when Bevin returned from his holiday. Their first plan did not meet with Cabinet approval, so it was sent back to them for greater amplification. Apparently, this instruction was misconstrued, because when the second plan was submitted to the Cabinet it proved to be less acceptable than the first. It was regarded as far too complicated. It was based on a points system and took into account length of service, period spent overseas, the marital status of each fighting man, and so on.

One morning Bevin sent for his lieutenant, who had become Sir Godfrey Ince by this time, and said excitedly, "I've got it. It came to me in the middle of the night." And there and then he outlined to Sir Godfrey the simple formula of age-and-length-of-service. Earlier in the war, Bevin had favoured the idea of "first-in, first-out," but the objection to this was that the last into the Forces had been skilled men who had been deferred because of their usefulness to industry, and as most of them were middle-aged and heads of families their retention in the Forces would mean personal hardship as well as a handicap to industrial recovery.

Now under his age-and-length-of-service idea, Bevin made an allowance of two months' service for every year of age above 18.

They, Bevin and Ince, decided, after working out the plan of the scheme, to secure the comments of the heads of the three service departments before submitting it to the Cabinet. This confirmed an experience the Ministry of Labour had accumulated throughout the war, that in matters of assessing the effect and implications of any proposal on their own men one of the fighting departments was far superior to the other two.

The most businesslike of the Service administrations in Britain proved to be, surprisingly, the War Office. It is usually the most maligned. The most praised, because of its long tradition, is the Admiralty. Its vanity in the prowess of its ships' companies seems to have led the administrators of the Admiralty to take a perverse pride in the inability of its officers to cope "with this office business and routine stuff and red tape and all that." Even the Admiralty, in its own good time, approved of Bevin's idea of release by age-and-length-of-service.

Armed with the support of the three Service Ministers, Bevin had no difficulty in getting Cabinet approval. Thus it transpired that Bevin not only fully mobilised the British, but organised their demobilisation also.

After finishing this great task, and getting the approval of the great majority of the men in the Forces for it as a practical scheme of rough-and-ready justice, Bevin started repeating in many quarters a very significant wise-crack. "They say," he grinned, "that Gladstone was at the British Treasury from 1860 to about 1930. They'll say that Bevin was at the Ministry of Labour from 1940 to 1990."

By that he meant that some of his works and principles would have their effect in Britain for fifty years. He may have been referring to his last acts in the Ministry.

He did two things. He prepared a scheme for the transition of Britain from war to peace. In this transitional period he provided for the control of labour for years after the cessation of hostilities. No man under 50, unless he had special qualifications, was to be allowed to be engaged or to find his own job without the approval

of the Ministry of Labour. The same control was to apply to
women under 40. Bevin had experienced the handicap of under-
manning in the nation's major industries, notably coal mining,
during the war. He felt that if all workers were given complete
freedom there was a likelihood that many of the older and vital
industries would be deserted for the newer and less-important
industries in modern factories, providing more pleasant working
conditions.

Yet now, barely six months after Bevin has left office, his old
colleagues on the general council of the Trades Union Congress
were so insistent on a reduction in the age of these controls that
George Isaacs, the printers' leader who succeeded Bevin as
Minister of Labour, has been forced to yield, and to abolish
completely all controls over women.

Bevin did another thing. He introduced, and carried, his Wages
Councils Act, which makes it imperative that all wages agreements reached between organised employers and workers must
be honoured even by firms which are not associated with any
federation in their industry. He gave individual workers the right
to appeal to a tribunal if they were underpaid, and the tribunal,
representing the State, has the authority to insist on recalcitrant
employers paying the agreed rates for their industry. In the first
instance, he intended this scheme to be tried as an experiment for
five years, and then reviewed.

Bevin, so obviously, was determined that he would play his
part in eradicating all traces of under-payment of workers.

It is quite likely that Bevin's own confidence in the permanence
of some of the principles he introduced at the Ministry of Labour
is based on their indirect value.

There are for example, many employers who were compelled
to introduce canteens into their factories, but who have found
such a good effect on production from the existence of such
amenities that it is sound business to make them permanent.

There are employers who found co-operation and consultation
with their workers such a useful contribution to smooth and
efficient working, and such a deterrent to strikes and industrial
unrest, that they will continue it voluntarily and permanently.

One of the features of the Essential Work Order was that
workers should be paid a guaranteed week's wages, and the old
system of instant dismissal prevalent in some industries was

abolished. The trade unions will obviously try to make this permanent.

And then, from the Ministry's point of view, Bevin's introduction of individual interviewing cubicles at local employment offices, and the new scope he gave to local officials so won public confidence and approval that all future Permanent Chiefs of the department will certainly try to retain the enhanced prestige which Bevin won for them.

Maybe, the close association which Bevin fostered on his joint consultative committee between representative employers and the principal trade union officials, and which he tried to initiate as far back as those remote Mond-Turner talks in 1928, has at last taken root and will flourish for all time.

Whatever the basis for Bevin's claim, one thing is certain. He was the first man in Britain's history to make a success of the job he took when he thought of retiring.

CHAPTER VIII

THE NEW VOICE OF BRITAIN

It was largely Mr. Bevin's own fault that Britain was surprised by his appointment as Secretary of State for Foreign Affairs.

Yet for some years he had given indications of his interest not only in foreign affairs but in the shortcomings of the Foreign Office in Whitehall.

But he had shown interest in many other aspects of government, and when he kept repeating during the six weeks of twilight indecision, in which Britain existed between the voting day of the general election in 1945 and the declaration of the results, that if his Party was successful he would elect to become the Chancellor of the Exchequer, or the nation's treasurer, he was taken at his word. On balance, his early interests were more emphatic on economics and monetary stability than on international relations. He has always been immensely proud of his work on the Economic Council of 1929 and, perhaps most of all, of his membership of the Macmillan Committee, whose report has always been recognised in Britain as the supreme example of clarity on such an abstruse subject as economics. True, its recommendations were not accepted by the MacDonald Government, but Bevin believed that if they had, much of the chaos which hit Britain a year later would have been avoided.

Bevin had other, more practical, reasons for desiring to become Chancellor of the Exchequer. He believes that a revision of interest rates on debts contracted generations ago is long overdue. He believes that future loans must carry low interest if Britain is to recover. And most of all he believes that only "cheap money" can make possible the provision of the millions of new homes needed in Britain. It was to play his part in the provision of these homes that Bevin set his heart on becoming Chancellor.

It seemed a reasonable development of Bevin's ambition. He had spent most of his life in raising the wages of people. Now he was going to use his energies to provide homes. He had worked out how much half of 1 per cent. on housing loans would mean in reduced weekly rents. He was all set for putting his theories into practice.

Now all this was going on in his mind when the result of the general election was unknown.

In spite of all that has been said since there was a landslide towards Labour in the general election of 1945, giving them a clear majority of nearly 200 in a House of Commons of 650 members and their first opportunity for real power in the history of Britain, the managers of all parties were in doubt right up to the declaration of results on July 26th, 1945. Polling had taken place early in July.

Earlier than that, in May, the annual conference of the Labour Party had taken place in Blackpool. It was there that the national government of Winston Churchill ended, just as it was at the Labour Party conference at Bournemouth exactly five years earlier that the famous wartime coalition had started.

There was desperate hope and courage in those dark days in Bournemouth; hope was tinged with misgiving in the even more complex days in Blackpool.

But there was one powerful factor operating in Blackpool. After five years of office the Labour leaders, Attlee, Morrison, Dalton and Cripps, who had rejoined the Party after six years "in the wilderness," had all enhanced their reputations as national leaders and administrators. Bevin had made, in five years, the most spectacular reputation of them all. Politically, Bevin's reputation up to 1940 had been as a great power behind the scenes.

Overshadowing all, however, was the tremendous reputation of Winston Churchill, the great war leader. If there was to be a general election the Labour Party leaders felt that their political rivals, the Conservative Party, had only one trump card. But what a card! The appeal of Winston Churchill, as "the man who won the war," was felt by Herbert Morrison, who is the natural manager of his party in a major campaign like a general election, to be one of those imponderables which it was safer to avoid than to face. Morrison was all for postponing the election until the late Autumn (fall) when the revision of the voters' registration lists was complete.

It was Winston Churchill and the Conservatives who forced the issue. They too, obviously felt that the appeal of the great war leader for continued support would mean electoral victory.

The clash between the parties came on a seemingly simple issue. Churchill asked Attlee for an assurance that the Labour men would remain in the Government until after Japan had been defeated—and that seemed quite a year away just then. Actually, Japan was knocked out within three months.

Attlee and his party colleagues felt that Churchill was deliberately "holding a pistol" to their heads. There was a note of asperity, they believed, in Churchill's request. There was an implication that they either stayed in his Government for a long time, or he would dispense with their co-operation quickly. In all this, they were in the hands of the Conservative party managers. The exchange of letters between Attlee in Blackpool and Churchill in Downing Street developed into a crescendo of counter-criticism. But it was not until Thursday evening, the night before the conference ended, that the break of the Government was certain and a general election inevitable.

For four days the conference had gone on in an air of uncertainty and unreality. In an atmosphere of rising emotion, little Ellen Wilkinson, who presided with charming efficiency, had introduced a note of wry and diffident humour from time to time by introducing the star speakers with a hesitant description of their ministerial offices. She would say, "Mr. Herbert Morrison —the—uh—Home Secretary, I think," or "Mr. Hugh Dalton, who is still President of the Board of Trade," or "Mr. Ernest Bevin, who, so far as we know, is the Minister of Labour and National Service."

It was universally agreed that the two great oratorical performances of the week were contributed by Herbert Morrison and Ernest Bevin. It is significant, however, that Clement Richard Attlee, that self-effacing, unspectacular model of integrity and high principles, was always accepted as the Prime Minister by the delegates who kept up an unceasing flow of speculation in the conference lobbies throughout the week. They always added, "if we win." That was the operative qualification throughout the conference.

These self-same mental speculators gave a gasp of delighted appreciation as Herbert Morrison sat down after analysing the major internal problems of the day, and added, "And he's the Deputy Prime Minister."

Ernest Bevin spoke later in the conference. He gave a remarkable performance. He was winding up a discussion on international affairs, and therefore was debarred from developing his views on the subjects which he had handled with such confidence and assurance during the preceding five years. Many of the delegates had never heard Bevin speak on foreign affairs. Many, indeed, were surprised that he had been selected by the executive of the Party to intervene in this debate. Usually, the role fell either to Hugh Dalton, who had been Under-Secretary of Foreign Affairs when the late Arthur Henderson was head of the Foreign Office, or Philip Noel-Baker, who was a specialist in these matters and had served for years with the League of Nations.

"We will have to form a Government at the centre of a great Empire and Commonwealth of Nations," Bevin declared, "which touches all parts of the world, and by means of diplomatic, commercial and labour machinery touches many races, every one of which has a different outlook on life."

He said that the tragedy in making the last peace was the failure to bring Russia into the peace conference. This brought an immense cheer from the many Soviet admirers in the conference.

"The security for peace," Bevin continued, "must be the United States, Britain and Soviet Russia. But we cannot remove the prejudices and economic differences, the effect of internal economies easily. The United States is a free enterprise country, the Soviet Union has a socialist internal economy, and Britain stands between the two. We will not weld these differing prejudices and conceptions into a power to prevent aggression by slogans, nor by saying that some people are all angels and others all devils. We have to show patience and toleration, and try to obtain understanding in order to come together for the common purpose of maintaining peace and developing a higher standard of living with a complete removal of fear."

He said, "It is difficult to decide what things cause war, whether they are economic, as some people say, or traditional emotion, or whether it is that nations get it into their heads that the only way to their prosperity is by domination. I believe it is a combination of all three."

Mr. Bevin said that the ordinary person who lived by his toil was the subject of speculation and financial monopolies, and this was the cause of most of our depression and unemployment. Labour, he announced, stood for a universal and orderly but sufficient distribution of food, taking away from any middle man the right to exploit it by monopolies and gambling on the world markets. They must stand for bulk purchase. They had done it during the war, and if it had not been for that the cost of living would have soared. They aimed at a unanimous wheat price. The farmer must have a guaranteed price, not only nationally but internationally. One thing they must fight—international combines, limiting production and causing scarcity to keep up prices. He wanted to have an immense flow of primary products going in plenty in order that the standard of living might be raised. The receiving and producing ends must be brought into harmony.

They must maintain Empire preference while tariffs were used against us by other countries, Bevin added. (This was said seven months before the terms of the American loan to Britain were decided.)

But, he went on, if there were a general lowering of tariffs in the world settlement, allowing a free flow of goods, and if in this the Dominions were with them, they would reconsider the problem. They recognised there had to be something devised to act as a balancing force in international exchange. They did not mind if the commodity was gold if it was used only for that limited purpose, but they would not be a party to going back to the gold standard where that commodity limited our own expansion and led us into the difficulty we had in 1931.

As Bevin went on to urge the establishment of international control over a wide range of raw materials, most of his hearers realised that here was the old economic student coming out in him again.

But he soon showed that he had well-developed views on international statesmanship. He declared, "We stand for collective security. This involves demands and I beg you not to bury your head in the sand. It is no use talking about an international police force if we do not devise the right means of supplying the policemen. I am certain that when we get to grips with this problem, Russia and the United States will want to know what our contribution is."

He forecast, "The centre of Europe may become a cesspool of disease unless we are very careful. While we must prevent Germany again developing a war potential, we cannot leave 60,000,000 people idle. They must grow food. We cannot feed them, neither we nor the United States, however sentimental we might be. We are trying to put the Germans back to till the soil

|Photo: Planet News

ERNEST BEVIN FLIES TO MOSCOW IN DECEMBER, 1945, TO RESTORE
THE FRIENDLY ATMOSPHERE AMONG THE "BIG THREE"
Here he is being seen off by Mrs. Bevin at Northolt Aerodrome

in the zone we are responsible for, and are telling them they must feed themselves. We are in favour of a peace conference. The problem of Europe cannot be settled by long-distance telegrams. Around the table we must get; but do not present us with *faits accomplis* when we arrive. In all the states of Europe, east or west, we are anxious to create a situation of settlement where there may be free and democratic elections, where they can choose their own government. We go further in order to give confidence. We pledge ourselves in our foreign policy never to use these small states to play off the big states, and so get advantage. If I may use a Cockney phrase, there should be 'cards on the table, face upwards'."

Bevin got a great ovation. Promptly, many tipped him as Labour's next Foreign Secretary, and quite as promptly many dismissed the idea on the ground that Bevin had too many prejudices, and would take little trouble to hide them. This was the talk that came from the extreme Left of the Party, from Communist sympathisers who recalled with facility how, throughout his years of domination in the Trades Union Congress, he had always thrown the massive vote of his union against all proposals designed for closer collaboration with or recognition of the Communists in Britain.

It is, however, important to emphasise that Bevin is against the Communists in Britain, but he has never criticised Russia's right to choose her own form of government. All that Bevin has ever hoped is that Russia should not include her creed among her exports to Britain.

In any case, while all these discussions were going on, the general election had yet to be fought.

Bevin was facing, in the Central Wandsworth Division of London, a particularly hard fight. The man who had last won the seat for Labour and who had given it up in 1940 on becoming Lord Nathan so that Bevin could secure an unopposed return to Parliament, had secured in 1935 a majority of only 2,000. Generally, the Labour Party managers felt before the election campaign opened that no seat could be considered safe for the Party unless it had a majority of at least 5,000 in the last election. So, by this reckoning, Bevin's was regarded as one of the "doubtful" seats. Besides, these overcrowded London boroughs do not offer the same facilities as provincial divisions for candidates getting to

o

know their constituents, and vice versa. Further, the Conservatives had chosen a gallant candidate with a fine military record, Brigadier Smythe, holder of the Victoria Cross, the nation's greatest award for valour, to oppose Bevin. And Bevin had never won a contested fight for Parliament.

Bevin enjoyed that election. He spoke in many parts of the country and the reception he got convinced him early on in the campaign not only that his Party would win but that he would hold Central Wandsworth. He won with a majority of 6,000. His Party swept home with an avalanche of victories. There was no doubt about the voice of Britain, however mysterious and far-off it might have sounded when all the Party chiefs entered the fight.

Attlee had been in Potsdam with Churchill, and Eden attending the conference of the Big Three. The British leaders had come home to receive the election results. President Truman and his entourage, and Premier Stalin and his advisers had suspended the conference to await the return of the British team.

It was not Churchill and Eden who went back, but Attlee and Bevin. Attlee sent for Bevin and invited him to name his post in the new Administration. Bevin asked for the Chancellorship. He was standing by the desire he had expressed after the Blackpool conference. Attlee acknowledged the request so non-committally that Bevin assumed it had been granted. He had arranged to go away for a short holiday with Mrs. Bevin, who at that moment was completing their holiday preparations in their Kensington flat. Later in the day, however, Attlee sent for Bevin again, and said, "Ernest, I want you to become the Foreign Secretary, and I want you to come back with me to Potsdam tomorrow. We fly."

That afternoon his appointment was formally approved by the King. He looked into the Foreign Office to have the principal officials presented to him. When he reached home that evening, he called out to Mrs. Bevin, "It's not Cornwall, but Potsdam." The next morning, his first flight ever, took him to Potsdam.

Dalton, who was most frequently tipped for the Foreign Secretaryship, went to the Treasury, which Bevin had asked for. Morrison was left in charge of the Government at home. There were many cynical references to "Government by triumvirate." I recall one commentator observing, "Attlee is called Prime Minister, Morrison thinks he is Prime Minister, and Bevin is the Prime Minister." This was a completely unreal picture of the new Administration, because rarely has the theory of the collective responsibility of the Cabinet become such a practical reality as in the Attlee administration. The comment is worth repeating only because it reflects the towering impression of Bevin which his wartime performance had created in the public mind.

All the same, there was a great deal of speculation at the time even among Labour Members of Parliament about Bevin's appointment to the Foreign Office. It was strongly held that but for the coincidence of the Potsdam conference Bevin might have had his own wish gratified. It was argued that Bevin had been chosen because of his toughness and his experience of delicate negotiations in the industrial field. Many politicians "in the know" added that as soon as the preliminary work of world resettlement had been completed, Bevin would go to the Treasury. There is not much likelihood of this. In the first place, the preliminary work of re-settlement threatens to take years, and secondly, Bevin has the habit of becoming intensely interested in anything he initiates.

His appointment caused the greatest flutter of all in the Foreign Office itself. Its senior members had barely seen Bevin. He was there for a moment and then he was whisked away to Potsdam. In the past Bevin had little to do with the Foreign Office, probably less than with any other Government department, and the diplomats had lived a life remote from the past world of Bevin. Indeed, he had been severely critical of them because of it.

He had announced, when he visited the Trades Union Congress as Minister of Labour in 1940, "There has been established, I think for the first time, a very close liaison between the Ministry of Labour and the Foreign Office. The object of that liaison is, in future, to get the whole of the Diplomatic Service to move and have its being in a new environment; to recognise that the limited Court Circular society of the Chancelleries will never return; that if there is to be a reconstruction of the world, then that reconstruction has to be brought about by harnessing and utilising the rising mass of labour to whom the future really belongs, and who must be the dominant factor in a new democratic world. There must be an absolute broadening of the curriculum, and of the right of entry into the Diplomatic Service. If the boys from the secondary schools can save us in the Spitfires, the same brains can be turned to produce the new world."

These were ominous words to the men in the Foreign Office, who had been brought up in an atmosphere of exclusivity and remoteness even from the rest of the British Civil Service, except the Treasury, whose officials regarded themselves as even more important than the Foreign Office men.

Nevertheless, this superior feeling did not prevent Foreign Office men making many anxious inquiries of Ministry of Labour men. Those who had worked closely to Mr. Bevin during the war were being pleaded with by those who were to work with Mr. Bevin in the peace for details of Mr. Bevin's idiosyncrasies and peculiarities. It is said that never have members of another department been entertained so frequently by officials of the Foreign Office as during the time when the inspiration of all this hospitality was away in Potsdam. The burden of the Ministry of Labour report was brief and direct. They said, "He's got decision and you'll have to work, too."

When Bevin finally returned and took over his duties in the Foreign Office, the gloom inside the austere building was quickly dissipated. Bevin set out to be his most natural and friendly self.

Within three days, he was calling the permanent head of the department, Sir Alexander Cadogan, the punctilious and the precise diplomat, by his abbreviated Christian name of Alec. Within a week he had toured the whole of his department, and had held sectional conferences with departmental heads, and had explained to them the general outlines of his policy.

He told it simply and straightforwardly. Although the Foreign Office has no authority over any part of the British Commonwealth and Colonial Empire, Bevin started his talk by emphasising how the whole economic level of peoples within the Empire must be raised. This process must go on, he continued, in all countries adjacent to British lands. He told his Middle East advisers, for instance, that Britain's allies in those lands were to be not their traditional rulers but the ordinary working folk. The standard of living of those who spin and weave, who dig the soil, and who fish the waters, must not only be raised but they must recognise instinctively that Britain is all out to help in this development.

Nearer home he insisted that Britain had to be friendly with all the countries of Western Europe. It was pointed out to him that there is a danger of this policy being misunderstood. "Of course, there is," he agreed, "as long as our motives are suspect.

We have got to kill suspicions, not only by what we say but what we do. Thank God, we have no bad past to live down." He was referring here to his own Party, whose practical record in foreign affairs was based almost entirely on Arthur Henderson's efforts to secure world disarmament.

Bevin toured the deepest recesses of his warren-like department. He was shocked by the crowded conditions in some of his sections, such as the despatch room, in which diplomatic bags are made up for dispatch to British embassies and consulates all over the world. He roared, "If this department was covered by the Factories Act, I would be prosecuted as a bad employer." He is now looking for an extension of premises so that those who work with him can do so in improved conditions.

He showed a rare sense of informality and innovation during the Foreign Secretaries' Conference in London.

He decided that all previous Foreign Office receptions and social functions to visiting diplomats had been too formal and stiff. He argued that when such visitors to Britain were entertained they should have an opportunity of meeting folk other than those whom they met in formal conferences throughout the day. So he instructed that invitations should be sent to typists and other clerical workers in the department. Let them come and enjoy themselves, he said, and if any Ministers from overseas want to dance or talk with them about conditions here, so much the better.

Mr. Molotov, the Soviet Foreign Minister, was unable to take advantage of this innovation because he was accompanied by his personal bodyguard to the most informal functions. Bevin was privately irked by this, because he considered it evidence of a curious Soviet mistrust and a reflection on the attempts of Britain to show all marks of friendship to Russia.

Bevin is well aware that the keenest critics he has inside his own Party are those who watch eagerly and ceaselessly for any sign of his supposed prejudice against the Soviets. Bevin has protested in Party meetings that he has no such prejudice. He says he is prepared to go half-way towards meeting the Russians on any topic. But not more than half-way. He says he does not believe in appeasement to anyone. Therefore, he is not afraid to refuse requests which he regards as unreasonable.

He was asked by Mr. Molotov to send back to Russia all Soviet citizens in Britain, except those whose presence in Britain was approved by the Soviet authorities. Mr. Bevin reminded Mr. Molotov that he, Bevin, knew such exiles as Mr. Maisky, former Soviet Ambassador to London and one of the most popular diplomats ever posted to the Court of St. James, when Mr. Maisky was a fugitive from the Czarist régime. Pointedly, but with great dignity, Bevin concluded, "I will do nothing to injure the reputation of my country as a sanctuary for exiles."

Early on in this series of social engagements arranged for the visiting Foreign Ministers, Bevin broke another tradition. He feared that one social engagement, which coincided with a period of great tension in the conference, would be marred by the too-early introduction of political topics. With complete disregard for the formality of the occasion, Bevin startled his guests by calling out, "Can anyone here sing ? Let's have a song."

Naturally, the first to respond to this mood were the Americans. Obligingly, Colonel Kelly, one of the advisers to Mr. Byrnes, the American Secretary of State, stepped forward, and in a slight tenor voice, sang "When Irish Eyes are Smiling."

Bevin was highly amused by the choice of Colonel Kelly's song. He knew there was no political significance in it, in spite of the traditional memory of past English misdeeds towards Ireland being so assiduously retained by the American-Irish.

Senior officials at the Foreign Office were charmed by the candour with which Bevin admitted that he did not understand the nuances of the more obscure terms used by the diplomats. He would have no hesitation in interrupting a report to ask for precise definitions. He would also acknowledge his inability to pronounce the names of some foreign potentates or cities, and would add with a great laugh, "You know what I mean."

Naturally, the success of Bevin with his new team of officials was soon talked of in wider circles than the civil service. With puzzling perversity, Bevin was immediately being criticised by some of his own Party for having "knuckled under" to the Foreign Office machine. They would not dare to say this to his face. But he was aware of the criticism all the same, and resentful of it.

Such critics were refusing credit to another aspect of his relations with his new department. Bevin proved quickly to his new associates that his reputation for quick and sound decision was well justified. He proved, too, that the new Administration was speedy in making up its mind. If there were decisions of major policy which had to be referred either to the Prime Minister or to the Cabinet as a whole, the answers were known inside the Foreign Office within 48 hours. So amazed was one senior official by this celerity that he blurted out to Bevin, "Up to now, Secretary of State, we have not been the Foreign Office for years. We have been merely a Post Office for No. 10 Downing Street." The implication was that Mr. Churchill had acted as Foreign Secretary as well as Prime Minister. This was a little unfair on Mr. Anthony Eden, who had kept up close consultation on major foreign policies with Mr. Bevin in the closing stages of the National Government.

It was not on his relationships with his staff, however, that Mr. Bevin was judged by his fellow-countrymen but by his public utterances. And the more outspoken he was the louder his critics cried, because it seemed to them that Bevin was reserving most of his criticism, open or implied, for Russia.

One of the ablest of the Labour Party critics, and one of the most courageous because his identity was known to Bevin, declared after the famous speech in which Bevin referred to Russian aspirations in the Mediterranean as evidence that she "wanted to go right across the throat of the British Empire," that, "Bevin's considered statements are better than his impromptu speeches. When he made his Palestine statement, announcing Anglo-American investigation into Palestinian troubles, he read from the carefully-prepared brief on the dispatch box in front of him. His review of the background against which his statement was made was short but illuminating. How different it was from his foreign policy speech. Once again the Foreign Secretary, standing at the dispatch box with a bundle of typescript before him, faced a packed House. He began to read; but after a few minutes he looked up and made an almost casual comment to the Conservatives opposite him. The comment was well received. He followed it up. Then, seemingly, warmed by Conservative cheers, he abandoned his script and launched into a fist-thumping tirade which brought the session's loudest ovation from the Opposition benches."

This commentator went on, "Throughout, his supporters sat silent—until the speech was over. Then they walked angrily out. They were not so much angry at what he had said as at the way

he said it. Many of them, like him, are irritated at Russia's
touchiness about a Western bloc at a time when she herself is
building an Eastern bloc. But they consider it hypocrisy for Bevin
to talk about putting cards face upwards on the table when everyone knows that Britain and the United States are holding the
atom bomb up their sleeves. They can well understand and
sympathise with Russian suspiciousness on that point; they
understand, even if they do not sympathise with, Russian
suspicions of longer standing. And they think that Bevin's sledge-
hammer treatment of Russia's present nervous state is about as
inept as it could be. As one back-bencher said in the Lobby,
"Ernest still thinks that he is the secretary of the Transport
Workers' Union and that Molotov is Lord Ashfield, boss of
London Transport. Why did he do it?"

The critic proceeds, "When he rose to speak, the House
expected no startling announcement. The experts said that in
view of Attlee's coming discussions with President Truman, he
was going to 'stall' for twenty minutes or so. One view is that
Bevin was led away by his audience. Inevitably, a speaker from
the Government Front Bench directly faces the Opposition
benches. His own supporters are behind him. He does not see
them. For many speakers, of whom Lloyd George was an outstanding example, the temptation to follow up a point that has
gone over is overwhelming. Perhaps that temptation took hold
of Bevin and Conservative encouragement playing on his natural
instincts, led him over the very precipice of indiscretion. If this
is even partially true, Bevin has been guilty of an irresponsibility
which will make difficult his continued tenure of the Foreign
Office."

They were talking of firing Bevin from his job! The man who
wrote the comment I have quoted is himself a Member of Parliament, and counted as one of the shrewdest observers in the
Labour Party. His bitterness reveals that Bevin's greatest offence
was not that he attacked Russian policy, but that he secured the
approval of his political opponents at home.

Generally, Bevin was praised by the general public in Britain
for "standing up for his country." But the most thoughtful
political observers in the country were disturbed by the trend of
his policy. One of the most balanced comments was, "True, the
Foreign Secretary, smarting from recollections of Russian

'awkwardness' at the London conference, was at pains to disavow any desire to do anything in Eastern Europe 'detrimental' to the U.S.S.R.; and he emphasised his wish to see an effective United Nations Organisation gradually built up. But he gave no support to the idea that its members should abate their sovereignty in the realm of armaments; and he spoke menacingly of Russia as wanting to go 'right across the throat of the British Commonwealth.' Praising Mr. Truman's 'healthy declaration,' he gave no sign of dissenting from the idea of an exclusive Anglo-American entente, based on the proposition that the atomic bomb should be the Entente's secret until better international relations had been achieved. These are the politics of international suicide. We had hoped that the British Government would have given, as it could have done, a moral lead to the world by offering to abandon all its aggressive weapons in favour of a World Authority and by appealing to the United States and Russia to do likewise. If Mr. Bevin, talking in Palmerstonian terms of the 'cheapness' with which the British Navy 'policed the world' has said the last word, the future is dark. For the sake of Conservative plaudits, the Cabinet will have forfeited a great chance for creative statesmanship."

There again is the note against winning Conservative approval. The Conservatives had a comment to make about all this.

Mr. Quintin Hogg, the Conservative Member of Parliament for Oxford, observed, "It is a mistake to suppose that Mr. Bevin has not the bulk of his Party with him. A few of the older men, brought up by the pacifist atmosphere of the 'twenties and 'thirties, do not like it much. The Communists, and near-Communists, not less, perhaps, than one in ten of the Labour Members of Parliament, but almost certainly not more, bitterly resent the slightest breath of criticism of Soviet Russia. A few more ardent spirits are angry with Mr. Bevin because he will not make ruder noises at Franco or whoever the newest Prime Minister is in Greece. Others again disapprove of the Government because it does not boldly advocate international control of the atom bomb. But none of this adds up to an alternative policy. The critics agree in abusing Bevin for his doctrine of continuity with the Coalition, but they agree on nothing else. In the meantime, Mr. Bevin can count on all the more solid, if less vociferous, elements in his Party."

The popularity of Bevin's pronouncements in the country, Hogg suggested, was due to the growing mood of the people of Britain that if there was to be any hope for the world it resided very largely in the unity and initiative of the British people, and particularly of the British people acting as the centre of a group of smaller nations, including the Dominions and those of Western Europe, who believe in the same ideals and practice the same way of life.

Now all this criticism and interpretation was particularly irksome to Bevin. He smarted from the adverse comments of members of his own Party. The suggestion that he should cease to be Foreign Secretary infuriated him.

He waited for Mr. Attlee to return from his conference in Washington with President Truman and Mr. Mackenzie King, of Canada, on the future of the atomic bomb, and after a full discussion in the Cabinet sat down to prepare the greatest speech, and the most important announcement of his life to that time.

As Bevin was preparing his notes late into the night at the Foreign Office, a group of his old union colleagues were gathered in Transport House, 400 yards away, the headquarters of the union which he had created, to count up the votes to decide on his successor.

There were six candidates. One of them was a Communist, popular hoarse-voiced Bert Papworth, the London busman who had become a member of the general council of the Trades Union Congress.

For weeks it had been whispered that Papworth was receiving considerable support from all parts of the country, and was likely to prove a menace to Arthur Deakin, the man who had carried on for Bevin while he was Minister of Labour. And nearer to the day of the declaration, the louder became the forecasts of Papworth's growing strength. There might have been some Communist propaganda behind it all. Bert Papworth himself, giving deep chuckles whenever he was asked what his chances were, said nothing.

And as we waited for the result, one of the most experienced officials at Transport House who had been with Bevin for more than 20 years, shuddered to think of the effects of a Papworth victory. "I have nothing against old Bert," he added, "but think of the effect in the annual conference of the Trades Union

Congress if the union's million votes were swung to the Left? Why, it would mean reversing most of the decisions they have taken in the last ten years. And look at all the work Ernie's put in. What will he say?" And the poor man shuddered in horror.

The result was announced next day. Arthur Deakin, the old steelworker who had spent exactly half his 55 years as an official of the union, won overwhelmingly. Papworth was third with fewer than a quarter of the votes cast for Deakin. It was the end of a chapter for Bevin; but his policy will live on in Deakin.

One hour later, Ernest Bevin rose to address the House of Commons. It was the second day of one of the most important debates of the session on foreign affairs. Mr. Attlee, the Prime Minister, had been welcomed back from Washington on the first day, and had been greatly cheered when he declared, "I am quite sure that in the United States it is fully realised that there is no difference in this House about our desire for the utmost co-operation in world affairs with the great Republic across the Atlantic." He was again cheered when he reminded Parliament that no international control of weapons could be effective unless there was mutual confidence among the nations, and added, "and over great areas of the world's surface this confidence is already established. War between Britain and any one of the Dominions is unthinkable. War between Britain, Canada or the United States is unthinkable."

But it was the ex-Foreign Secretary, Anthony Eden, as immaculate as ever, who caused the greatest sensation in the debate by declaring, "Every succeeding scientific discovery makes greater nonsense of old-time conceptions of sovereignty. It is yet true that national sentiment is still as strong as ever, and here and there it is strengthened by this further complication—the differing conceptions of forms of government and differing conceptions of what words like freedom and democracy mean. So, despite some stirrings, the world has not been ready to abandon or to modify its old conceptions of sovereignty."

"Now," continued Mr. Eden, "atomic energy has come to enforce the call for something more, because the world family is smaller today than was the European family at the end of the last war."

He concluded, "We have somehow to take the sting out of nationalism. We cannot hope to do this at once. But we ought to start working for it now, and that, I submit, should be the first duty of the United Nations. We should make up our minds where we want to go. I know in this respect where I want to go. I want to go to a world where the relations between nations can be transformed in a given period of time, as the relations between England, Scotland and Wales have been transformed." One of the Parliamentary wits observed that Mr. Eden, the Conservative, had made "the principal speech for the Government."

But Bevin was still to come into the debate. The House was crowded as he rose to speak. The diplomatic galleries were full. Hardly a member moved from the Chamber throughout the whole speech, and it was long by modern standards. Bevin spoke for nearly two hours, and he constructed his speech with more care than usual. Its beginning and ending were especially carefully phrased.

He opened, "If the Great Powers which are primarily concerned will say exactly what they want, either in territory or in bases or any other form, then it can be examined and there is no need to take any action of any kind which will cast reflection on the action of one another. I really think that if any large or small nation in the world is suspicious of Great Britain, I invite—I repeat, I invite—them to tell me frankly what their suspicions are, and I will frankly face them."

He continued, "Equally, I say to other countries nothing can remove suspicion but the utmost frankness as to our respective policies. I cannot see why there should be suspicion still. We have agreed to the United Nations, and we know our obligations. Great Britain will not be afraid, and will not in any way decline to have anything it does, or wants, or seeks to promote, discussed in open assembly. I do not think I can be franker to remove suspicion than that."

Members listened intently, hanging on every word, as Bevin said, "I cannot accept the view that all my policy, and the policy of His Majesty's Government, must be based entirely on the Big Three. I cannot allow myself, if an ambassador, or representative, or a Foreign Secretary sees me, to discuss a matter between his nation and ours, I cannot allow myself for one moment to consider whether he represents a great nation or a small one. I should be failing in my duty if I did not try to decide the issue on the basis of the facts, and do right because it is right, and not because of what might happen. That is a principle on which we must work, and I hope it will not be interpreted as being antagonistic to anybody. It does not matter whether it is a big nation or a small nation; to me they represent human beings. The fact that they are divided into large or small countries may be an accident of power or an accident of geography; but it does not alter the value of the contribution they can make to humanity as a whole. May I say that civilising influence is not determined by the value of the armaments you have, but it is determined by the cultural development you possess?"

The House was interested, but not startled by these comments of Bevin.

It was towards the end of his speech that members really sat up.

"We are driven relentlessly," Bevin declared, "to the necessity for new study for the purpose of creating a world assembly, elected directly from the people for whom the Governments who formed the United Nations were responsible, to make a world law which the people would then accept, and be morally bound to carry it out."

"You may invent all sorts of devices," Bevin continued, "to decide who is the aggressor, but the only repository of faith I have been able to find to determine that is the common people. There has never been a war yet which, if the facts had been put before the common folk, could not have been prevented."

He went on passionately, "The common man is the great protection against war, and the supreme act of government is, after all, the horrible duty of deciding matters which affect the life and death of the people. That rests on the House of Commons as far as this country is concerned."

He paused to wipe his forehead, and then said with great deliberation, "I would merge that power into the greater power of a directly-elected world assembly in order that the great repositories of destruction and science, on the one side, might be their property, to protect us against their use, and, on the other hand, it could easily determine whether a country was going to act as an aggressor or not."

He paused again, and looked around as if to see that all present were paying attention to him. Then he said, "I am willing to sit with any body, of any party, or any nation to try to devise a franchise or a constitution for a world assembly for a limited objective—the objective of peace. When we get to that stage we shall have taken a great progressive step. From the moment that is accepted, the words 'international law,' which presuppose conflict between nations, will be substituted by 'world law,' with moral world force behind it, rather than case-made law. It will be a world law, with a world judiciary to interpret it, and world police to enforce it. It will be the decision of the people, with their own fate resting in their own hands, irrespective of race or creed. The great world sovereign-elected authority will hold in its care the destinies of the people of the world."

Quickly the assembly emptied. Groups of members stood talking animatedly about Bevin's proposals in the lobby.

In one group were three members of Parliament who happened to be members of Bevin's trade union. One of them called me over. Solemnly, he asked, "Do you know why Ernie is convinced that this idea of world federation can be made to work?" I asked him for his theory. He replied " 'Tis no theory. Quarter of a century ago Ernie pulled nearly thirty unions together, and most of them hated each other like hell. He got them to work together, yet he devised a means of letting each one of them look after all the things that are of concern to itself only. But on all the things that concern all of them, why, they just work together like one happy family. There's more in what I'm telling you than you appear to think. Next time you see Ernie you ask him if the principle is not the same."

Just then Bevin appeared. He was surrounded by members patting his back and shaking his hands.

Bevin walked away from the little group for a moment, and looked out through the gloom of a November dusk across that River Thames, which men after John Burns call liquid history.

Bevin is rarely left alone long these days. One of the Conservative back-benchers came up to him, and said, "That was a great and noble speech, sir."

Quite simply and without pretension, Bevin replied, "If I never do or say anything else, I am glad I had the chance of making it." Then he walked through the hall in which Charles the First, King of England, was sentenced to death, across gloomy Palace Yard to the room in the Foreign Office where he would study whatever response might come from the outside world to his appeal for the common man of all nations.

POSTSCRIPT

PRECISE dates cannot matter so much to a man like Ernest Bevin, whose life has been part of the history of great movements, as they would to a man who has resigned himself to the orthodox custom of his class.

Yet, on March 9th, 1946, Bevin faced, and with sombre satisfaction rather enjoyed, the supreme irony of his career. It was a date which more than marked a milestone ; it divided Bevin's life into chapters.

It was the day of his 65th birthday. The day of the formal ending of his career as general secretary of the world's largest trade union. The day of his retirement from his life's work. His retirement.

Bevin, in the years before he had been called to the great offices of State, had frequently envisaged the day. There had been times when his health had forced him to consider advancing it by five years ; when the vision of answering to no man on how he spent his days seemed alluring ; when the ease of pottering about a garden in the West Country offered comfort.

And now the day had arrived, bringing with it, rather surprisingly, better health and a more contented confidence than he had known for years. He needed them both—in full measure.

The tasks ahead seemed colossal and disheartening. Peace was frighteningly elusive. His own desire for a World Parliament of Man appeared to be merely the dream of an unworldly visionary. It was so remote from his own recent and bitter experiences.

Immediately behind him were the nightly tussles with Andrei Vyshinsky, of the Soviet Union, before the delegations of fifty-one nations of the world at the assembly of the United Nations at Westminster. These tussles revealed only too painfully the rift between two great States.

Within his own Party were bitter, earnest critics who feared that his old prejudices against the Communists of Britain would continue to throw up barriers against co-operation with the Communists of the Soviet Union towards world peace; critics who accused him of too readily accepting the traditions and forms of the Foreign Office and its career diplomats; critics who said that he was throwing away golden opportunities of proving to the

223

world that a new Britain had been born from the will of its people.

And the reports from all parts of the world seemed to give substance to this uneasiness.

Skirmishes and the ambushing of British soldiers in Indonesia. Famine over India. Riots against Britain in Egypt. Mysterious Russian troop movements in Iran. Cabinet resignations in Greece. Armed raids in Trieste. Confusion and plague in Manchuria. Intransigence in South America. Resettlement troubles in Australia. Problems in every Continent in the world.

No wonder Bevin said sardonically to his colleagues in the Government, "If peace breaks out anywhere, I'll let you know."

In all this there was little to account for the confidence which Bevin displayed in public and to his own private circles ; little to explain the strength with which he embarked upon the "Indian Summer" of his life.

Obviously there are explanations. Some of them have forced a re-assessment of Bevin's mental processes. For example, Bevin showed a detachment in his sizing up of the efficiency of the machinery of his new department which was alien to his earlier prejudice against the restricted field from which recruits to the diplomatic service had been drawn for generations.

He retained, and promoted, many career diplomats not out of perversity towards Socialist Members of Parliament who demanded wholesale changes in the overseas representation of the new Britain, but because these diplomats convinced Bevin that they were men of extreme perception and of selfless devotion to the interests of their own country. Bevin, a critical chief in this respect, was satisfied. And that is a tremendous compliment to the quality of the diplomatic service.

Secondly, Bevin, who had never accepted criticism of his actions or doubts of his intentions with equanimity, showed a refreshing readiness to discuss his policy with the many groups formed inside the Parliamentary Labour Party to emphasise specific aspects of Britain's foreign relations.

Many of these back-bench members were experts. Men like Zilliacus and Tom Driberg, William Warbey and Phillips Price, Michael Foot and Seymour Cocks had spent years in studying foreign affairs. Some of them proved disconcertingly well-informed on last-minute developments in foreign lands. They were outspoken in their criticism of their Foreign Secretary. He accepted their challenges, and, more often than not, rebutted their conclusions to his own satisfaction.

But the most satisfying comfort to Bevin was his conviction that he was correctly interpreting the desires of the great majority of his fellow-countrymen. There was much evidence of this.

While the thoughtful Phillips Price might say openly in the House of Commons that he had his doubts about the wisdom of Mr. Bevin's attitude to Russia, Bevin's own assertions that he was showing a masterful restraint in the face of irritating provocation from the Soviets struck the deeper responses from the great majorities inside and outside Parliament.

Phillips Price had said, "Mr. Bevin had an easy task in dealing with Mr. Vyshinsky before the United Nations. He had a chance to speak his own mind and to stand no nonsense, but when all the applause for this has died down, one is left with the uncomfortable feeling that this by itself does not constitute a foreign policy which is leading us anywhere. Mr. Bevin must not allow his dislike of Communist activities in the trade unions to colour his attitude to the Russian state." This was a restrained version of what the British Communists were saying.

But in Parliament and before enthusiastic audiences in the country Mr. Bevin declared passionately that he is for friendship with Russia—fifty years of it, for a start—an offer made to the Kremlin which the rulers of the Soviets were curiously reluctant to pass on to the Russian peoples.

After the fourth major foreign affairs debate of his "reign" at the Foreign Office (it was in February, 1946, and the fact that there had been four debates in seven months revealed the deep concern of Parliament with world affairs), a London newspaper conducted a poll on Mr. Bevin's popularity. It showed a remarkable result. Eighty-five per cent. of those who took part in the poll stated they considered Mr. Bevin was making a success of his job. His "stock" had risen 26 per cent. since a similar poll had been taken six months earlier. True, this disparity suggests public fickleness. But the later result, taken after the publicity which had been given to the debates of the assembly of the United Nations and the implications of the disagreements there, was significant of the mood of Britain.

It was, however, in the letters he received from his old trade union colleagues in March, 1946, when he formally ended his

trade union career, that Bevin realised the depth of the faith he
had inspired in his own people.

Most of them, naturally, spoke of his earlier days. They were a
spur to his prodigious memory. Most valuable of all, they were an
incentive to self-analysis.

Bevin, after the strain of a winter in which a journey to Moscow,
conferences with foreign secretaries of the great allies, and the
meetings of the United Nations and its security council, had
jostled with his enormous and continued interest in Britain's
complex internal affairs, had been forced to take a brief holiday
in Cornwall.

It lasted barely a week. But it came at the right time. It restored
his physical health, and, as was revealed on his return to office, it
had given him an opportunity of crystallising his philosophy.

Bevin believes in Britain. And that explains why he has trans-
cended party divisions in his supporters. He believes that Britain's
contribution to world sanity is based on a new, much sharper,
appreciation of economics as it affects the common man. He
would not mind being remembered as "the bread and butter"
statesman. He believes that bread means more than boundaries.

In a way, this attitude, this outlook, is the perfectly logical
climax to his own career. It is the field in which Bevin feels most
natural and most confident.

It may be argued that one man, particularly in a Labour
Government, does not make the foreign policy of his country.
That is to forget the great secret of Bevin.

Throughout his long career as a representative of the people,
the dominating, adroit industrial negotiator, who had known
when to be aggressive and when to be conciliatory as long as
principles were not sacrificed, had been highly successful. He had
formed thousands of committees in his time, had paid full attention to such bodies as the executive council of his own union, the
general council of the Trades Union Congress, and the executive
of the Labour Party, but he had discovered that in emergencies
one man, and one man only, is frequently called on to make
decisions. And in Bevin's experience that one man had so often
been Ernest Bevin.

No one had accused him openly, and with evidence, of being a
dictator for the simple reason that when Bevin made a decision it
was found that the overwhelming majority of his fellows agreed

with it, freely and sometimes wonderingly. That has been proved consistently true in nearly forty years of trade union life. The same mould can be expected now.

Will this approach ensure peace? Bevin is no easy-going, slap-dash optimist, going around trying to persuade himself and convince others that the world has turned its back on war. Peace, he realises, has got to be fought for, with the weapons of toil, of courage, of probity, of honesty, and of the understanding of the needs of other peoples. It may demand concessions, but, he believes, it will never justify appeasement to an aggressor.

It may take five years of anxiety, of patience, of adjustment, of appeals and of distractions to lay the foundations for a century of peace. And, if a century, why not an immortality? It is a bold conception. It makes temporary barriers seem trifling.

The old world has gone. Bevin realising this, has an advantage over many other world statesmen. He says, "If we can get confidence in each other we can grow together. I repeat that, we can grow together. It is the task of growing together that is the purpose of my policy."

That is his policy. For his outlook he can with accuracy and with pride adopt the final words in an Order of the Day issued to his troops on the eve of the Burma campaign by the late General Wingate : "Our aim is to make possible the Government of this world in which all men can live at peace, and with equal opportunity of sacrifice. Finally, knowing the vanity of man's effort, and the confusion of his purpose, let us pray God that he may accept our services, and direct our endeavours so that when we shall have done all, we shall see the fruit of our labours and be satisfied."

INDEX